ARID DOMAIN

By William S. Greever

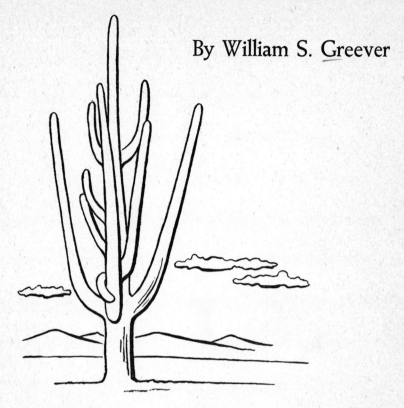

ARID DOMAIN

THE SANTA FE RAILWAY AND ITS
WESTERN LAND GRANT

Stanford University Press • *Stanford, California*

STANFORD UNIVERSITY PRESS, STANFORD, CALIFORNIA

Published in Great Britain, India, and Pakistan by Geoffrey Cumberlege,
Oxford University Press, London, Bombay, and Karachi

The Baker and Taylor Company, Hillside, New Jersey
Henry M. Snyder & Company, Inc., 440 Fourth Avenue, New York 16
W. S. Hall & Company, 457 Madison Avenue, New York 22

Library of Congress Catalog Card Number: 54-6172

To My Parents

PREFACE

IN 1866 Congress passed an act incorporating the Atlantic and Pacific Railroad, authorizing it to build from Springfield, Missouri, to the Pacific Ocean and offering it the right to earn a land grant to help cover the cost of construction. The purpose of this study is to find out what happened to the land. The railroad actually earned and received title to very little acreage outside New Mexico and Arizona. The land there was arid, in a few places covered by forests, and almost everywhere unsuited for agriculture. The Atlantic and Pacific, and its successor the Santa Fe Pacific, fostered livestock and timber operations on the grant, but never conducted a colonization campaign and hardly ever gave any encouragement to farmers to settle in the region. Only very gradually did they persuade trespassing stockmen to lease railroad acreage. Their sales of grazing land were never large except during the booms of the first and second World Wars. They also marketed some town lots and vended a little rural property for miscellaneous purposes. They conducted an extensive series of land exchanges, surrendering sections the federal government especially desired and receiving in return the right to pick tracts elsewhere. Their management of the arid land was of necessity almost entirely different from the policies of the railroads handling land in the fertile midwestern United States or in Canada.

This study was originally undertaken as a Ph.D. thesis at Harvard University. Subsequent to earning the degree, I have done much additional research and have completely rewritten the text. The present version is a general discussion of the railroads' policies, up to the middle of 1946, for the curious layman and the average historian. The relatively few experts who will wish complete, minute details are referred to the thesis, deposited in the Harvard College Library, for the material covered in Chapters V–XI and XIII.

I am indebted to Santa Fe Presidents E. J. Engel and F. G. Gurley for permission to study the company's records. The late E. O. Hemenway, land commissioner, did everything possible to facilitate my examination of the records and made me welcome as well. C. B. Mc-Clelland, former field examiner and present land commissioner, patiently and thoroughly answered many questions. Other railroad people who helped me include Mildred H. Balch, Clyde E. Davidson, H. B. Fink, J. R. Hubbard, Ralph Sellards, J. P. Reinhold, and the late Lee Lyles. For special courtesies while using the libraries of their organizations I am indebted to Mrs. May Briggs of the Southwest

Museum, Mrs. George Kitt of the Arizona Pioneers Historical Society, and Mulford Winsor of the State Library of Arizona. Frederick Merk, my adviser for the thesis, not only offered helpful advice but through the example of his scholarship and of his human understanding also gave inspiration. Garland Greever, my father, made many suggestions regarding style. The *Pacific Historical Review* has allowed me to republish that portion of Chapter V which originally appeared in that magazine. The maps for the book were executed by James H. Cheek.

WILLIAM S. GREEVER

MOSCOW, IDAHO
June 1954

TABLE OF CONTENTS

A. Estimated Cost of Reproducing the Isleta-Needles Line, 1896—B. Net Profit from the Land Grant—C. Dividends Declared by the Santa Fe Pacific Railroad—D. Gross Receipts from Rentals—E. Gross Receipts from Land Sales, Including Interest and Lieu Rights—F. Gross Receipts from Town Lot Sales—G. The Size of the Grant

MAPS

CHAPTER I

THE BACKGROUND

PART of the fulfillment of the American dream about a transcontinental railroad to the Pacific was the construction of a line running from Isleta, just south of Albuquerque, to Needles, California, and thus traversing northern New Mexico and Arizona. The laying of track on that portion of the projected Atlantic and Pacific Railroad located between the Rio Grande and Colorado rivers had important economic consequences for the region. This book is devoted to a study of how the railroad handled its land grant and how that management affected northern New Mexico and Arizona. Before plunging into the problems of administering thirteen million acres of land, however, it would be well to recall briefly facts already known to specialists about the Pacific railroad problem, the topography of the two states, the Indians of the area, the history of the area, and the operation of the livestock industry. To these matters this first chapter will be devoted.

As early as the 1830's some people envisioned a carrier to link the established East with the undeveloped West, but not until about 1845 did the first really important advocate appear, Asa Whitney. Convinced by two years' residence in China as a tea merchant that a transcontinental railroad would do much in furthering America's participation in the increasingly lucrative Oriental trade, he returned to the United States and zealously championed his idea. Knowing that in times past the nation had made grants of land to aid states or corporations in their canal or highway projects, he naturally requested for his project similar assistance. Whitney lacked a realistic approach to practical problems, such as those of engineering, but by his boundless enthusiasm roused much interest about the project.

Congress discussed Whitney's proposals from 1845 to 1852; it never acted on them. In 1850, however, it authorized to another type of enterprise, the Illinois Central, the first federal grant of alternate sections of land for a railroad project. Meanwhile it continued to debate with much energy various new plans broached for a Pacific railroad. Most legislators agreed that San Francisco was the logical western terminus, but they championed a variety of routes and a multiplicity of eastern starting points. Usually when a new session of Congress met, somebody would introduce a bill concerning the federal construction of a railroad along the central route. Since sectionalism

1

was so dominant in the political picture during the 1850's, inevitably southern congressmen, objecting that a central route would not benefit their section of the country, would force an amendment to authorize construction of another line along the southern route. Either as part of a political deal or as an additional manifestation of sectional forces, soon a similar amendment would appear concerning the northern route. Although most observers believed the federal government could not afford to finance more than one transcontinental railroad and Congress could not agree on less than three, midwestern cities battled to be the eastern terminus or, if unsuccessful, at least to be on a branch line of the transcontinental. The cities and the sections waged such a vigorous struggle over the Pacific railroad that Congress did not authorize one until the Civil War prevented effective southern opposition. In 1862 the federal government provided a land grant and financial assistance for the line from Council Bluffs to Sacramento. In 1866 it approved two additional transcontinental railways, the Atlantic and Pacific, which would build in part through northern New Mexico and Arizona, and the Northern Pacific. It authorized for these two roads land grants only.

The discussions in the 1850's induced Congress to have the army make the so-called Pacific Railroad Surveys covering five possible routes from the Mississippi to the Pacific. It directed that one survey be through the northern area, one approximately along what became the Central Pacific–Union Pacific line, another about on the mountain passage of the Rio Grande company, another through northern New Mexico and Arizona (nearly the present route of the Santa Fe), and another close to the southern border. The results, published in 1856, demonstrated that transcontinental railroads could be built along as many routes as the traffic warranted.

The survey most significant to this present study is that of Lieutenant A. W. Whipple from Fort Smith, Arkansas, along the 35th parallel to Tehachapi Pass and San Francisco. Whipple found the first 650 miles could be located easily in the valley of the Canadian River. From Isleta on the Rio Grande to Cajon Pass in California his survey was for the most part identical with the route the Santa Fe now follows. Although he had to cross several mountain ranges in New Mexico and Arizona, Whipple found suitable passes through them; west of the Colorado River he struck no obstacles until he reached the coastal ranges.

When the explorer crossed the Rio Grande at Isleta, he was at an elevation of 4,897 feet. As he continued westward across the high region known to geologists as the Colorado Plateau, he was seldom below 5,000 feet until, two-thirds of the way across Arizona, he started the long descent to the Colorado River, where he was at 480 feet. Shortly after leaving Isleta he entered a region of low mesas and erosion valleys dominated by the Zuñi Mountains. Beyond he traversed the Navajo section of the Colorado Plateau, which was a series of mesas, rock terraces, retreating escarpments, shallow canyons, and dry washes. At the western edge of this area he encountered the Painted Desert, a scenic but barren territory where the annual rainfall was sometimes as low as three inches. He then climbed onto the San Francisco Plateau, another division of the Colorado Plateau, which contained about 2,500 square miles centered around the present town of Flagstaff. The San Francisco Plateau was a gently rolling region with a few steep slopes and a few abrupt canyons cut by streams. Above its tableland, sometimes as much as 5,000 feet, towered the San Francisco Mountains. At the south end of the plateau there was, in contrast, a rapid drop-off. Moving westward, Whipple crossed two-thirds of Arizona and then began a steady but gradual descent into the Colorado River desert country.

In the high region which Whipple traversed, the temperature seldom gets above 90° during the summer, but in the desert it can reach 125°. The soil is really fertile in some of northern New Mexico and Arizona but virtually nowhere, even yet, is there agriculture without irrigation. The rainfall, which varies greatly from year to year in any particular spot, is annually three to fifteen inches. Obviously water is so scarce that it is much more important in the region's development than minerals, soil fertility, or capital. Lack of water determines that 85 percent of all Arizona's land and 98 percent of New Mexico's is useful only for grazing. It also means that often forage plants grow less than luxuriantly and that the average capacity of the range adjacent to the Santa Fe Railroad is about forty acres annually for one cow.[1]

The more important livestock feeds to be found in the belt include alfilaria, grama grasses, mesquite, blue stem grasses, mountain bunch grass, saltgrass, sages, yuccas, snakeweed, and greasewood. In the mountains there are important stands of timber, almost all yellow pine but with a scattering of spruce and Douglas fir, which form the basis of a large-scale lumbering industry now flourishing at Williams, Flag-

[1] Unless ranchers actually own the land they use they can hardly afford to spend money for water development. They know how to take advantage of springs and small streams but realize they have little opportunity of finding well water in quantities. Sometimes, by building earthen tanks to catch the natural runoff, they preserve a year-long supply despite the high rate of evaporation.

staff, and McNary. At Jerome there is much copper, and Gallup marks the center of very extensive deposits of coal for which there is little foreseeable demand. Mohave County, Arizona, contains a number of minerals, generally of too low a grade to be yet commercially valuable. Petroleum companies have discovered a few pools of oil in northern New Mexico and Arizona, but no large fields.

The Indians of the region, inhabitants since prehistoric times, are important to this study because of the problems they created for the railroad's land department. Of the smaller tribes, the Hualpais, living in the Kingman–Ash Fork region, have clung to their ancient ways rather than adopt the white man's, and since the turn of the century their number has steadily declined. The Hopis, whose tribal name was formerly translated Moqui, are north of Holbrook. Before the Americans came they lived a precarious life in their pueblos, their unirrigated fields being parched by frequent droughts and their ill-protected sheep offering constant temptation to roving bands of Navajos. In New Mexico, the Pueblo Indians occupy mostly the Rio Grande Valley from Taos to Isleta but have a few settlements such as Laguna and Acoma elsewhere. Had it not been for the systematic raids the Navajos and Apaches organized against them, the Pueblos with their fertile irrigated farms and their sheep would have been prosperous. They were so well organized in self-government that the Spanish did scarcely more than make them grants of land. When the Americans came, the Pueblos asked little besides the confirmation of their land titles and, after much discussion about precise locations, this was finally granted.

Of the large tribes, the Apaches generally roamed south of the Santa Fe land-grant area but were important in the history of the two states. A fierce, warlike tribe, they inflicted much damage upon whites and greatly hindered the development of Arizona especially, until in the 1880's the American army for the last time subdued them.

The Navajos were as important as the Apaches but since the American occupancy have been more peaceful. Their traditional hunting grounds, which form their present reservation, occupy the northeast quarter of Arizona, the northwest sixth of New Mexico, and adjoining areas in Utah and Colorado. In the early days they built up large herds of sheep by constantly making raids on the Pueblo Indians and the Spanish. When the Americans took over the region and forced them to sign a treaty, the Navajos did not observe its terms. In 1858 the United States army destroyed the tribe's livestock "as a lesson," thus compelling the red men to starve or go on further raids. After a temporary peace during the Civil War, the army in 1863 again seized the initiative and by force moved nearly all the Navajos to a reservation, the so-called Bosque Redondo, near Fort Sumner in central New Mexico. Supervising them there the army discovered its expert drill sergeants were quite inept at teaching the Navajos to farm. More serious was the poor land and bad water. Clearly the whole experiment failed and in 1868 the government returned the Navajos to their traditional territory. It gave them 15,000 sheep and these so prospered that during the 1870's the red men fast became a pastoral people. Between 1870 and 1900 the Navajo tribe doubled in size. Their reservation, seemingly adequate upon their return from Bosque Redondo, proved too small for the increasing tribe and additions made in 1878, 1880, 1884, 1886, 1900, 1901, and 1934 failed to provide all the acreage necessary. The Navajos, owning an ever increasing amount of livestock, had so overgrazed their land that by 1928 the damage was serious. Under the New Deal, they were forced to reduce sharply the number of their animals. Although this was sometimes tragic for the individual, only drastic action saved the reservation pastures from total ruin. Still the Navajo tribe increased in numbers and after World War II they again faced a serious crisis, enduring much suffering. The future of the tribe apparently lies in greater education which will gradually permit many to leave their reservation and take their place in the white community.

The Navajos were fortunate to secure the beginnings of their reservation early, for not all the tribes in New Mexico and Arizona had one until 1887.[2] All were under the jurisdiction of the Department of the Interior and, more directly, the Bureau of Indian Affairs. The Bureau suffered from frequent changes of its commissioner and from repeated shifts in the location assigned to subordinate officials, so that continuity of action was difficult to secure, and long established Indian traders on a reservation often had more influence than the parade of government agents. While there were some dishonest federal officials, most were honorable, conscientious, and at least reasonably efficient.

The government made slow progress in educating the Indians of the Southwest. Many parents, especially of the pastoral tribes, did not want to send their children to day schools on the reservation and they objected more strenuously to boarding schools, which were operated on the theory that the best way to teach a red youngster the white man's way was to prevent his having any contact with Indians until he

[2] Although on many reservations in the United States the land has been divided up into individual allotments of 160 acres and the surplus sold, this procedure was followed little, if at all, in New Mexico and Arizona because the land was so arid and because some tribes, like the Pueblos, preferred common ownership.

had completed the long education process. When the government took a critical look at its Indian schools in 1929, it discovered that methods of 1900 were still used and that conditions in general were bad. It began reforms even before the New Deal period, but such changes naturally take time; much still remains to do. One important milestone that demonstrates solid achievement is that the Navajos, once averse to education, are now bitterly complaining of the shortage of schools.

The Bureau of Indian Affairs attempted to provide health and medical service for its charges, but generally lacked sufficient funds. In 1874 it could furnish no doctor to several agencies in the Southwest and only one, with little equipment or means of travel, to others. In the late 1920's it was still providing service far below the standards of such agencies as the army and the navy. The chief diseases of the southwest Indians were trachoma and tuberculosis.

The Bureau underwent its greatest change when John Collier became its commissioner in 1933. He was backed by the vigorous support of the President and of Secretary of the Interior Ickes. Serving more than twelve years, he battled the dead weight of past traditions among the Indians and the Bureau itself to achieve his objective. He believed the Indians should develop in their own way rather than imitate the white man. He urged through Congress in 1934 the Wheeler-Howard Act which authorized the voluntary revival of the Indian tribe as both an agency of self-government and a business enterprise. It granted the red men authority to negotiate through the tribe with federal, state, and local government on policies affecting them or on actions believed to infringe on their rights. Some Indians of the Southwest hurried to organize their group under the new legislation while others, such as the Navajos, refused to take any action. Whatever they did, the red men found themselves administered in the spirit of the act. Collier continued educational reform, expanded the health work, and fostered desirable elements in the Indians' own culture. While it is too early for a definite appraisal of his work, the many changes he made are manifest.[3]

White occupancy of New Mexico and Arizona, while not as long as the Indians', dates from the late 1500's. Father Marcos first explored the region, returning to Mexico with reports of seven rich cities. Coronado set out to find these depositories of wealth but, after traveling over considerable portions of the two states and as far east as Kansas, correctly concluded the towns were chimerical. The Spanish

[3] In writing about the Indians the author has made considerable use of Everett Edward Dale, *The Indians of the Southwest* (Norman, Okla., 1949).

made their first permanent settlement in New Mexico in 1598. They continued to colonize both that region and Arizona during the seventeenth century but, lacking the lure of easy gold, made but slow progress. The Catholic Church actively established missions, leading to constant friction over minor matters between ecclesiastical and civil authorities. They agreed enough over exploiting the Indians to cause the Pueblo Revolt of 1680, in which the red men excluded all Spaniards from New Mexico for thirteen years but eventually met decisive defeat. The Spanish policy in New Mexico and Arizona, as elsewhere in their colonies, was to isolate the settlements and prevent any foreigners interloping in their trade territory.

In 1821 Mexico revolted and forced Spain to grant her independence. She reversed the traditional isolationism, welcoming outlanders. The next year the first United States trader drove a wagon from Missouri to Santa Fe; an annual caravan developed. This famous trade of the Santa Fe Trail gave New Mexicans a much closer outlet for their goods than the long routes southward and excited American citizens' imagination about the West.

When United States expansionists forced a war on Mexico by methods akin to those of Hitler and his *Lebensraum* advocates, the American army promptly struck westward to the Pacific Coast in California. General Stephen W. Kearny made a bloodless conquest of New Mexico, but after he went farther west there was a revolt which was vigorously put down. The Americans encountered slight trouble in taking Arizona, although the well-known Mormon Battalion had to fight a little before entering Tucson. The United States organized the whole region as "New Mexico Territory" in 1850. The next year the Catholic Church made a separate diocese there and sent out Bishop Lamy, whose important reforms produced much lasting good. The United States extended the national system of land laws to its new possession. It shortly added a little to the province, making the Gadsden Purchase to secure an excellent railroad pass, but also sliced away some acres in organizing Colorado Territory. It finally heeded the complaints of Arizonans weary of difficult communications with the distant capital of Santa Fe and in 1863 created two separate territories with the same boundaries as the present states. After the Civil War a problem of gradually increasing seriousness in New Mexico was America's promise to recognize the land grants made there by the Spanish and Mexican governments. The numerous, intricate, and highly technical disputes arising over these estates finally forced the national government in 1891 to hand solution of the questions over to an especially established Court of Private Land Claims, which by 1904 succeeded in settling most of the difficulties. New Mexicans and Arizonans started agitating for statehood as early as the turn of the century, but did not achieve it until 1912.

Livestock handling in the two states has since earliest times been the most important industry. Before the United States captured the region, ranchers mostly ran sheep. The early Spanish explorers and missionaries brought the first of these animals into the region. Despite Indian troubles, the sheep gradually increased until by the early 1800's they were frequently found in southern Arizona and almost overran all New Mexico. A very large number of them in the latter state were owned by about a dozen families, each of whose male members often grazed a quarter or a half million sheep. Some large owners had elaborately organized ranches with a hierarchy of supervisors to oversee the work of the so-called *pastores*, who handled a flock of about two thousand sheep. They paid their shepherds such low wages that they often had to lend these *pastores* money in an emergency and, since the salary was often not sufficient to allow repayment, held the herdsmen in a debt slavery until old age. Other large owners preferred the *partido* system, putting out a flock of sheep on shares for five years. To them this method was quite profitable, but their partners, if they encountered a serious accident which destroyed many sheep, found themselves in debt for life. Their animals were far from purebred stock, growing an inferior wool and yielding little good meat. Their chief worry was to protect their flocks from thieving Navajos, Apaches, and Comanches. The sheep were marketed in old Mexico.

The American conquest of New Mexico and Arizona itself caused little change in sheep ranching, but when shortly the gold discovery brought throngs to California there was an unprecedented demand there for sheep. Starting in 1849 New Mexicans drove herds of them across Arizona to the miners; between 1852 and 1860 probably 551,000 head hoofed it to California.

After the Civil War the sheep industry in the United States started expanding. Flockmasters found a surplus of animals in California and started moving them eastward, especially when the southern part of the state in 1870 and 1871 experienced serious droughts. Some found northern Arizona largely unoccupied and moved sheep into the eastern two-thirds of the region. Others trailed their flocks of highly bred rams to New Mexico, where they disposed of them at a tidy profit to ranchers wishing to improve their stock. The New Mexican shepherds themselves had the only other large surplus of animals in the United States. Before the railroad came, they drove their sheep overland to markets in Kansas, Nebraska, Missouri, Colorado, and Wyoming. From 1870 to 1900 they exported three or four million sheep. The increasing number of sheep in Arizona prompted the Mormons to establish several woolen mills, the first in 1879, but all eventually failed because they could not compete successfully with California establishments.

The sheepmen's prosperity lasted from the Civil War to 1893, when they encountered a severe drought in the two states, the removal of tariff protection on wool, and the national financial panic. They did not begin to recover from these blows until 1896, with the abandonment of free trade in wool. During the First World War they enjoyed high profits. In the decade of the 1920's they, along with cattlemen and farmers generally, conspicuously failed to share in the general prosperity. Their difficulties increased in the great depression era, forcing most of them to turn for aid to the New Deal's refinancing agency, but they made good profits during the Second World War.[4]

The flockmasters in the early days of New Mexico and Arizona ran sheep that were inferior producers of wool and meat but were adept at hunting feed, at finding water, at resisting storms, and at escaping predatory animals. About 1880 shepherds began gradually to import better breeds of sheep. Today most of them have in their herds only the hardy, long-lived, prolific Rambouillet, which produces a maximum of high quality wool and meat, which readily travels long distances for nourishment, and which manages easily in a herd.

A single shepherd generally handles a flock of about two thousand sheep. Completely responsible for their health, safety, and nourishment, he usually is very loyal to the animals even when he has a low opinion of their owner. Generally he is a Mexican or an Indian. His life is solitary but far from monotonous, for today seldom presents the same problems as yesterday. His day starts at sunup when the sheep begin to graze; to prevent damage to the range he urges them to spread out for a mile or more. The shepherd allows them to seek shade in midmorning and to rest in a compact body until late afternoon, when they again feed. His constant companion and very faithful assistant is a collie, whose instincts and training from puppyhood have made him almost as wise as his master in handling sheep.

A good shepherd does not keep his sheep in any locality too long, lest their sharp hoofs wear permanent pathways as they graze the vegetation so close they obliterate it. He leads the flock to water every

[4] Regarding the history of sheep the author has especially used two works: Bert Haskett, "Early History of the Sheep Industry in Arizona," *Arizona Historical Review*, VII (1936), 3–51; and Edward N. Wentworth, *America's Sheep Trails; History, Personalities* (Ames, Iowa, 1948).

three or four days. He prevents his sheep from grazing on loco weed, whose effect on them is about like opium on a human being, but he knows they will not eat other poisonous herbage unless there is nothing else available. The shepherd keeps a sharp lookout for coyotes, the greatest of the seven animal enemies of sheep; perhaps he wishes the New Mexico and Arizona grasses grew rank enough to make coyote-proof fences economically feasible. He is alert to protect his flock from diseases, of which by far the most common is scabies, but thanks to the work of state sheep sanitary boards formed about the turn of the century these now are seldom to be found.

The most critical period of the year in handling sheep is lambing time. Before the turn of the century lambing took place on the range, but increasingly owners have provided special sheds to make possible better care to mothers and to new twins. The ranchers hire traveling bands of experts to shear their sheep, by hand in the old days but now almost always by machine. The flockmasters move their herds into the high altitudes during the summer and return to the lower plains in winter. In New Mexico they seldom have to travel far, but in northern Arizona some do and others don't. Some Arizona owners, leaving the heights of the San Francisco Plateau, take their flocks the short distance to the feed grounds of the Little Colorado River. A larger portion of them prefer to winter far to the south in the Salt River Valley, more often driving the sheep down federal government stock trails than traveling on the railroad. By deciding whether they will stay north, go south only to the foothills, or migrate all the way to the valley floor, they also determine whether their lambing period will be May, February, or November.

Sheepmen financed themselves during the great depression era to a considerable extent with government loans, but in ordinary times they relied upon banks. Two additional methods they used were the *partido* system, almost unchanged from the old Spanish days, and taking sheep on shares from a mercantile house. In the middle 1930's Arizona sheepmen secured about 65 percent of their income from lambs, 25 percent from wool, and 10 percent from such miscellaneous items as pelt sales.

Sheep of the Navajos presented some special problems. The Indians eliminated scabies from their flocks much more slowly than did the whites, although by the middle 1920's much had been done. Their failure to pay close attention to modern ideas of proper grazing methods and their overstocking inflicted much damage on the range. Their animals, far from purebred, increasingly produced fleece that was short and greasy. In 1930 the Bureau of Indian Affairs began steps to correct these defects in the wool and to produce a fleece more suitable for the hand spinning and weaving industry which is such an important source of income for the Navajos.

Although sheep were predominant in Spanish times, more recently cattle have become equally important. In Arizona Father Kino established a mission herd of cattle in 1700. From this start a number of ranches run by laymen grew, but the Apaches became so bold in their thefts that by 1843 most of these ranches were abandoned and the remaining animals drifted into a wild freedom. Despite various efforts it was not until the middle 1860's that more than temporary ranches again were established in southern Arizona.

The cattle industry of New Mexico and Arizona began its major growth after the Civil War from the impetus of Texas. This neighbor accumulated during hostilities a huge surplus of animals, worthless there but valuable at market centers. After Appomattox, Texans headed a horde of cattle in the long drive northward, seeking two objectives. One of these was the packing houses, reached either direct or by such famous railheads as Dodge City. The other was the Great Plains, so recently cleared of their chief animals, the buffalo, and their chief human inhabitants, the Indians. Upon the plains a greatly expanded cattle industry gradually arose, which for many years imported more animals than it marketed.

One enterprising Texan who sought the northward market was Charles Goodnight. With a partner he drove his animals to New Mexico, where he sold some to the government at an Indian reservation, and then continued on to Colorado, where he found purchasers for the remainder. His route attracted the attention of other Texans, who increasingly followed what came to be known as the Goodnight Trail.[5] This roused to ever greater activity Indians engaged in the "comanchero" trade of stealing cattle from Texans and selling them in New Mexico. The red men seized cattle traversing the trail and also made raiding expeditions into Texas. Although the Bureau of Indian Affairs attempted to eliminate purchases of stolen cattle, the army officers of at least one New Mexican fort succumbed to the ob-

---

[5] When Goodnight on his original journey came to Raton Pass, he consulted the owner of the toll road across it, "Uncle Dick" Wootton, who declared there was no alternate route and demanded 10 cents a head for passage, with no reduction for quantity. The resourceful drover scouted around until he found Trinchera Pass and thus bypassed Wootton. Most writers have commented that if only "Uncle Dick" hadn't been so "greedy" with Goodnight, he would have earned a golden harvest from the Texans who followed him. One old-time cowman, however, has cast serious doubts on this theory, "for there is nothing will knock hell out of a mountain road quicker than a trail herd." (J. H. Culley, *Cattle Horses and Men of the Western Range* [Los Angeles, 1940], p. 78.)

vious profits in a trade where they could purchase a cow from red thieves for a loaf of bread and a good-sized herd for a keg of whisky. Texans sought without much success to eliminate the "comancheros." Few met with the success of John Hittson who repossessed ten thousand head of his own and his neighbor's cattle "by authority of Judge Colt." The trade broke up only when the United States confined all Indians to reservations.

Stocked from various sources, legally and illegally, the cattle industry of New Mexico and Arizona grew during the 1870's, although by the end of the decade there were still comparatively few cattle in the region. One of the most active ranchers was John Chisum, who gradually increased his range until he occupied 150 miles on the Pecos River in New Mexico. He was an admirable pioneer in many ways but had an unfortunate habit of purchasing Texas cattle with promissory notes he never pretended to redeem, and a few times he knowingly traded in stolen cattle.[6] His clashes with the small-scale neighboring ranchers finally resulted in the Lincoln County War of 1876, famous for the activities of Billy the Kid, which it finally took the territorial governor to stop. In Arizona Colonel Henry C. Hooker established in 1872 an important pioneer cattle ranch.

In the 1870's the range cattle industry of all the West began a boom period. Immediately after the Civil War, prices of cattle started to rise and this attracted many to enter the business. The double demand of normal consumption and stocking new ranches forced prices still further up, resulting in annual profits to cattlemen of as much as $33\frac{1}{3}$ percent. This attracted the eye of foreigners, especially the English, and of wealthy American capitalists who rushed into the business, sometimes on a small scale and sometimes with a corporation controlling a huge enterprise.

All this expansion increasingly crowded the range until, though few realized, the ranchers were seriously overgrazing the land with animals that were better beef producers than the original Texas Longhorns but less able to care for themselves. In the winter of 1886–87 came weather of unprecedented ferocity. When ranchers finally could venture out in the spring, they discovered that large herds had been obliterated. The losses were so tremendous that few cattle outfits escaped bankruptcy.

New Mexico and Arizona experienced the same type of expansion and disaster as did the Great Plains region. Especially with the com-

---

[6] In one famous instance Chisum delivered a large herd to a purchaser and, to his dismay, then had to accept in payment a bundle of his Texas notes, bought there at considerable discount.

pletion of the railroad across northern Arizona did the cattle industry grow. By the middle 1880's most of the range was occupied by stockmen. As in the Great Plains, a few large cattle outfits arose such as the Aztec Land and Cattle Company, the so-called Hashknife outfit. Many small-scale operators appeared, some stocking their ranches legitimately while others helped to make the tradition that all a man needed for a start in the region of the Hashknife ranges was a good stout rope and a branding iron.

One rancher sought to discourage rustlers by inserting, with the customary notice of his brand and range in the local stock newspaper *Hoof and Horn*, the following statement:

To whom it May Concern:

Any person caught Monkeying with any of my Cattle, without permission, will catch HELL!

YOURS IN CHRIST,
"Grizzly" Callen

After this warning had run in *Hoof and Horn* for about half a year, the issue of February 17, 1887, contained the following letter:

Philadelphia, Pa., Jan. 25 '87

Pubs. Hoof and Horn, Prescott, Arizona—Gentlemen: A copy of your issue for January 6th has been received in Philadelphia, and people who profess to be Christians, and who, to say the least, are shocked that you would allow an advertisement to appear in your paper worded as that of "Grizzly Callen," top of column, sixth page [*sic*]. Profanity is bad enough, but when put in type, and, you might say, blasphemy added, in what we suppose to be a respectable paper like yours, we blush for the state of society in your section of Arizona. It does not give much encouragement to any Christian young man to make Arizona his home, or to a man of family to settle there; and it would seem that your paper, which should be a pioneer of civilization in the far west, when it admits an advertisement like the one we speak of, goes square back on the first principles of civilization and Christianity, and would, if it continued to accept and publish such advertisements, soon degenerate into a heathen sheet, not admissible to families where profanity is looked upon as a sin. We trust, however, that our feeble remonstrance, made with the kindest of feelings and best wishes for your prosperity, may have the desired effect, and that you "will sin no more." Would be pleased to see such a promise in your next issue.

Yours very respectfully,
A Friend

The letter prompted the editor to comment on the difference between eastern and western outlooks. He thought that "A Friend" had never experienced the things that try men's souls in the cattle business. He pointed out that, although using an unorthodox method, Callen was trying to promote the Christian virtue of honesty and that "stall-fed" divines in the East promised their listeners "an unlimited supply of exactly what Grizzly threatens, for monkeying with the ways and wickedness of the unconverted."

When ranchers first went into the virgin grasslands of New Mexico and Arizona, their annual animal increase was sometimes as high as 90 percent. They encountered no particular reversals until 1891, 1892, and the first half of 1893 brought a continuous drought. This disaster, quite comparable to the winter of 1886–87 in the Great Plains, inflicted losses on herds of 50 to 75 percent. Coupled with the panic of 1893, it struck ranchers a staggering blow. They gradually recovered, although never again to operate in a bonanza style. They encountered peaks of great prosperity during the two World Wars but suffered difficult times in the 1920's and especially in the 1930's. After the turn of the century the size of individual operations declined; previously a "big" cattleman had been one who owned fifteen to thirty thousand head, but by 1951 few herded more than three thousand.[7]

New Mexico and Arizona ranchers at first ran Longhorn cattle, which could travel long distances without harm and under all but the most extreme conditions could rustle for themselves. Unfortunately they also took four years to mature, were regrettably gaunt where the choice cuts were, and produced a "teasingly tough" meat. The stockmen gradually turned to the Hereford, starting in 1883, and now use them almost exclusively. These animals, quickly responding to a fattening ration, produce a high quality beef and are good rustlers on the range. Ranchers also learned it was good business to care for their animals better. Once, in handling cattle, the cowboy frequently ran them at a gallop and, in branding, threw the calves with earthshaking jars. Such practices are now confined to western movies, for fast-moving herds destroy profit-making beef, and calves are gently led between the confining walls of the special branding chute. Ranchers still turn their cattle loose to wander over the range, but they exercise more control over their movements than formerly, casually inspect them more frequently, and look after them better during winter storms. They round up their stock once, frequently twice, a year and often do it in co-operation with their neighbors.

---

[7] Of the various books and articles consulted on cattle, the most useful single reference was Bert Haskett, "Early History of the Cattle Industry in Arizona," *Arizona Historical Review,* VI (1935), 3–42.

Ranchers, seldom attempting to regulate the breeding season, often keep one bull for twenty-five cows and one and a half to two cows for each calf raised. Their average annual calf crop is between 33 and 48 percent. They try to guard their herd from death, but a 1928 investigation in New Mexico and Arizona placed losses at 11.5 percent where the stockman had exclusive use of a range and 18.5 percent where he didn't; deaths were largely from starvation. Unless willing to exist in a rural slum, ranchers must own 350 or 400 head of cattle to make a reasonable profit and, with feed on the range so sparse, this would require undisputed control of almost three-quarters of a township. Prior to the 1920's cattlemen relied upon private banks and capitalists for their funds, but during the postwar slump and the great depression of the 1930's they turned to the federal government.

Cattlemen and sheepmen all have faced serious problems of range control and use. At first they followed the traditional western practice of establishing their ranches entirely upon the public domain. Technically they were trespassers but nobody complained of the universal practice. When one man occupied an area, others kept their animals out of it and respected his "range rights." As increasing numbers of ranchers entered the region it became more difficult to find an unoccupied area, and eventually newcomers began to argue that mere priority was not enough. They expected the old-timer to use his range to the maximum, and if he failed to utilize all the grass, then they turned their own livestock into his area to finish the job. Established ranchers generally undertook to forestall interlopers by stocking their area so heavily that nobody else would seriously consider competing. If any of them failed to overgraze, they were enjoying the luxury of sound range management at the potential expense of sharing their exclusive control with less idealistic newcomers. Often they built fences, illegally enclosing public land but protecting their "range rights."[8] This competition continued until 1934 when Congress in the Taylor Grazing Act established the United States Grazing Service (later renamed the Bureau of Land Management). The agency designated just where established ranchers could for a nominal fee occupy the public domain and prevented their overgrazing it.

Some stockmen tried to protect their range rights by leasing land from private owners or from the states. Others sought the same objective through purchases. In the railroad land-grant area they might buy the company's alternate sections to give them legal jurisdiction over half the area, and perhaps they could exercise unofficial control

[8] In 1885 President Cleveland ordered all fences enclosing the public domain removed. Most of them were, but only until the excitement died down.

over the rest. They might purchase a solidified area of land from a homesteader or the owner of an old Mexican or Spanish grant. They might buy acreage from New Mexico or Arizona, to whom the federal government had granted it to support various worthy purposes. Ranchers realized, however, that most of the land still belonged to the United States. Under the terms of land laws long ill-adapted to arid regions, they could secure legal title to national land by filing homestead claims. In the earlier days they could obtain only 160 acres; after 1909, 320 acres in an "enlarged" homestead; and from 1916 till the New Deal closed almost all land to entry, 640 acres in a stock-raising homestead. Obviously ranchers could never make a living on areas so small in a region so arid under the terms of laws so impractical for grazing country, however wise for eastern farming regions. They often resorted to dishonest devices in obtaining under the homestead law more acreage than was legal. Ranchers also might acquire government acreage by purchasing from private sources various relatively expensive rights, called scrip, to stated amounts of available federal land; scrip was originally issued to certain war veterans or to those surrendering private tracts the United States especially wanted. Stockmen generally could not afford to purchase all the land they used and frequently bought strategic tracts, such as those bordering a stream or occupying a canyon mouth, with the intent of automatically controlling the adjoining public domain. They found that if they purchased too much land their fixed charges were high and their competitive market position with those owning no acreage was poor in times of stress.

Difficulties over range rights, so frequently unsolved by purchases or leases that there was no permanent settlement till the Taylor Grazing Act of 1934, often involved traditional quarrels between cattle-men and sheepmen. They clashed for various reasons, one of which was that sheep eat grass much closer to the ground than do cattle, and for a long time ranchers incorrectly assumed the two could not be run profitably over the same area. Their most publicized clash, whose causes are obscure, was the Pleasant Valley War which almost eliminated the entire Graham and Tewksbury clans. Arizona stockmen had arrived by the end of the 1880's at a satisfactory adjustment on what precise regions should be occupied by which type of animal. Outside sheepmen, however, in the early 1890's began to crowd into northern Arizona, upsetting the previous tacit understanding and awakening the cattlemen's vigorous opposition to additional flocks. In one celebrated instance the cattlemen invaded 25,000 head of bedded-down sheep by driving in one hundred wild horses, some with cowbells and others with strips of dried rawhide attached to their tails; this annihilated the flock. Stockmen again gradually adjusted their differences. Today research has proved that if a rancher handles both sheep and cattle on his range he will make more profit than if he runs one to the exclusion of the other.

Another land problem, slow to achieve the recognition due it, was proper range management. Pioneer ranchers in the arid West, unlike farmers in the East, had no body of precedent to follow in determining their practices. Deceived by the initial lushness of the virgin grasses, they crowded more and more livestock on the range without apparent ill effect until they used what subsequently proved to be three or four times its normal carrying capacity. Many sincerely believed statements like the following:

Nor need he have any fear about "eating up" the range. After being grazed down to the roots, the sweet grama grass shoots up next season with fresh vigor and luxuriance. Ranges over which cattle have roamed for years show no falling off in the quantity or quality of feed. In fact, it is claimed by some that the ground is enriched by the cattle, and that the native grasses attain a stronger growth after being pastured for a few years.[9]

From such disasters as the winter of 1886–87 in the Great Plains and the droughts of 1891–93 in New Mexico and Arizona, ranchers eventually realized that they were overstocking the range. By a process of trial and error, they gradually learned how many animals they ought to keep in their area and how to handle them to secure the maximum nourishment from the vegetation available. Often, however, they could not put their knowledge to use because they must preserve their "range rights" without proper regard for the grasses or some interloper would push into their territory. Sometimes even when they felt no danger from outsiders the temptation to recoup previous losses or to profit from unusually advantageous market conditions led them to overstock.

Overgrazing eventually produces erosion. The absence of many bunches of grass allows the water, running off too rapidly, to carve its own passageway or to follow animal paths. This process obviously destroys what once had been good pasture land. It also permits such fast drainage that the water fails to soak properly into the soil; eventually two or three good rains are necessary to produce the same results on the forage that once one would have.

The destruction of the ranges, partly through ignorance and partly through greed, caused almost irreparable damage to a most important economic asset of New Mexico, Arizona, and the other states west of

[9] Patrick Hamilton, *The Resources of Arizona* (San Francisco, 1884), p. 261.

the 20-inch rainfall line. A 1936 comparison of all these regions with their original condition reached the still disputed conclusion that the range on the public domain had been depleted an average of 67 percent; on Indian reservations, state lands, and private property, 51 percent; and on national forests, 30 percent.[10] For years no important steps were taken to remedy this depletion. In recent times both the United States Grazing Service, founded in 1934, and the Soil Conservation Service, created in 1935 to help protect privately owned as well as public land, have done conservation work in the arid West; it is too recent to be appraised.

The first government agency to attempt proper range management was the United States Forest Service. With the establishment of the initial national forests primarily to protect their timber reserves, the Service at first entirely excluded sheep; but in 1902 it definitely adopted a policy of allowing at least some flocks in its forests. The Service engaged in a more or less continuous controversy with stockmen over what amount of grazing would furnish nourishment to the greatest number, and to what kind, of animals without damaging the range or the trees. Both at times were wrong, and there will probably always be differences of opinion, but the net result was more sound economically than that produced elsewhere in the arid West. The Forest Service charged ranchers a moderate fee for their grazing licenses. It argued with stockmen who wanted licenses for ten years, but has periodically granted them wholesale. Since the demand for grazing rights in any national forest almost always exceeds the supply, it has occasionally reduced the quantity allotted to each established permittee in order to have space to accommodate newcomers. Some say this practice is true democracy; others that it prevents long-range planning by private enterprise and will eventually produce rural slums.

The American ranchers first started using large portions of the New Mexico and Arizona ranges in the 1880's. Although Indians, Spaniards, and Mexicans had previously grazed many sheep during the long history of the region, the area was never entirely filled with livestock until the boom days climaxing in the early 1890's. Ranchers then began operating on a smaller scale and improving the breed of their animals. Their informal "range rights" gave way to more vigorous if unofficial means of control and to actual land purchases, but they seldom could afford as individuals to practice proper range management. Part of their prosperity depended upon the railroad completed from Isleta to Needles in 1883. To the early history of the Atlantic and Pacific we shall turn in the next chapter.

[10] "The Western Range," *Senate Documents,* 74th Cong., 2d sess., No. 199, p. 7.

CHAPTER II

ATTEMPTS AT LAUNCHING A TRANSCONTINENTAL RAILROAD

CONGRESS, although pausing in the midst of the Civil War to authorize a transcontinental railroad along the central route, partly as military necessity and partly as political opportunism stimulated by the absence of the Southerners, waited until 1866 before approving other lines to the Pacific. It sanctioned construction of two other routes much discussed in the ante bellum debates, that of the 35th parallel by the Atlantic and Pacific Company and that of the north by the Northern Pacific. Congress had encouraged the original transcontinental line with both land and financial aid, but in 1866 it proffered to the two additional companies only land. Apparently most of the discussion and maneuvering before the measures were passed took place in the Committee on the Pacific Railroad or through unofficial channels; just as in the history of land-grant railroads studied by other historians, the debates published in the *Congressional Globe* seem routine.

B. Gratz Brown of Missouri, reportedly chiefly responsible for the passage of the Atlantic and Pacific's charter, introduced the necessary legislation for that road into the Senate.[1] When reported from the committee to the floor for debate, it was twice amended. The senators, apparently influenced by the so-called Big Four, who wished to preserve a California railroad monopoly for their Central Pacific, authorized a new creation of these financiers, the Southern Pacific, to connect with the 35th parallel route at the Colorado River. Seeking to protect the rights of the red men in the Indian Territory through which the Atlantic and Pacific must operate, they amended the clause ordering the United States to extinguish tribal title in conflict with the company's land grant as rapidly as possible by providing the additional requirement of Presidential approval for any donations the Indians might make the company. In the House of Representatives the only important change was the elimination of a clause often found in similar legislation providing that within the grant area the government must sell its remaining land at double the minimum price. The House passed the measure sixty to forty-four, with eighty-two not

[1] Speech of ex-Governor T. C. Fletcher of Missouri in *Opening of the Atlantic and Pacific Railroad and Completion of the South Pacific Railroad to Springfield, Mo., May 3, 1870* (Springfield, Mo., 1870), p. 17.

19

participating, and the Senate vote was not recorded; signed by the President, the bill became law.[2]

The act, a federal charter incorporating the Atlantic and Pacific Railroad, named seventy-five men to organize the company, including such notables as John C. Fremont, John Edgar Thomson, Thomas A. Scott, Levi Parsons, John W. Garrett, J. B. Eads, Edward F. Beale, and Frederick Billings.[3] It authorized construction of a continuous line from Springfield, Missouri, through Albuquerque, along the 35th parallel to the Colorado River, and then "by the most practicable and eligible route, to the Pacific." It approved a branch from

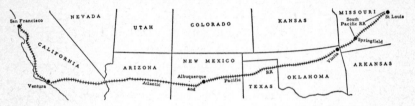

PROPOSED ROUTE OF THE ATLANTIC AND PACIFIC RAILROAD

Van Buren, Arkansas, to the main line at the Canadian River in Texas. It forbade charging the government a higher rate than other customers and required co-operation with any other railroad connecting with the new line. For financing it authorized issuance of one million shares of stock, par value one hundred dollars, and acceptance of any gifts or loans, those from Indian tribes to be approved by the President of the United States; but it stipulated that the federal government would never furnish any funds.

To aid construction the United States gave the railroad a right of way one hundred feet wide, with additional space where stations or shops proved necessary, all exempt from taxation in the territories. More important, it authorized the company to earn a land grant, justified as necessary to encourage a route for the mail and the military, of alternate, odd-numbered sections for twenty miles on either side of the line in the states and forty miles in the territories. Since it had previously disposed of some acreage in these so-called place limits to homesteaders and others, as replacement for acreage so lost it established an additional strip ten miles on either side of the place limits in which the railroad could pick so-called indemnity land from the odd-numbered sections. It would not allow the company to select any

[2] *Congressional Globe,* 39th Cong., 1st sess., pp. 1100–1102, 4182.
[3] *Statutes-at-Large,* XIV, 292.

mineral property, with the customary exception of coal or iron. It stipulated that the railroad must earn the land by actually building its line, with the right received from three inspecting federal commissioners to additional property with each twenty-five miles of road accepted as finished. To enable the company to obtain title for its acreage promptly, the President of the United States was to have the area of the land grant surveyed "as fast as may be required by the construction of said railroad." Concerning the Indian Territory, the law provided, "The United States shall extinguish, as rapidly as may be consistent with public policy and the welfare of the Indians, and only by their voluntary cession, the Indian title to all lands falling under the operation of this act. . . ."

Congress, seeking prompt action, allowed the company two years for accepting the law and beginning construction. Stipulating that building once commenced must progress at least fifty miles annually, it set the required date of completion at July 4, 1878. If the corporation failed to meet these provisos, then Congress was to have power for "any and all acts and things which may be needful and necessary" to ensure prompt construction of the entire line.

The Atlantic and Pacific law of 1866 also authorized the Southern Pacific Railroad of California to build eastward from San Francisco to a junction with the 35th parallel route near the state boundary and as encouragement offered the opportunity to earn a similar land grant. Thus there were to be two western terminals, one of the Southern Pacific at San Francisco and the other of the Atlantic and Pacific at an indefinite point. It is hardly likely, although no evidence remains, that the backers of the new venture welcomed this interference from the Big Four.

Another unfriendly enterprise, in addition to that of the California financiers, appeared. The Kansas Pacific, which basically is today's Kansas City to Denver line of the Union Pacific, promptly cast longing eyes on a route along the 35th parallel. It was so interested in a line through Kansas, Colorado, New Mexico, and Arizona to California that in 1867 it sent out a surveying expedition in charge of General William J. Palmer, later to gain fame with the Denver and Rio Grande Railroad. He followed the Santa Fe Trail to Albuquerque, then appointed an assistant to head a party to investigate the 32d parallel route while he himself led a group almost retracing surveyor Whipple's footsteps and following the present rail line along the 35th parallel. The general published a report enthusiastically describing the railroad construction possibilities and traffic potentialities of the route he had traversed, but he expressed doubts over the region his assistant had surveyed.[4] Fortunately for the Atlantic and Pacific, Palmer's book failed to stimulate the Kansas Pacific into following his recommendations favoring a line to southern California.

Even before Palmer began his expedition, twenty-five out of the seventy-five men Congress named to organize the Atlantic and Pacific met at Turner's Hall, St. Louis, on October 1, 1866. They elected General John C. Fremont to the presidency of their interim commission and for one day threw open stock subscription. Fremont, for himself and as trustee, purchased 2,750 shares. Frederick Billings of California subscribed for 1,000, and Levi Parsons of Kansas for 1,000. The stockholders, meeting in New York City at the end of the month, approved purchase of the South Pacific Railroad, also headed by Fremont, which was already building from Pacific, just west of St. Louis, to Springfield. Through this move they made possible a through route under one ownership from the Mississippi River to the West.[5] Having selected members of the Board of Directors, these new officials in November completed work of organizing the new transcontinental by electing Fremont as permanent president, an office he certainly held no later than 1870, and Levi Parsons as vice president. They also promptly accepted officially the terms of the 1866 act.

The Atlantic and Pacific first completed the South Pacific to Springfield, next constructed as a joint venture of the two companies the line from Springfield to Pierce City, Missouri, and then in 1870 laid fifty miles of its own rails. When it requested a federal inspection of this last trackage, a necessary requirement before it could obtain title to its adjacent land grant, the Atchison Topeka and Santa Fe Railroad unsuccessfully objected without giving any justification for its complaint, and the three commissioners reported the line acceptable.[6] Doubtless the Atchison even at this early date had its eye on the 35th parallel route for itself, because in 1870 a bill was introduced into the Senate but never left the hands of the Committee on the Pacific Railroad, which would have approved such an enterprise and appropriated a land grant.

Further opposition in 1870 harried the Atlantic and Pacific before the Senate. It sought an extension until 1872 of the time within which

[4] W. J. Palmer, *Report of Surveys Across the Continent in 1867–68 on the Thirty-Fifth and Thirty-Second Parallels for a Route Extending the Kansas Pacific Railway to the Pacific Ocean at San Francisco and San Diego* (Philadelphia, 1869), pp. 151–61, 187.

[5] Report of the Board of Commissioners of the A&P, December 5, 1866, the National Archives, Washington (hereafter cited as NA), Railroad Package No. 9.

[6] Francis B. Hayes, President of the A&P, to the Secretary of the Interior, April 1 and August 1, 1870, NA Railroad Package No. 10.

it must build through Missouri and requested authority to mortgage all its property, including land, as security for a bond issue. It encountered two crippling amendments, one forcing it to build through the Indian Territory as soon as the national government secured the necessary right of way and the other eliminating entirely the land grant in the red men's preserve. The first of these might have been prompted by the general hostility already arising against all railroad corporations, by a genuine desire to force speedy construction, or by the machinations of some rival line; the other was advocated by the Committee on Indian Affairs. The company doubtless felt great relief when the Senate, adjourning eight days after the debate on the matter, failed to act on the bill.[7]

The Atlantic and Pacific in 1871 continued construction work until it reached Vinita, Indian Territory, 361 miles from St. Louis. It attempted to connect there with the Missouri Kansas and Texas Railroad, already running north and south, but that entrenched line persistently ran all its trains "rapidly past the place of crossing, without stopping them." Since the newcomer's objective was to short-haul the older line on through traffic, the latter's reluctance to co-operate is understandable. Early in 1872 the two made a satisfactory agreement.[8]

Another 1871 achievement was securing congressional approval, with almost no debate, to mortgage all the Atlantic and Pacific's property to bondholders with the stipulation that if the creditors foreclosed prior to the completion of the route, they could obtain only that segment of the land grant adjacent to the finished portion of the line.[9] The railroad's progress induced the Committee of One Hundred, a San Francisco commercial club, to explore with the company the possibility that the line would soon reach the Bay area. It began some kind of negotiations but finally decided to do nothing because some of its members favored instead the Southern Pacific or the Texas and Pacific.[10] During the time of these discussions, the Atlantic and Pacific leased the Pacific Railroad of Missouri, the predecessor of the present Missouri Pacific extending from St. Louis to Kansas City, and by thus creating a system totaling 844 miles secured a virtual railroad monopoly of southern and western Missouri.

The company considered additional construction in the Indian

[7] *Congressional Globe,* 41st Cong., 2d sess., pp. 4570–71, 4636–37, 4705–7, 4916–18, 5147–48.

[8] James Baker to C. J. Hillyer, December 3, 1871, NA Railroad Package No. 11.

[9] *Statutes-at-Large,* XVII, 19.

[10] Glen Bradley, *The Story of the Santa Fe* (Boston, 1920), pp. 212–13.

Territory, but the prospect for local traffic and, as we shall see shortly, for securing any land there was so dismal that it began seeking from Congress an extension on the time limit for completion of the line through to the Pacific. It failed both with a separate measure and with an attempt to tack the desired proviso onto a law concerning the Texas and Pacific. It found slight relief in an interpretation of the 1866 act, elicited from the Department of the Interior, that the requirement to build fifty miles of line a year started July 28, 1870, rather than earlier, and that if the company constructed more trackage in any twelve months, then the unused balance might be applied toward the next year's requirement. Perhaps the railroad or perhaps the welfare of the Indians prompted Senator James Harlan, chairman of the Committee on Indian Affairs, to protest additional work because construction workers "beyond the usual restraints of civilized life" might have an evil effect on the red men, but the Secretary of the Interior, seriously discounting the possibility, placed upon the company itself the burden of deciding whether it would comply with the fifty miles a year requirement.[11]

The Atlantic and Pacific by 1872 had acquired sufficient information about the territory beyond Vinita to file with the government a map of definite location for its route as far as San Francisco. When the United States accepted these maps, it would then take the important step of withdrawing from entry all acreage within the place limits and indemnity strip of the railroad's land grant until, presumably, the company had acquired title to all sections earned by constructing the entire line. The company's president, apparently apprehensive, inquired whether the map covering the portion of the route into San Francisco had been approved. Yes, replied the Acting Secretary of the Interior, since the 1866 act sanctioned it and ". . . there is no doubt of their right to construct the road on that line."[12] The government withdrew the land along the entire proposed route to San Francisco.

The decision regarding San Francisco met prompt opposition from the Southern Pacific, which claimed the sole right to build west of the Colorado River and attacked the proposal for the A&P to touch the ocean at Ventura and thence follow the coast to the Bay area. The Atlantic and Pacific, seeking to justify its interpretation of the clause "by the most practicable and eligible route to the Pacific," claimed that

[11] C. Delano to James Harlan, June 14, 1872, NA Department of the Interior Letter Book "Pacific Railroad No. 2."

[12] B. R. Cowan to Francis B. Hayes, April 11, 1872, NA Department of the Interior Letter Book "Pacific Railroad No. 3."

Congress substituted these words for a phrase in the original draft authorizing lines to both San Diego and San Francisco; hence it interpreted them as approving a railroad to one of the two places but not both. Obviously, it believed, "eligible" meant "desirable and attractive to us." It discounted its rival's opposition to the projected route along the coast since the Big Four interests had abandoned their original plans to follow an almost identical survey in favor of actually building down the San Joaquin Valley. It charged that the Southern Pacific, allied with the Texas and Pacific, sought to exclude it entirely from California.[13] These conflicting arguments drove Secretary of the Interior Delano to seek the advice of Assistant Attorney General W. H. Smith, who upheld the Atlantic and Pacific's right to claim its proposed route. He thought the company could not make a strained interpretation of the debated clause, such as asserting it could build to Puget Sound, but he viewed as reasonable the selection of San Francisco, California's chief trading post on the Pacific. Fortified with this opinion, Delano upheld the Atlantic and Pacific.[14] In 1877 a new Secretary of the Interior, Carl Schurz, refused to reconsider the ruling because those who objected presented no new evidence. Between 1874 and 1880 congressmen introduced five bills forfeiting all or part of the railroad's land grant, but each of these measures died in committee.

The Atlantic and Pacific meanwhile suffered two serious blows. It fell into the hands of its enemies, for by 1873 Thomas Scott, a leading promoter of the Texas and Pacific, was president, and the next year his associates had majority control. They apparently planned to unite the two projects, building the Atlantic and Pacific to a junction with the Texas and Pacific somewhere in Texas, thence jointly to the West. Scott even went so far as to secure congressional consideration of a measure surrendering the western portion of the A&P's land grant and containing other provisions benefiting the T&P, but he met defeat at the hands of C. P. Huntington, who spent $200,000 securing passage of an entirely different law favorable to the Southern Pacific.[15] The second serious blow was that the Atlantic and Pacific, overexpanded when the panic of 1873 struck, defaulted on its bond payments that year and two years later plunged into bankruptcy.[16] In 1876 a group of bondholders purchased the completed

---

[13] J. P. Henderson to C. Delano, March 10, 1873, NA Railroad Package No. 11.
[14] W. H. Smith to C. Delano, March 16, 1874, NA General Land Office files; Delano to Commissioner of the General Land Office, April 15, 1874, NA Department of the Interior Letter Book "Lands No. 16."
[15] *Congressional Record*, 48th Cong., 1st sess., pp. 789–90.
[16] By the fall of 1873 the company had secured a total of $19,760,000.00 from the sale of stock, issued $15,133,860.36 worth of bonds, and contracted a floating debt

road and adjacent land grant, forming a new corporation entitled the St. Louis and San Francisco, the so-called Frisco. The new company retained control of the original charter, valuable for both its authority to build west and its land-grant provisions.

One serious problem which plagued the Atlantic and Pacific from inception through bankruptcy to completion of the isolated segment in New Mexico and Arizona was the Indian Territory. The national government, originally intending always to preserve the region for the red men by excluding white settlers, did not survey the area or establish there the usual public land system. It transferred title in much of the acreage to four tribes who exercised full control of affairs within their boundaries subject only to mild federal supervision. The red men stipulated that only a few railroads might cross the Territory in certain specified directions. The approximate route for one of these the Department of the Interior gave the Atlantic and Pacific. The company deposited with the federal government a $500,000 bond to protect the rights of the tribes through whose areas it built.

When the railroad sought to claim its land grant within the Indian Territory it discovered the prize was more theoretical than actual. The 1866 act proffered it land, situated in a state or territory of the United States, to which the federal government held full title that had not been otherwise granted, sold, or appropriated on the date the railroad filed a map of definite location. But before 1866 the government had set acreage aside for the red men, thus obviously creating a prior disposal of the land. Furthermore, the region named Indian Territory actually was a special reserve area and not an ordinary territory within the obvious meaning of the words of the 1866 act. The Atlantic and Pacific, while still abuilding in Missouri, realized there were grave doubts whether it could ever secure title to the land theoretically given it. When the company asked the Cherokees to present it with a belt of land similar to that described in the 1866 act, the red men flatly refused.

The railroad, impatient by 1871, proposed that the Department of the Interior completely change the national policy toward the Indian Territory. It advocated establishing a government similar to that which had prevailed under the celebrated Northwest Ordinance, making Indians as subject to the new regime as any other citizen. It proposed giving each tribal member 160 acres and selling what remained to white settlers at $1.25 an acre, thus financing a fund to benefit the

---

of $2,758,025.38. The total cost of building the line from Pacific to Vinita was $36,262,322.70. (Andrew Pierce, Jr., Vice President of the A&P, to the Secretary of the Interior, September 24, 1873, NA Land and Railroad Division Railroad Package No. 308.)

red men. It maintained that since the Indians cultivated only one-fifteenth of their preserve they were hindering the traditional government policy of land for the landless. Denying that they had ever owned the continent, it alleged that any wrongs the Indians might have suffered arose from their unreasonable refusal to recognize the superior claim of the United States to their land. It described their use of any area as only a political right sanctioned by peace treaties whose terms ought to be altered with changing conditions.[17] The railroad arguments failed to impress the government at the time, although public pressure forced a somewhat similar plan when the federal authorities sanctioned formation of what was to be the state of Oklahoma. Thus during the 1870's the company's management came to feel that the Indian Territory would remain unchanged forever, a region affording almost no traffic as partial offset to the company's unsuccessful claim for the grant. Beyond the red men's preserve it saw Texas, open to white development but with all unoccupied land owned by the state as a successor to the Lone Star republic rather than by the federal government. Obviously the United States could not offer the railroad a land grant where it did not hold title to any acreage. If the company could ever build this long stretch of line without assistance, it would claim federal land in New Mexico, Arizona, and California. But financiers shied away from investing in so large an enterprise in backward Indian Territory and undeveloped Texas. Probably this was the most important reason why the Atlantic and Pacific, as envisaged in the 1866 act, was never completed. Another was the strong opposition of the Southern Pacific and the Texas and Pacific.

Meanwhile in Missouri the railroad received title to considerable land. When the Atlantic and Pacific took over the South Pacific it also acquired the rights to an 1852 federal grant, originally to the state of Missouri but assigned to the South Pacific, extending from Pacific to within fourteen miles of the boundary line of Indian Territory, or, in other words, to about two miles west of Neosho. This grant, contrary to the usual practice, was for the alternate even-numbered sections rather than the odd-numbered ones. In addition, the Atlantic and Pacific in its own name received under the terms of the 1866 act a grant for odd-numbered sections starting at Springfield, extending the eighty-nine miles to the state border and beyond, which obviously overlapped the South Pacific's for seventy-five miles. The Department of the Interior, citing a passage in the 1866 act eliminating from the total to which the transcontinental road would be

---

[17] C. J. Hillyer, *Atlantic and Pacific Railroad and the Indian Territory* [Washington, D.C.], 1871.

entitled the acreage the local line would acquire, decided Congress had knowingly created the overlap.[18] It ruled that the Atlantic and Pacific might file claims in the grant area of either for the total net acreage both companies had earned. It allowed a situation, probably unique in the history of railroad land grants, where a corporation could acquire both even- and odd-numbered sections in the same area. Despite the seemingly large area from which to pick, the Atlantic and Pacific discovered the region had been so filled with homesteaders prior to the completion of its construction that it could not secure all the acreage to which it was entitled in the place limits and found some acreage in the indemnity strip so inferior that it did not bother to claim it. The final figures on the company's grant were as follows:[19]

Gross area under the 1852 and 1866 grants.......... 1,062,141.15 acres
Deducted because of the overlap 431,347.25
Net to which the railroad was entitled.............. 630,793.90
Amount to which company received title............ 510,497.86
Deficiency (never made up) 120,296.04

Little is preserved in the government records to show how the railroad handled the land it acquired. The 1868 stationery of the South Pacific advertised land between St. Louis and Springfield at $2.50 to $10.00 an acre. In 1870 the Atlantic and Pacific complained that, in the interval between its selection of certain tracts and the arrival of final title, thieves often destroyed the principal value of the property by removing all the timber.

Any good fortune in Missouri was, as we have seen, more than matched by ill fortune elsewhere. The original Atlantic and Pacific, despite its federal charter authorizing construction of a major transcontinental line, was so beset by its troubles in the Indian Territory, the panic of 1873, and the opposition of competing lines that it got no farther than Vinita before being overtaken by bankruptcy. Its completed railroad, reorganized as the St. Louis and San Francisco, eventually developed as a north and south carrier.

The so-called Frisco retained as one of its assets the Atlantic and Pacific corporate framework, bulwarked by a federal charter and the offer of a land grant if it built west again. Part of the proposed route along the 35th parallel was never completed. A major segment in New Mexico and Arizona was to be finished in time by a corporate device the original founders of the Atlantic and Pacific could never have foreseen.

[18] William F. Vilas to Commissioner of the General Land Office, NA Land and Railroad Division Letters Sent No. 89.
[19] Enclosure to letter, T. C. Havell to T. P. Littlepage, April 11, 1931, NA General Land Office files.

CHAPTER III

THE ATLANTIC AND PACIFIC'S WESTERN DIVISION

THE Atchison Topeka and Santa Fe Railroad, which at least as early as 1870 had enviously eyed the route along the 35th parallel, was vigorously expanding, and in 1880 its track reached Albuquerque, New Mexico. It then turned south to connect with the Southern Pacific's transcontinental line at Deming, but it disliked depending permanently on another company for through California traffic. With the Frisco, which now used the mileage to Vinita and still owned the 1866 federal charter, it shortly joined in reviving the Atlantic and Pacific. Each would furnish money necessary to construct additional trackage. They agreed in 1880 to build at once the so-called Western Division from Isleta, just south of Albuquerque, along the 35th parallel to the Pacific Ocean, and planned later to lay track on the so-called Central Division from Vinita to Isleta. Pending completion of the latter, the Atchison would haul all through traffic eastward to Wichita, then turn over the St. Louis–bound cars to the Frisco while retaining the Chicago freight for itself. If the Atlantic and Pacific failed to earn enough to make necessary payments on its bonds, the two parents would advance for that purpose not more than 25 percent of their gross earnings on through traffic from the Western Division. Neither of the two would build any additional lines in Kansas without the prior approval of the other.[1]

The Frisco and the Atchison divided securities of the revived company between them. Apparently the Atchison resold these to its own stockholders and perhaps others; what the Frisco did is not clear. The two each took half of the A&P stock. They also shared equally in handling the 6 percent first mortgage bonds, which had as security the property, including the land grant, of the Western Division. Issued at the rate of not more than $25,000 per mile, the bonds were to be redeemed in 1910. Their holders, in addition to the right to foreclose if any payment was six consecutive months overdue, had the protection of retaining control over the selection of the railroad land commissioner.[2] Although the Atlantic and Pacific might sell portions of its land grant, it must use money thus obtained in repaying

[1] The so-called Tripartite Agreement between the three roads, January 1, 1880, as amended April 15, 1880, and October 5, 1886, records of the land commissioner at Albuquerque (hereafter cited as LCA), A&P Document Box No. 2.

[2] Indenture, Atlantic and Pacific Railroad and the United States Trust Company, July 1, 1880, LCA A&P Document Box No. 1.

STATE OF ARIZONA AND THE RAILROAD LAND GRANT

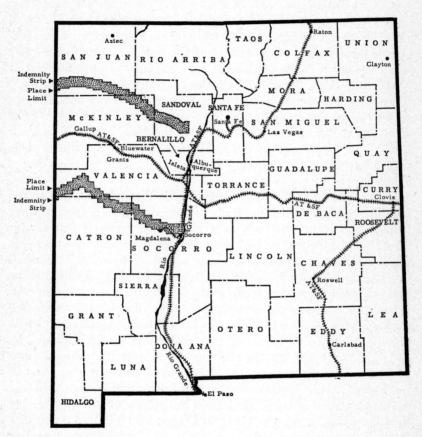

STATE OF NEW MEXICO AND THE RAILROAD LAND GRANT

31

its debts to bondholders. The revived company obtained further financial support from the general public by marketing 6 percent income bonds, issued at the rate of not more than $18,750 per mile, with repayments of principal and interest to be made only from earned income.[3]

When under this arrangement the Atlantic and Pacific began construction at Isleta late in 1880, it intended to extend its line into San Francisco but encountered the vigorous opposition of C. P. Huntington's Southern Pacific and Jay Gould's Texas and Pacific. These two financiers purchased stock control of the Frisco. They forced their unwilling partner, the Atchison,[4] into halting the new railroad at Needles on the Colorado, where the Southern Pacific would build to meet it. The tracks joined there to form a "continuous through route."[5] The Southern Pacific from Needles to Mojave earned the adjacent land grant under the terms of the 1866 act; it still owned almost all this acreage in 1945. Having apparently excluded their rival from California, the two financiers sold their holdings in the Frisco.

The Atlantic and Pacific received little through traffic from the Huntington lines, which naturally preferred to earn a greater profit by hauling freight over their own rails to two gateways farther east than Needles, Ogden, or El Paso. The Atchison and the now independent Frisco faced either allowing a highly unprofitable situation to continue, abandoning their new line, or building through to the coast on a route directly parallel to the Southern Pacific. Huntington, fearing such expansion, actually sold the Atlantic and Pacific his trackage from Needles to Mojave in 1884 although legal technicalities prevented him from delivering title until later. He also granted an option, never exercised, on running rights over his railroad from Mojave to San Francisco. The Atchison, as part of the agreement, surrendered to the Southern Pacific its mileage from Benson, Arizona, to Guaymas, Old Mexico. By 1885 it had secured its own track from Barstow into Los Angeles and San Diego; by 1900, into San Francisco.

[3] Indenture, Atlantic and Pacific Railroad and the Boston Safe Deposit and Trust Company, October 11, 1880, LCA A&P Document Box No. 2.

[4] The Atchison Topeka and Santa Fe Railroad was known to the general public as the Santa Fe and in financial circles as the Atchison. The latter term is used in this book to distinguish the parent company from its important subsidiary with which we shall have much to do, the Santa Fe Pacific.

[5] Between 1882 and 1886 the A&P constructed 77.9 miles on its Central Division in Oklahoma and had plans, never executed, to build at least 86 more. All this trackage eventually became part of the Frisco.

Financial difficulties, mostly caused by insufficient traffic, beset the Atlantic and Pacific during the entire time it operated the Western Division. By 1884 it had borrowed $2,774,513.64 to pay the interest on the first mortgage bonds and for other purposes from its two parent railroads and the banking house of J. & W. Seligman and Company. Valuing the land grant, its only readily available asset, at 50 cents an acre, it turned over 5,424,800 acres to Edward W. Kinsley as trustee. He was instructed to sell the tract within five years and liquidate the $2,774,513.64 debt.[6] He asked the railroad land commissioner to continue active management of the acreage under the trusteeship and consequently it was administered in the same fashion as the remaining grant. Kinsley, after selling relatively few acres, in 1890 terminated the trusteeship when further financial adjustments involving land proved necessary. Meanwhile, with the outlook growing bleaker in 1886, the Atchison assumed direct management of the Western Division and the Frisco of the Central Division. They arranged for an exchange of the 6 percent first mortgage bonds for 4 percent second mortgage bonds and, seeking to keep their child out of bankruptcy, promised each to underwrite half of its future deficits.[7] In 1890, with ever increasing financial difficulties facing it and no cash available, the Atlantic and Pacific liquidated the advances its parents had made for bond interest by giving them title to practically all the surveyed land in its grant. It handed the Atchison 2,277,641.15 acres, valued at approximately 75 cents each, to erase a debt of $1,708,230.86 and surrendered 1,215,043.75 acres to the Frisco covering advances of $911,282.81. The Atchison's property, which quickly became named the Frost lands, lay untouched until 1897, when a newly organized corporation we shall later hear much of, the Santa Fe Pacific, started managing it. The Frisco, keeping its acreage quite apart from that of its ally, established the New Mexico and Arizona Land Company; this tract will virtually disappear from our discussion.[8] The Atlantic and Pacific, through

[6] Trust deeds, A&P RR Co., the United States Trust Co., and Edward W. Kinsley, June 27, 1884; deed of release, same parties, January 2, 1890, LCA A&P Document Box No. 2.

[7] Joint bond agreement, the three railroads, October 5, 1886; indenture concerning the 4 percent bonds, same parties plus the Mercantile Trust Co., October 5, 1886, LCA A&P Document Box No. 2.

[8] Since an 1887 federal law forbade any corporation owning more than five thousand acres in any territory of the Union, except for railroad operating purposes, the Atlantic and Pacific officially transferred the land to individuals, Jacob Seligman as "dummy" for the Frisco and George F. Crane (later succeeded by John Frost) for the Atchison. (James A. Williamson to Allan Manvel, February 17, 1891, A&P outgoing Letter Books stored at the Stationery Warehouse at Topeka [hereafter cited

this device and the previous sales under the Kinsley trust, had used its grant directly in paying its debts.

Financial problems were not the only dangers facing the struggling railroad. It fought unsuccessfully to ward off seizure of the unearned grant adjacent to its projected but unbuilt mileage. It struggled to stop the revocation of the withdrawal from entry of the indemnity strip from Isleta to Needles—a withdrawal which prevented other possible claimants from seeking acreage there. It encountered a public attitude toward land-grant railroads in general which had altered gradually from generous encouragement in the 1860's to suspicious opposition. This change was prompted partly by the Grangers' complaints of high rates, of discrimination between patrons or localities, of free passes, of shady financial manipulation, and of poor service; partly by the companies' failure to observe the dates set for completing construction of their lines; partly by the growing shortage of good tillable acreage available in the public domain; and partly by reformers' fears of an alleged developing American land monopoly. Although a few called for forfeiture of unearned railroad grants as early as 1867, not till ten years later did the movement gain momentum. Meanwhile the Supreme Court decided that, until Congress took action on the companies' failure to comply with their time limits, they still might earn their grants. Prodded by reformers, Congress between 1884 and 1890 first passed laws regarding certain corporations and then declared a general forfeiture of grants adjacent to uncompleted portions of all lines. The federal government regained possession of about 33,600,000 acres.

The Atlantic and Pacific as early as 1881 fought off a congressional attempt to recover its unearned land east of Isleta and west of Needles. In 1884 it faced the most serious threat yet. Its spokesmen argued, much as did those of the Northern Pacific and the Texas and Pacific when similarly threatened the same year, that the problem was so involved the courts rather than Congress should assess its merits and that previous failure to declare a forfeiture automatically granted an extension for "a reasonable length of time." Its opponents criticized Secretary of the Interior Delano's approval of the extension from Ventura to San Francisco and characterized building the isolated Western Division as a violation of the original concept of a through, independent, transcontinental railroad. The two sides argued the perennial problem of the land in the Indian Territory and

as TLB]; agreement, Jacob Seligman and SL&SF Ry. Co., January 2, 1890, LCA A&P Document Box No. 1; deeds, A&P RR Co. to George F. Crane, 1890, LCA A&P Document Box No. 3.)

debated whether, despite clear wording to the contrary, the 1871 congressional permission for the railroad to mortgage its land grant established a permanent, irrevocable trust fund for the construction of the line.[9] The company escaped passage of the hostile legislation in 1884 because the House would not agree to an amendment proposed in the upper chamber. Senator J. T. Morgan of Alabama, who introduced it, wanted the forfeiture to be suspended until the courts could rule on the rights of the Atlantic and Pacific. Railroad Land Commissioner J. A. Williamson, present in Washington during at least part of the battle, reported that railroad representatives talked with three members of the Senate-House conference committee on the bill and quoted Senator P. B. Plumb of Kansas as opposing any railroad through the Indian Territory which might divert through transcontinental traffic from his state. Williamson, without amplification, declared the forfeiture had become so "purely political" that the company could not for long prevent it.[10]

In 1885 the railroad suffered a serious defeat on the same matter at the hands of William Andrew Jackson Sparks, the newly appointed commissioner of the United States General Land Office. He set about with such uncontrolled vigor to reform all at once the admittedly numerous evil conditions in his bureau that shortly not even the support of the Secretary of the Interior or President Cleveland could save him from the great pressure for his resignation. Sparks, catching the railroad without warning, seized upon a routine homestead case before his office, in disregard of established procedure. He ruled that the company was not entitled to any land from Ventura to San Francisco. Secretary Lamar, sustaining him, declared it beyond the power of either the corporation or Delano to make an extension 380 miles northward from the legal terminus at the point of first reaching the Pacific Ocean and dismissed complaining railroad mortgage holders with the observation that they should have investigated the security for their bonds more carefully.[11]

But the railroad lost more than its grant from Ventura to San Francisco in 1895. When Congress met late that year, Plumb promptly introduced a bill forfeiting all the railroad's remaining unearned land. Soon he stated he was going to call the measure up from the Committee on Public Lands for consideration by the entire Senate, which led Williamson to comment, "This may or may not be so,

[9] "Forfeited Grants Atlantic and Pacific Railroad Company," *House Reports,* 48th Cong., 1st sess., No. 1663, *passim; Congressional Record,* 48th Cong., 1st sess., pp. 4619, 4883–88, 5861–68, 5942–62, 5965–66.

[10] J. A. Williamson to H. C. Nutt, president of the A&P, January 7, 1885, TLB.
[11] *Land Decisions,* IV, 458.

as it may be his policy to threaten loud and openly. Perhaps you know better than I do."[12] Much more serious was the measure proposing the same thing which T. R. Cobb of Indiana, chairman of the House Committee on the Public Lands, advocated. Williamson appeared at a hearing before the committee and judged he was winning converts among its new members. Then Cobb "took alarm" and after "much talk and some feeling among themselves" got the group into an executive session which automatically prevented the commissioner from appearing further.[13] When the debate on the measure began on the floor of the House itself, the chief opponent, T. C. McRae of Arkansas, wanted instead to forfeit all land unclaimed on the original date for finishing the road, July 4, 1878. Cobb resisted this proposal as contrary to the 1871 act approving the company's mortgage. Williamson, left by his superiors to his own devices, repeatedly sought through his own efforts and those of a Northern Pacific man to stifle the bill by referring the legal question involved to the House Judiciary Committee for discussion. At first he succeeded, but the Committee on Public Lands forced the measure back onto the floor. It was passed in the almost deserted House with a dozen approving and no opposing votes.[14] The Senate, considering the measure, rejected Morgan's familiar stall to leave the matter to the courts and struck out a proviso retaining whatever rights the United States might yet have in the remaining, supposedly earned, portion of the grant. It passed the bill. McRae, still eager to forfeit more, created a sensation in the House with a speech attacking such moderation to any railroad, but his colleagues quickly agreed with the Senate. Williamson commented upon senatorial approval of the act as follows: "Southern Pacific combining with other influences did it. I will verbally explain the influence [*sic*] I refer to."[15] His only hope now lay in persuading the President to veto the bill. He learned of a "certain gentleman," reportedly a close friend of the Chief Executive, who would present the situation in a light favorable to the railroad upon payment of a $1,000 retainer and promise of $10,000 to $15,000 additional if a veto resulted.[16] Whether this was attempted is not clear, but the President's signature soon made the bill into law.

The Atlantic and Pacific then tested the validity of this measure through legal action up to the United States Supreme Court. The

[12] Williamson to Nutt, December 15, 1885, TLB.
[13] Williamson to Nutt, January 29, 1886, TLB.
[14] Williamson to E. F. Winslow, February 5, 1886; Williamson to Nutt, February 15, 16, and 24, 1886, TLB.
[15] Williamson to Winslow, May 26, 1886, TLB; *Statutes-at-Large*, XXIV, 123.
[16] Williamson to J. & W. Seligman & Co., January 8, 1886, TLB.

judges there cast aside its arguments based on the absence of any express passage about forfeiture in the 1866 act, discounted complaints over the government's failure to survey parts of the grant area, thought the railroad must take its own chances in the Indian Territory where the United States had prior commitments, and denied that the 1871 approval of mortgaging was an extension of time for completing the road. They upheld the forfeiture as legal.[17]

Meanwhile, in 1887 the railroad received a blow from Secretary of the Interior Lamar. He shared the growing public resentment against the previous withdrawal from occupancy by ordinary citizens of the indemnity strips adjacent to land grants of all railroads. He thought it once justifiable to have reserved this acreage till the corporations learned whether they wanted any of it, but now, with the increased shortage of land and the delay in railroad construction, resolved to throw the tracts open to anybody. In 1887 he made his key decision by revoking the withdrawal of the indemnity strip from Isleta to Needles and then turned to other railroads until he had restored about 54,000,000 acres to general occupancy. In the Atlantic and Pacific case, reversing a previous Secretary's act of administrative discretion in originally setting aside the land, he chided the company on its "ill grace" in complaining of the government's failure to survey its earned land grant when it had built only such fragments of the transcontinental line as pleased it.[18] His revocation did not prevent the railroad from claiming land in the indemnity strip but did place a premium upon making prompt requests before others obtained all the choice tracts. The company feared rivals would promptly flood into the area, but during the first year only ten persons filed application for acreage, and government officials approved none of these.

The railroad also encountered difficulties within its place limits. Others had secured the right to certain acreage there before it established its own claim to the area in 1872 by filing the map of definite location. Although eventually replaced by selections in the indemnity strip, the company lost in its place limits 785,825.68 acres from Spanish grants, 36,063.00 from military areas, 595,761.35 from Indian reservations, and 7,006.87 from homestead entries, making a total of 1,424,659.90 acres.[19]

[17] A&P v. Mingus, 165 US 413.

[18] Williamson to Nutt, May 26, 1888, TLB.

[19] Howel Jones, land commissioner of the Santa Fe Pacific Railroad, to Edward J. Engel, February 12, 1919, LCA 3131. These figures exclude 486,564 acres involved in the Hualpai controversy discussed in Chapter XII.

Very important, obviously, were the problems involved in the grants made when Spain or Mexico controlled the Southwest. The grants were recognized by the United States if valid at the time of the treaty of Guadalupe-Hidalgo ending the Mexican War. Some were entirely legal, others supposedly correct had been inadvertently made by those no longer authorized to dispense such gifts, and others were either dishonest attempts to magnify greatly the size of relatively small tracts or else clearly spurious. The most famous of the frauds was the Peralta-Reavis claim to 12,467,456 acres outside the railroad's territory in southern New Mexico and Arizona, for which a former St. Louis streetcar conductor, Reavis, so cleverly altered numerous documents in Mexican and Spanish archives that for years many important lawyers accepted the claim as genuine. Despite his marvelous ingenuity and magnificent audacity, his hoax was conclusively exposed in 1895. The knotty problems involved in testing the validity of these old grants prompted the United States in 1891 to establish a special Court of Private Land Claims to handle the disputes. When dissolved in 1904 it had examined demands for title to 35,491,020 acres and had upheld as valid only those to 2,051,526 acres. Some applicants then appealed to the regular courts, but by 1915 almost all cases had been settled. Genuine Spanish or Mexican grants obviously took precedence over the Atlantic and Pacific's 1872 claims. But the railroad could hardly remain idle when faced with a combination including most of the region's leading lawyers to secure wholesale approval of the most doubtful claims.[20] While it is certain the company took protective steps, the exact measures are not clear.

The railroad had to protect itself against improper homestead entries on its base lands. Those made prior to the 1872 filing of the map of definite location it could not oppose, but later ones it promptly protested. The company had to scrutinize claims critically under the pre-emption law, which allowed those who had squatted on acreage before 1872 to claim it later. The corporation contested such claims as that of a man who testified he had lived continuously on a certain tract since 1870 but actually during the period had been a well-known saloonkeeper in Santa Fe. It tried to detect government surveyors who were bribed to report falsely that especially valuable tracts fell in even-numbered sections, open to any claimant, rather than in odd-numbered ones the company had earned. Since understaffed government offices perforce accepted as correct all material submitted if

[20] Williamson to J. D. Springer, February 24, 1892, TLB.

apparently reasonable, the Atlantic and Pacific had resort to vigorous action and, in 1890, Williamson reported such success that it had lost few, if any, acres through the frauds described.[21] It also investigated the question of certain military and Indian preserves but did not seriously dispute their validity. To the army it lost the region of Fort Wingate and Camp Mohave; to the red men, that portion of the Navajo and Laguna reservations established before 1872. It successfully and correctly claimed land within Indian reservations founded after that date; indeed, the government recognized this right by establishing the reservation over only the even-numbered sections. But what of land within the Camp Verde reservation, opened in 1871 and closed in 1875? The company could claim nothing there, ruled the government, for the region had already been appropriated before 1872.

Although the railroad did not lose its rights to any land because of interlopers, it suffered from their activity. Some, sincerely doubting the validity of the whole grant, actually inquired of Williamson "if the Atlantic and Pacific Company is engaged in procuring money on spurious title and if I am aiding and abetting said Company in so doing."[22] Others, actually well enough informed, served their own ends by proclaiming "that the damned railroad has no title."[23] But the majority of white trespassers, so accustomed to the western system of range rights, gave almost no thought to who owned the land, and the company was helpless in the face of existing territorial laws to take any effective action against them. The railroad felt vexed with Indians grazing their livestock outside reservations on its land because it believed they prevented an influx of white interlopers, to whom it might eventually sell some tracts. It suffered most from the Navajos, who occupied in 1893 almost two million of its acres. High company officials rejected Williamson's recommendation that it employ Willshire and Cooper, apparently lobbyists, to hamper another tribe by securing revocation of the Zuñi reservation. They later authorized him to spend not over $2,500 in agitating for the federal government to confine all the red men within their own areas; the measure was of no avail.

The Atlantic and Pacific's troubles with interlopers on its place limits lands, serious enough, were more than matched by difficulties

[21] T. S. Sedgwick to H. L. Waldo, May 26, 1884; Williamson to W. C. Hazeldine, June 25, 1890, TLB.

[22] Williamson to J. H. Hoskins, January 25, 1888, TLB.

[23] Williamson to Nutt, March 8, 1888; Williamson to H. W. Gardiner, December 7, 1893, TLB.

in obtaining legal title to that acreage from the government. It constantly faced the problem of how legally to identify specific tracts when the United States neglected to survey large portions of its grant between Isleta and Needles. Initiative lay with federal authorities, who could order a surveying expedition if they chose and invoke an 1876 law requiring land-grant railroads to pay half its expenses. The Atlantic and Pacific knew that an individual settler might deposit money covering the cost of a prompt survey in an entire township where he held a claim and receive, in return for his financial assistance, certificates applicable in payment on government land. The company proposed to make similar advances to hasten work it especially desired, but the federal authorities refused on the ground that a railroad was certainly not a settler.

The corporation made vigorous efforts between 1888 and 1892 to obtain a congressional appropriation for the survey of its property but failed despite Williamson's long sojourns in Washington. It received support from various territorial and county officials, including Arizona's governor. They protested that local governments were losing possible tax revenue and complained that uncertainty of section lines prevented homesteading. But when the railroad asked the territorial legislature to pass a resolution favoring the desired appropriation, it refused. It feared it might give the company a stronger hold on its grant, and the disappointed Williamson exclaimed, "The venom and the stupidity of some of the people of Arizona is without a parallel in all my experience with men."[24] In 1895 the company, completely reversing its policy, decided it did not want the work done because the territories could not tax unsurveyed, unclaimed land even though the railroad's eventual possession of it was reasonably certain.

In those areas where the government did finish surveys during the 1880's and 1890's, the railroad still encountered difficulties. It applied for possession in the prescribed fashion, but Sparks, the reforming commissioner of the General Land Office, refused to issue title. To justify his action he cited the company's failure to build within the time limit originally set in the 1866 act; this despite an opinion in 1880 by the United States Attorney General that until the government called a forfeit or took steps to hasten construction the railroad might still leisurely obtain its land. Williamson, irritated, complained, "His prejudice and enmity against railroads is boundless and controlling."[25] Delay continued after Sparks's resignation. By

---

[24] Williamson to Hazeldine, March 23, 1891, TLB.

[25] Williamson to Nutt, December 15, 1885, TLB; *Opinions of the Attorney General*, XVI, 572.

1892 the government had given the railroad title to some of the land it claimed but had not yet taken action on additional requests totaling 2,668,299.21 acres.

The Atlantic and Pacific also encountered difficulty in making selections in its indemnity strip. In requesting those sections it was supposed to point out the specific tracts it had lost in its place lands but often could not because they were not surveyed. To correct this disability the company in 1885 made a blanket application for all the odd-numbered sections in the entire indemnity, alleging its total losses would exceed the area available there, but the government rejected the request. In 1887 the railroad again made an unsuccessful attempt, specifically describing all surveyed indemnity and approximately locating the unsurveyed. In 1889 it described lost land correctly but sought to obtain indemnity sections on unsurveyed tracts and again failed. About this time it encountered another difficulty in a new government ruling that indemnity selections must be in the strip nearest the lost land, but this was later modified to read "the nearest available surveyed tract."[26] Faced with all these problems, the Atlantic and Pacific obtained title to relatively little indemnity land.

A problem closely related to the company's obtaining title to its grant was taxation. In 1886 Congress passed a law allowing states and territories to tax all surveyed land which railroads might claim within their grants whether or not they yet had obtained legal possession of it. The Atlantic and Pacific, fuming at such a law when faced with Sparks's delays in giving it title, decided to pay the taxes levied within the place limits but not on land in the indemnity. This proved generally acceptable although sometimes the road encountered difficulties because of an entirely separate controversy with counties over a levy on its right of way.[27] A few other relatively simple tax problems arose, such as Mohave County's attempt to assess unsurveyed acreage; this was at first mistakenly upheld on the remarkable reasoning that the decisions of the United States Supreme Court did not apply in the territories. In local newspapers of the grant area there were occasional protests about the company's taxes; usually these were directed against the government's failure to survey the land or involved the controversy over the right of way.

To handle all the problems arising under its grant the Atlantic

---

[26] *Land Decisions*, VIII, 373; XVII, 313.

[27] Williamson to Nutt, August 3, 1887, and March 9, 1888, TLB. The controversy centered around the interpretation of the 1866 act's clause which exempted the railroad right of way from taxation in the territories. Did this include all equipment and fixtures on that real estate? Yes, finally said the United States Supreme Court. (New Mexico v. United States Trust Company, 172 US 171.)

and Pacific early needed a competent specialist. It found him in James A. Williamson, commissioner of the United States General Land Office from 1876 to 1881. It appointed him in November 1881 to the dual position of railroad land commissioner and general solicitor; by 1892 his annual salary was $10,000. He at first divided his time about equally between his two jobs but after 1886 concentrated considerably on land activities. He resigned in 1894, certainly with anger and probably under compulsion caused by "age and infirmity." His successor, busy railroad attorney C. N. Sterry, entrusted the grant mostly to subordinates. Among Williamson's assistants for lengthy but varied terms were Thomas S. Sedgwick, previously active with the initial surveys to determine the road's precise route to the West; J. W. Donnelley, once chief of the Division of Accounts in the United States General Land Office; William F. Taliaferro, first an office boy in 1886 but eventually chief clerk; and C. H. Fancher, originally hired as an expert on timber. The railroad always maintained a land office in Albuquerque. At times Williamson's headquarters was also there; at other periods it was in Chicago, Boston, or Washington. Since the Western Division was in financial difficulties, correspondence between land department employees contains repeated reference to economies and occasional complaints about the difficulty of purchasing supplies on credit.

Williamson led the battles to prevent forfeiture of the grant adjacent to the uncompleted portion of the railroad, resisted Lamar's revoking the withdrawal of the indemnity strip, planned general strategy on claiming the land which the company had earned, and worried with the broad aspects of tax problems. At first his assistants concentrated on such routine chores as making up tract books containing the legal description of all the land the company had earned, yet claimed or not; quite correctly they boasted ". . . our books will be models of neatness and legibility. . . ." They tried to learn from government surveyors and other informed sources about the specific nature of the property and for about eighteen months employed a land examiner, but there was as yet no practical business reason why they should learn the details about all the grant. Their most important task was helping Williamson in his attempts to sell land, a problem so involved it requires a separate chapter.

CHAPTER IV

EARLY EFFORTS TO SELL THE LAND GRANT

THE Atlantic and Pacific made vigorous efforts to sell its land, but various circumstances prevented it from accomplishing satisfactory results. The famous winter of 1886–87, dealing a serious blow to the cattlemen of the Great Plains area, burst the bubble of unsound speculation so thoroughly that investors felt loath to put funds even into enterprises outside that area. Unaffected by the great blizzard, New Mexico and Arizona suffered much damage in the droughts of 1891, 1892, and 1893, whose climax coincided with the nation-wide financial panic of 1893. The possibilities of land sales were lessened when Congress in 1887 passed a law prohibiting aliens from owning land in the territories and forbidding any corporation, other than a railroad, from acquiring more than 5,000 acres.

The most serious handicap to sales was interlopers. Bolstered by traditional range rights and by their ability to prevent the territorial legislatures from passing any effective trespass laws, ranchers constantly used the company's land without hindrance. They obtained free pasturage and often prevented anybody else from attempting to use the region where they had located. They could, over the short term, obtain little additional benefit from leasing or purchasing railroad land, but would have assumed heavy fixed charges to pay for it. Few felt inclined to spend money for what during the immediate future they could certainly use gratis. Their attitude hamstrung the land department, but at least their presence pleased the railroad's traffic department.

When the company first built west from Isleta, there was very little livestock in the region, but by 1888 there were fully 150,000 head of cattle and a considerable number of sheep. Animals of both kinds increased annually until the whole range was overcrowded and the droughts of the early 1890's caused a reduction of 50 percent. This increase has been described by a pioneer cattleman as follows:

I well remember in 1885 the disgust which fell upon my own outfit, then located upon the Little Colorado River in northern Arizona, over the advent of a neighbor. Our nearest had been twenty-five miles distant and the newcomer had the temerity to turn loose 1,000 head of west Texas heifers at a point fully twenty miles above us. Our cattle seldom wandered more than five miles away from the rough camp where we had established ourselves. Between us and the new neighbor was an almost untouched stretch of grass land, and back of us lay a virgin country fifty miles wide with not a settler or domestic animal on it. Nevertheless, we felt much aggrieved at the nerve of the newcomer to crowd in on us in that fashion, and for several months there was hostile feeling between the two outfits. As the newcomer had been squeezed out of his Texas ranges by nesters, our lack of cordiality made no impression whatever upon him.

This was the beginning of the end of our delightful isolation, and we lived to see stockmen's cabins at every water hole and available location all over the country. Where we felt crowded by 2,000 cattle, 50,000 were hunting grass and water on the same range a few years later.[1]

Transporting livestock came to be an important source of revenue for the railroad. Sometimes the animals presented problems to the operating department, however, as illustrated in the following news item:

The wreck of the No. 3 westbound passenger train, which occurred about fourteen miles west of Winslow last Sunday, was a most disastrous one, considering the apparently trivial cause. That a common ordinary brindle bull, running before a rapidly moving train of cars, could derail half the string of coaches and smash the engine into smithreen [*sic*] seems almost miraculous, yet such was the case. And the most wonderful part of it all is that no one was serious[ly] injured.[2]

Since the railroad faced such a discouraging prospect for selling tracts to those already in the grant area, it sought purchasers living in other parts of the country. It insisted they should not buy without seeing the land and urged them to make inspection tours. It kept, between 1883 and 1889, a team and wagon which it moved by train to points where potential customers wished to start a free exploring trip. At first it was quite generous with passes, but in 1884 one group "so abused their privileges" that the company then required the purchase of half-fare tickets, the cost to be credited on any land purchase made. To sell its lands, the company at first followed the example of railroads holding grants to the east; it enrolled a considerable number of commission agents scattered in various parts of the United States. These it offered between 2 and 6 percent of the prices they secured. They produced only a single sale; this involved 75,000 acres of grazing land. In 1889 the railroad abruptly terminated all arrangements because it felt competition between various authorized agents caused it to lose an important timber sale.[3] It

[1] W. C. Barnes, *Western Grazing Grounds and Forest Ranges* (Chicago, 1913), p. 82.

[2] *Coconino Sun,* October 11, 1894.

[3] Williamson to A. H. Neidig, February 11, 1889, TLB.

then made five experiments by giving options for 6,000 to 350,000 acres of grazing land to various promoters who sought to peddle the tracts in the East. None of them were successful, perhaps because the railroad fixed its prices in these areas higher than those it charged elsewhere. The company's only land advertisements appeared in local newspapers strung from Albuquerque to Kingman and were discontinued in the middle of 1889. It issued a pamphlet describing its acreage in 1893, but apparently no copy has survived.

The railroad attempted to interest various British investors in its property, finding great difficulty in explaining to them such unfamiliar phenomena as alternate odd-numbered sections, surveying practices, and pre-emptions. It could not compete with the sales campaigns of those who peddled inexpensive Mexican land or those who offered acreage even cheaper since they had no title at all to the tracts they hawked. Williamson once summarized his efforts with the British in the following acid fashion:

My experience . . . in trying to do business with English and Scotch people has resulted only in their securing free transportation and board and on occasions wine, where they never had the slightest intention to purchase anything. It is one of the English-Scotch methods, so far as I know, of dead beating unsuspicious American property holders.[4]

Although the railroad sold most of its land for 50 or 75 cents an acre, its publicly announced price was never less than $1.00 and generally $1.25. The Atlantic and Pacific actually considered on their merits any offers received but took the precaution of inspecting the desired tract lest customers misrepresent what it was like. The company would not sell less than its land in a township because it did not wish to dispose of the choice tracts and have to retain indefinitely the undesirable ones. It would not sell any acreage in its indemnity strip until it actually held title from the government, but in its place limits would make sales on any tract which it might reasonably expect to obtain eventually. These rules were occasionally violated, but with no unfortunate results except in two indemnity land contracts. The company considered developing the water resources of its grazing land through wells, windmills, and dams, believing this work would increase marketability more than enough to repay the cost of construction. But funds to undertake such projects were never available.

The railroad used a standard form of contract for all sales. After extracts from the 1866 act, the first mortgage, and the second mortgage, the agreement contained a legal description of the land. It

[4] Williamson to L. W. Dennis, September 7, 1892, TLB.

exempted from sale the 100-foot right of way on either side of the track, the necessary station grounds, and whatever else might be useful "to protect the main line." Should the company, for reasons beyond its control, fail to provide a legal title, the contract was void. If the purchaser failed to make payments when stipulated, the railroad might secure all profits earned from the land after the default; if this continued for more than three months, all the remaining purchase price was due at once and the company might foreclose. The written contract ended with the land commissioner's certificate that the price was reasonable, the United States Trust Company's release of the acreage from the first mortgage, and the Mercantile Trust Company's release from the second.

The railroad's first sale, comprising most of the area on the south side of the track from Holbrook to Flagstaff, was for 1,000,000 acres at 50 cents each. The purchaser was the Aztec Land and Cattle Company. This corporation had been organized in 1884, shortly after the creation of the Kinsley Trust, by the Atchison and others interested in the Atlantic and Pacific.[5] It paid such a low price because the two parent railroads and the Seligmans forced the Atlantic and Pacific to raise the money due them. Although the Aztec bought 1,000,000 acres, its contract actually covered 1,059,560 acres with no extra charge for additional land. By 1894 it had received from the railroad deeds to 572,950.27 surveyed acres but had not yet secured title to 427,049.74 unsurveyed acres. It attempted to enforce a refund provision in the sales contract covering the undelivered land, but although an arbitrator decided in its favor the Atlantic and Pacific soon went bankrupt and the Aztec received no money. It then sought deeds to its land direct from the United States government and received most of them. It failed, however, to get possession of all the area it had purchased because the Atlantic and Pacific had not established a valid claim to some land in the indemnity strip.

The Aztec, promptly upon signing the sales agreement with the railroad, shipped in about 40,000 head of cattle and established a ranch generally known as the Hashknife outfit. It encountered many difficulties with trespassing stockmen who formerly had occupied the

[5] The capital stock of the Aztec, originally set at $963,100, was owned as follows: Atchison, $215,500; certain members of the Atchison Board of Directors, $200; J. & W. Seligman and Company, $241,000; some people connected with the Seligman firm, $4,000; and others (in large part Texas ranchers), $502,400. The Atchison in 1928 sold its Aztec stock, receiving over the years from its investment a final total of $233,780.25. It also made cash advances and purchased Aztec bonds, but on both these did not get all its money back. (W. E. Davis to Charles H. Woods, December 30, 1942, LCA 13490.)

range unmolested and resented the company's purchase of the odd-numbered sections within their traditional range. It was certainly at fault if the charge is true that it threatened death to anybody claiming even-numbered sections of government land in its area. The Aztec went into temporary bankruptcy about 1900, apparently the victim of wholesale cattle rustling. It then increasingly turned to selling off its land and about 1928 came under the domination of the New Mexico and Arizona Land Company.[6] The Aztec always was entirely independent of the department of the railroad which handled the railroad's New Mexico and Arizona land grant; hence it now virtually disappears from this history.

Next to the Aztec, the Atlantic and Pacific's most important sale was to Dr. E. B. Perrin, a sheepman and land speculator. By 1887 it had sold him a total of 258,873.08 acres around Flagstaff for 70 cents each. In the initial transaction, taking advantage of Kinsley's hastily drawn option, he selected an irregularly shaped tract which included the best land in the region and omitted the worst. Dissatisfied with the results of his bargaining, he twice surrendered portions of his purchase to the railroad and received in exchange acreage he believed more desirable; his proposal for a third swap was rejected. When a new land survey by the national government made changes in the legal description of the area, the railroad drew up a new contract to define correctly his property and obtained his signature only after great difficulty. At various times he asserted that he held an option to purchase additional land at 70 cents an acre and had been promised he could buy a valuable water supply, Supai Pond; but the company denied these claims. He grumbled about trespassers on the government land within his range and asserted, without ever submitting proof, that people were jumping his odd-numbered sections. He periodically made bitter complaints about land title, since the railroad had sold him acreage in the indemnity strip to which it had not yet established a right under the 1866 act, as well as to some unsurveyed land in its place limits. Land Commissioner Williamson always insisted that the difficulties involved in deeding Perrin these tracts had been fully explained before he signed his first contract. In any event, Perrin made prolonged arguments against his "unfair treatment" and refused to make his last payment of over $50,000 until the com-

---

[6] Decision, Edward Lauterback, September 26, 1894, records of the land commissioner stored at the Stationery Warehouse at Topeka (hereafter cited as TSW) 1109; "Cattle Grazers on Public Lands," *House Executive Documents,* 50th Cong., 1st sess., No. 232, pp. 22, 161; W. C. Barnes, *Apaches & Longhorns* (Los Angeles, 1941), pp. 130–31.

pany gave him title to the last acre. Meanwhile the Saginaw Lumber Company had purchased the railroad's rights to timber on some of Perrin's land, subject to a time limit. Discovering it could not complete work as rapidly as anticipated, it made his final payment for him in return for a twenty-five-year extension. In 1896 Perrin claimed he had overpaid $2,914.40; the railroad was so weary of his controversies and "very much vexatious correspondence" that it gave him some additional land. He, however, had not yet secured title to all his acreage, and, as we shall see later, argument continued into the 1920's.[7]

The Atlantic and Pacific made seven additional sales of grazing land totaling 252,760.17 acres. To the Arizona Cattle Company, partly owned by officers at Fort Wingate, it sold 121,490.65 acres at $1.00 each; to S. G. Little and Company, 75,748.99 acres for a net of 70 cents each; to the Cebolla Cattle Company, 41,592.19 acres at 50 cents; to Charles Zeiger, 11,528.34 acres at 80 cents; and to three others a total of 2,400 acres. With those not offering cash the railroad agreed to accept a quarter down and the rest in four equal annual payments with interest at 6 percent. Later it had to give several purchasers extensions but they eventually paid all that was due. The only serious difficulty arose over extracting a deed for the Little property from the red tape surrounding the Kinsley Trust; Williamson secured it only after writing plainly that he was tired of being called to his face "a swindler."[8]

The company clearly did not meet with much success in selling its grazing land. It disposed of 511,633.25 acres through its own efforts; it was forced to let the Aztec Land and Cattle Company have 1,000,000 acres at a low price; and finally it turned over to its two parents, to satisfy debts, 3,492,684.90 acres. Ostensibly the Atlantic and Pacific sold a total of 5,004,318.15 acres of grazing land, but the actual amount voluntarily placed under contract through the work of the land commissioner was about a tenth of that figure. Its comparative failure stemmed from trespassers, lack of water, difficulties over unsurveyed land, the droughts of the early 1890's, the severe winter in the Great Plains in 1886–87, and the financial panic of 1893.

Two other railroads attempting to sell the same type of arid land elsewhere also encountered difficulties. In Wyoming the Union Pacific tried unsuccessfully in 1883 to convince the United States it should

[7] Williamson to E. W. Kinsley, January 3, 1886; Williamson to Thomas De Witt Cuyler, February 11, 1889; Williamson to J. W. Donnelley, September 24, 1889; Williamson to William A. Bissell, January 17, 1894, TLB.

[8] Williamson to Kinsley, December 3, 1887, TLB.

give the company a solidified area on only one side of the tracks, or should allow joint sales of the property each owned, or should approve long-term grazing leases of government sections intermixed with railroad land. The company then launched a campaign to dispose of its tracts for about $1.00 an acre, with annual payments for ten years and interest at 6 percent. Many purchasers promptly erected fences to establish control over the intervening public domain.[9] Farther toward the border the Northern Pacific in 1882 sought to dispose of its grazing area quickly before trespassers overran all the region. It publicly refused to sell anything but large tracts including both good land and poor.

The Atlantic and Pacific, unable to persuade many ranchers to purchase its property, failed even more signally in its attempt to rent them grazing rights. In 1887 it announced that anybody using its acreage must take out a lease, but nobody did; under existing laws, the company could take no effective action against trespassers. In 1892 the railroad again attempted to interest renters but succeeded in making only one small lease for one year. After the turn of the century, as we shall see later, ranchers very gradually and with much reluctance began to rent railroad land.[10]

The company early faced the problem of whether to colonize farmers on its grant. The area was fertile enough but unless irrigated would almost never produce a profitable crop. At first Land Commissioner Williamson refused to "take the responsibility of inducing persons of little means" to undertake such a doubtful venture as farming arid lands. In 1888 he persuaded himself that in some areas agriculturalists could grow crops without irrigation. He encouraged them but never launched a colonization campaign such as those the land-grant railroads to the east used. By 1895 the Atlantic and Pacific had sold 4,000 acres of alleged agricultural land at prices from $2.50 to $8.00 an acre; likely very little of it could actually be dry-farmed.

Irrigation offered real prospects of success, but the railroad never made a systematic engineering survey to find possible locations for such projects. Though nine places seemed obviously suitable, it lacked the capital necessary for the undertakings. Two promoters, J. E. Saint and S. M. Folsom of Albuquerque, devoted much effort to a scheme involving the railroad land adjacent to the Little Colorado River near Winslow but failed to interest financiers. Williamson himself finally undertook a project in 1894 at the most promising location, along

---

[9] E. S. Osgood, *The Day of the Cattleman* (Minneapolis, 1929), pp. 210–14.

[10] *Arizona Champion,* July 9, 1887; C. H. Fancher to Williamson, September 6, 1892, TLB. The rental proposed in 1892 was 2 cents an acre annually.

the Colorado River in western Arizona, but could not raise the necessary capital. W. E. Pedley actually completed a small dam near Prescott, whether primarily for irrigation or livestock is not clear; but at any rate it washed out almost at once and was never rebuilt. The railroad itself spent a considerable amount of money on a less expensive type of development, artesian wells, but even today nobody has ever obtained water from such a source in the grant area.[11]

The company sought town lot buyers as eagerly as it did farmers and ranchers. In 1882 Williamson, doubtless thinking of the profitable experience of some other lines, declared that all villages must be located on the corporation's odd-numbered sections if they expected any railroad service.[12] He never carried out this threat and some towns arose on government land. The Atlantic and Pacific established Ash Fork, Williams, Winslow, and Gallup, as well as making an extensive addition to the older city of Flagstaff. It charged from $25 to $250 a lot, most prices being near the lower end of the scale. There are no records remaining to indicate the volume of sales, except the comment that in 1888 its gross income from urban property was $10,791.84.[13] It handled sales from the Albuquerque office and, until 1893, also through local part-time representatives. It donated some lots for schools and churches. In the early days especially it had considerable difficulty with people building on its property and then absolutely refusing to purchase, which forced it to take legal action against them. About one case Williamson received the following report:

. . .[He] has two houses on the lots, one occupied as a saloon and the other by a house of ill-repute and I have tried frequently to get him to buy them and, failing in that, have exhausted every remedy short of suit, to have him remove his buildings. No one would buy them, although the lots have been offered to a number of people. The character of the two houses is of the worst and has given the neighborhood a very bad reputation.[14]

In 1888 fire destroyed all of Holbrook, a town laid out on an even-numbered section, and Williamson proposed moving the depot a half-mile to a railroad odd-numbered section. This, he said, would either inflict much inconvenience on the townsmen or, more likely, force them to purchase lots at the company's new site.[15] Fortunately

[11] Williamson to Oliver D. Cram, January 2, 1892, TLB.
[12] Williamson to T. S. Sedgwick, February 14 and March 11, 1882, TLB.
[13] Williamson to F. E. Hancock (1889), TLB.
[14] Donnelley to Williamson, January 31, 1891, TLB.
[15] Williamson to Nutt, July 17, 1888, TLB.

for the good reputation of the Atlantic and Pacific, his scheme appealed neither to his superiors nor to his colleagues in the operating department. Otherwise he handled town development wisely and obtained a reasonable profit for the company.

The railroad profited by selling timber from its rural property. Its first customer was Edward E. Ayer, an important lumberman in Chicago, who erected a large mill in Flagstaff and started cutting trees on company land shortly before the railroad was completed to that point. Late in 1883 he paid the railroad $27,440.89 for timber chopped under an oral understanding and signed a contract for the trees on 77 of the company's sections in that region. At this time he was selling about 75 percent of his finished product to the Mexican Central Railroad, 10 percent to the Atlantic and Pacific, and 15 percent to the general public. In 1886 he signed a contract covering 84 additional sections. He shortly sold his Ayer Lumber Company to its local managers, the Riordan brothers, who renamed it the Arizona Lumber Company. In 1887 the railroad made a new agreement covering 853 sections in either the original areas or sundry additional tracts. The Arizona Lumber Company, combining these areas with others covered in contracts it was making with the Aztec Land and Cattle Company and the Arizona Cattle Company, now had a timber monopoly of the Flagstaff region. In 1892 the Atlantic and Pacific flatly canceled this large agreement. Three years later the company sold the Arizona Lumber Company the timber on 26 sections and this contract was never altered. Obviously the timber outfit cut a considerable number of trees on railroad land, but surviving records do not indicate the quantity actually removed or how much the Atlantic and Pacific received for it.

As early as 1887 the railroad had received reports that the Arizona Lumber Company was using improper lumbering methods. The company had also chopped 12,847 crossties out of 9 sections not covered in any purchase contract. By 1892 the firm's conduct left railroad authorities with few illusions. It did not report the full number of trees cut from railroad land until the Atlantic and Pacific hired an expert who inspected the mills and kept a correct tally. It grossly violated its promise to fell all the merchantable timber on any given group of sections before going on to the next. It went wherever it wished, cutting the choice trees and pretending it had taken everything of any value; actually it left, sometimes standing and sometimes rotting on the ground, a considerable amount that could have been marketed. It thus slashed and destroyed almost as much as it paid for; yet there remained enough timber on its "completed" areas for other lumbermen to make offers to purchase the wood.[16]

Although the Arizona Lumber Company was the Atlantic and Pacific's most important customer for timber, the railroad also marketed forest property to others. In 1888 it sold the trees on 120,000 Arizona acres to the Arizona Cattle Company, which had already purchased the grazing land there, for $20,000. In 1892 it disposed of the timber on 199,439.33 acres around Williams to the Saginaw Lumber Company for $75,000. Part of the actual land belonged to Perrin, and the purchasers paid off his debt to the railroad in return for a twenty-five-year extension on the time within which they must cut the trees. In 1896 the railroad sold the lumber on 9 sections to J. M. Dennis and on 16 to Greenlaw Brothers, at $1.25 per thousand feet of timber cut. In all the last three transactions the railroad agreed to accept finished lumber products in lieu of cash. It made one contract for New Mexico forest property, in 1890 selling both 314,668.37 acres of land and the timber on it to Mitchell Brothers for a total price of $1.425 an acre. The railroad sold a small amount of firewood, generally where lumbering operations had already been completed, at 25 cents a cord. Somewhat related to these activities was a unique sale, that of petrified wood on 1,860 acres at $2.00 a ton; there is no record of how much was actually removed.[17]

The railroad, diligent in disposing of its timber resources, preferred not to develop its coal property at Gallup. It wished to keep this in reserve since operators on the even-numbered sections produced more than enough to meet the current demand. Three mines removed coal from railroad acreage, apparently in deliberate attempts at theft, but the company forced them to stop and to pay it a royalty of 12.5 cents a ton for what they had already stolen.

The Atlantic and Pacific experienced difficulties in selling its assets in the land grant to advantage. Its officials seem to have done all possible under the circumstances, but the profits were small at a time when the struggling company needed additional income badly. Including forced "sales" to its parents, it secured a total net profit from the grant of $3,853,336.17. The substantial profits from the acreage came to the Atchison after its subsidiary went bankrupt.

[16] Donnelley to Sedgwick, September 23, 1887; Williamson to Fancher, January 5, 1892; Williamson to Manvel, February 20, 1892, TLB.

[17] Telegram, Donnelley to Williamson, May 1, 1888, TLB; contracts, A&P RR Co. with Greenlaw Brothers, August 13, 1896, and with J. M. Dennis, October 15, 1896, and with F. A. Trittle, January 22, 1887, and with E. B. Perrin and the Saginaw Lumber Company, January 5, 1894, LCA A&P Document Box No. 2.

CHAPTER V

THE FOREST LIEU LAND EXCHANGE

THE Atlantic and Pacific went bankrupt in 1894; so did the Atchison and the Frisco. When these two had been reorganized, they divided up their subsidiary. The Frisco took for itself the trackage in Oklahoma. The Atchison in 1897 secured the property from Isleta to Needles and had already created a new subsidiary, the Santa Fe Pacific Railroad, to manage the acquisition. The fledgling corporation needed a federal charter and sought it from Congress. During the debate in the House of Representatives, H. Henry Powers of Vermont, who favored the desired bill, charged that W. E. Barrett of Massachusetts was acting for security holders of some enterprise antagonistic to the Santa Fe Pacific. He sneered that the Bay State had furnished Webster, Sumner, and the two Presidents Adams, all of whom were dead, and now Barrett had come to shed his light in Congress. "He was born, Mr. Speaker, to be a rose, with the destiny of blooming and blushing upon this floor, but his fate has been to wither and waste his beauty on a desert air." Barrett bitingly replied, "I trust I shall never serve so long as to try to cover up a bad case by an attempt at ridicule of a new member who is trying to do his duty." He declared that Powers was a member of the Vermont Supreme Court during the time its decision wrecked the Central Vermont Railroad and that the matter was ". . . about the biggest stench in the nostrils of honest men ever recorded in this country."[1] Despite these recriminations, the measure was passed with little debate.

The newly incorporated Santa Fe Pacific operated the Isleta-Needles railroad line, handled that portion of the adjacent land grant to which the Atlantic and Pacific had always retained title, and also managed, as agent for the Atchison, the so-called Frost acreage which the parent company had previously acquired. It treated these two parts of the grant as an inseparable unit except for accounting purposes. By 1944 all practical reasons for keeping separate books on the two had long since vanished, and the railroad land commissioner persuaded the Atchison, which would eventually receive all the profits anyhow, to relinquish all further revenue from the remaining Frost land to its subsidiary.[2] The land department's chief clerk was so delighted

---

[1] *Congressional Record*, 54th Cong., 2d sess., pp. 1331–32.

[2] Memorandum, F. G. Gurley to R. G. Rydin and W. E. Davis, October 29, 1944, LCA 8757.

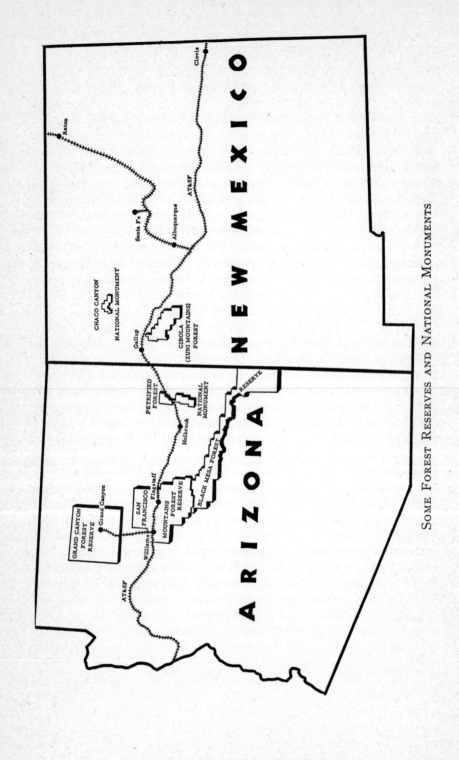

Some Forest Reserves and National Monuments

with this elimination of red tape that she gave the staff a celebration dinner at Albuquerque's leading hotel.

In 1903 the Atchison attempted to eliminate the Santa Fe Pacific Railroad, operating the railway line in its own name and deeding the grant over to a new subsidiary named the Santa Fe Pacific Development Company. This new corporation functioned less than a year, chiefly because the United States General Land Office feared it might not complete an exchange of forest land already in progress.[3] The development company deeded back the grant to the Santa Fe Pacific Railroad, which despite its title has ever since remained merely a land management subsidiary.

When the Santa Fe Pacific first took responsibility for the grant, it could not have sold the entire area even at 50 cents an acre. It first placed management of the property in the hands of A. P. Maginnis, who as Atchison Tax Commissioner in Los Angeles had a variety of tasks. His two important acts were to commence the campaign to exchange forest land with the national government and to help secure rejection of the offer made by a man named Addicks to purchase the entire grant for half a million dollars.

In 1901 Maginnis relinquished management of the grant to the first official land commissioner the Santa Fe Pacific had, Howel Jones. Jones held the position until his sudden death from a heart attack in 1928 at the age of eighty-four. Jones in 1872 hung out his shingle as an attorney in Topeka. Concentrating on land law, he became an expert; in his region of Kansas, Jones's ability to clear title within twenty-four hours in all but the most complicated cases was well known. He read a great deal, the material ranging from a detailed study of the Roman soldier to Nick Carter detective stories. For a time he conducted a Sunday morning class in Shakespeare. Jones was first employed by the Atchison prior to 1880 in certain law suits, and his success in untangling knotty legal problems favorably impressed high company officials. In 1900 he was elected to the Board of Directors and served until his death. There is an entertaining tradition that he opposed Addicks' offer to buy the grant, claiming even he could make more than half a million dollars out of it, and that he talked so much the other directors challenged him to try. However that may be, once Jones had become land commissioner he wanted "to die in harness," and the company valued his services enough in 1920 to increase his annual salary to $9,000. Since he was also a member of the Board of Directors, other company officials interfered little with

[3] J. H. Frimple to the Secretary of the Interior, February 13, 1904, TSW 552.

his handling of the grant although he was under the supervision of W. B. Jansen until 1910 and then of Edward J. Engel. Jones established the land office in his home town, Topeka, rather than in New Mexico or Arizona. Since he concentrated during the early years on the land scrip business, which could easily be carried on by mail, this location was a suitable one.[4]

Jones was ably assisted by William F. Taliaferro, chief clerk from 1901 until his death in 1926.[5] To "Tally" fell the chief responsibility for handling taxes and the mechanics of land selection. He had started as an office boy under Williamson in 1886, from the first making a special effort to understand and remember transactions about the grant. His knowledge of the details of the business is reported to have been considerably greater than Jones's. It is impossible to determine just how much credit should go to Taliaferro for the success of Jones's administration, since he always acted in the name of his chief, but there is no doubt he was a valuable man.

Much of the legal business connected with the grant lands was handled in Washington by the law firm of Britton and Gray. It had performed a similar service for the Atlantic and Pacific, starting in 1880, and its sole surviving partner, Lawrence Cake, now under his own name still represents the Santa Fe Pacific in certain matters. The firm for many years specialized in land law, numbering the Northern Pacific and the Missouri Kansas and Texas among its regular clients. It ably handled special cases before the Washington law courts for the Santa Fe Pacific and was equally valuable in seeing routine business through Department of the Interior channels.

The railroad's first important profits from the grant came through its forest lieu land exchanges. The background for these lay in the many changes in land policy made by the national government during the administrations of Cleveland, Harrison, and Theodore Roosevelt. For the first time, the United States devoted much attention to the conservation of forest resources. Congress took the initial step in 1891 by authorizing the President to set aside permanent forest reservations. Fifteen reserves in western states, totaling about thirteen million acres, were established within three years. Cleveland, in the fall of 1893, refused to proclaim any more because there were no laws then existent to give any protection to those already founded. The matter drifted for three years, until the Secretary of the Interior called

---

[4] *Topeka State Journal*, April 7, 1928; J. R. Hubbard to author, February 14, 1942; interviews with M. H. Balch and C. B. McClelland, April 15, 1946; LCA 11670, *passim.*

[5] TSW 11227, *passim.*

upon the National Academy of Sciences to recommend changes in the nation's forest policy. The academy appointed a commission of six, whose tour of the West resulted in the establishment of thirteen additional reserves containing over twenty-one million acres. The proclamations were issued so abruptly as to be unfair to those in the region. Westerners, either actually injured by the hasty action or else hampered in their plans to exploit the public domain, presented strong opposition. Congress, debating the matter during two sessions held in 1897, finally changed the effective date of the proclamation to March 1, 1898.

An important section of the act making this alteration concerned lieu lands and read as follows:

That in cases in which a tract covered by an unperfected bona fide claim or by a patent is included within the limits of a public forest reservation, the settler or owner thereof may, if he desires to do so, relinquish the tract to the Government, and may select in lieu thereof a tract of vacant land open to settlement not exceeding the area of the tract covered by his claim or patent. . . .[6]

This lieu land provision, explained in all the congressional debates as merely aiding the small settler, actually benefited much more the railroads which had previously received land grants within the areas where forest reserves were established. It clearly authorized all who surrendered acreage to select in lieu any other federal land, regardless of value.[7] Years later politicians declared a corporate lobby pushed through this section of the act; if so, there is no written evidence to demonstrate the fact.[8] However that may be, speculators quickly realized that the law gave them a means to acquire valuable public domain at relatively small cost. The net result proved the various exchanges were disadvantageous to the government and in 1905 Congress tardily forbade any more.

Within the area of the Atlantic and Pacific land grant were forests the government desired. In 1893 President Harrison established the Grand Canyon Forest Reserve, close to the scenic wonder of that name,

[6] *Statutes-at-Large*, XXX, 36.

[7] *Congressional Record*, 55th Cong., 1st sess., pp. 899–902, 908–25, 962–71.

[8] If there was a lobby, the chief corporation discussed in this history, the Santa Fe Pacific, did not belong to it. The company could not take advantage of the act until its forest lands were surveyed. At the time there was no way to force a survey. In 1899 Congress passed an act saying that if a land-grant railroad paid in advance half the cost, the government would make the survey. Santa Fe Pacific officials did not learn the law existed until a private attorney called it to their attention. Had they been lobbying for the 1897 act, they certainly would have been actively seeking a law similar to that of 1899.

in a solid body without giving any consideration to the railroad's prior claim to the odd-numbered sections. In 1898 President McKinley acted differently. When he established the San Francisco Mountains Forest Reserve, near Flagstaff, Arizona, he included only the even-numbered sections. He had been advised by Binger Hermann, commissioner of the General Land Office, to exclude the odd-numbered sections owned either by the Santa Fe Pacific or those to whom the Atlantic and Pacific had sold land, and thus to prevent them from ever proposing a lieu exchange.[9]

Unfortunately the checkerboarded, unsurveyed San Francisco Mountains reserve proved to be a serious problem to the government and the various property owners. No lumber company could afford to log only the private property. The United States could not successfully administer its forest according to scientific principles because the intermixed patches were managed altogether differently. Nobody could graze sheep or cattle on only the even- or the odd-numbered sections unless fences were built. But fencing was economically prohibitive and, unless all the owners agreed, would likely have been an illegal enclosure of public or private property. The fundamental difficulty was that a single section was an economic absurdity in a region where it required thirty to forty acres to nourish one cow for a year.

To solve these problems, as early as 1899 the federal superintendent of the reserve recommended at least partially eliminating railroad land through an exchange. About the same time the Santa Fe Pacific attempted to obtain lieu rights under the 1897 act but, as its lawyers forewarned, failed because McKinley had literally established 1,502 separate reserves on even-numbered sections and none on the company's odd-numbered sections.[10] The company learned at this time of a new law enabling railroads to secure a survey of whatever portions of their land grant they desired by depositing half the estimated total cost with the national government; it promptly made such arrangements for the Grand Canyon Forest Reserve.

Soon an acrimonious discussion, at first entirely independent of the lieu lands proposal, arose over the grazing of sheep in the San Francisco Mountains Forest Reserve. Those who opposed such grazing included these groups: farmers in the Salt River Valley of southern Arizona, who believed it injured their watershed enough to reduce their irrigation supply; canal companies in the valley, who were

---

[9] *Statutes-at-Large*, XXVII, 1064; XXX, 1781; "San Francisco Mountains Forest Reserve," *House Documents*, 59th Cong., 1st sess., No. 613, pp. 2-3.
[10] "San Francisco Mountains Forest Reserve," *loc. cit.*, p. 4; *Land Decisions*, XXI, 597.

charged by some with selling water rights greatly in excess of what was available; cattlemen in the north, who coveted all the grass in the reserve for themselves; cattlemen in the south, who saw northern shepherds trespass on their unofficial range rights during the winter months; reformers honestly interested in timber preservation, who believed sheep damaged the forest; and a rich sheepman, Dr. E. B. Perrin, who apparently hoped to get all sheep but his own excluded from the reserve since he owned some of the odd-numbered sections.[11] The Arizona Wool Growers' Association with great vigor championed the right of its members to use the reserve. The controversy was but one of many regarding sheep and forest reserves in the Far West. In this particular discussion, the Secretary of the Interior in 1900 and 1901 decided to allow only a limited number of sheep in the San Francisco Mountains reserve.[12]

Meanwhile, in 1900 the Santa Fe Pacific and other private owners within the reserve sought to solve the difficult problem of checkerboarded land by requesting the United States to acquire their odd-numbered sections and as payment give them lieu rights under the 1897 law. They conducted their negotiations orally in Washington. There is no way of knowing whether, at this time, they discussed the problem of sheep grazing. While requesting regular lieu rights, good anywhere, for most of their land, they agreed that in payment for some unwooded tracts they would accept 180,000 acres of restricted rights, good only on untimbered, nonmineral land located south of the Tehachapi range and the 37th standard parallel.[13]

The proclamation extending the reserve over the odd-numbered sections had actually been prepared for the President's signature when opposition arose. The citizens of Coconino County in northern Arizona, where the reserve was located, held a mass meeting and sent a delegation to Washington to protest. The railroad's attorneys in the capital at once telegraphed that the Salt River Valley advocates of the extension ought also to call a mass meeting and hurry representatives east.[14] This they did. Whether they would have without prompting is a question.

[11] N. O. Murphy to E. A. Hitchcock, March 15, 1900, NA L&R Div. Files, Letters Received No. 589; *Coconino Sun*, March 3, 1900.

[12] E. S. Gosney, "The Arizona Wool Growers' Association, 1898–1909," MS deposited with the Arizona Pioneers' Historical Society, Tucson, Arizona, pp. 12–13.

[13] E. D. Kenna and E. B. Perrin to Hitchcock, January 11, 1901, marked approved by Hitchcock; memorandum of agreement between the Santa Fe Pacific Railroad Co., William F. Baker, E. B. Perrin, Robert Perrin, and the Aztec Land and Cattle Co., January 11, 1901, TSW B-SF.

[14] Telegram, Britton and Gray (hereafter cited as B&G) to A. P. Maginnis, January 24, 1901, TSW B-SF.

At a hearing in Washington in February 1901, the two delegations presented their views to the Secretary of the Interior, the commissioner of the General Land Office, and the chief of the Lands and Railroad Division of the Department of the Interior. It is not clear to what extent the men represented the actual opinion of their respective regions and how much they were merely presenting the case for interested parties. The views of the Salt River Valley contingent, from the irrigated regions of southern Arizona, were helpful to the owners of the property within the reserve, while those of the Coconino County group, from the north, were an aid to the sheepmen. The northern men declared that the removal of so much property from the tax rolls would increase threefold the burden on the remainder and alleged that the livestock industry, totally excluded from the reserve, would be cut in half. The southern men pictured the reserve as vital protection for the water supply of 150,000 acres actually and 250,000 additional acres potentially under irrigation; they attributed the decreased water supply to sheep grazing in the forest area and did not mention the general drought in the state. Railroad attorney Alexander Britton pointed out that owners of private land within the reserve would be surrendering their "virtual monopoly" of timber land in the Southwest. Of course, each speaker sought to refute the assertions of his opponents.[15]

The northern men, returning home, complained to Secretary of the Interior E. A. Hitchcock that some of the land would be released subject to the right to cut the timber off it. This startled him into demanding an explanation from the owners and announcing that negotiations must start again from the beginning. Surprised in turn, they pointed out that they had clearly stated their plan both orally and in writing. Railroad officials assured each other that if blame for the misunderstanding belonged to anybody, it belonged to the government. Hitchcock admitted he had not read all the written material given him but insisted the owners had been unfair. With such a condition attached, he vowed never to approve the exchange.[16] This misunderstanding created a delicate state of affairs in Washington. Dr. E. B. Perrin, one of the owners, made the situation worse; for in his overanxiety to secure approval he had almost daily interviews with Hitchcock's subordinates, who grew so weary of him they felt the easiest solution would be to revoke entirely the reserve already existing. The Secretary flatly refused to see him further.[17]

[15] "San Francisco Mountains Forest Reserve," *loc. cit.*, pp. 20–72.
[16] Maginnis to Jones, April 10, 1901; B&G to Kenna, June 4, 1901, TSW B-SF.
[17] B&G to Kenna, April 20, 1901, TSW B-SF.

Negotiations dragged along. Hitchcock made the vital point regarding irrigation in southern Arizona that three-quarters of the forest area tilted northward and nobody could prove the direction of underground drainage.[18] In November 1901 the railroad expressed willingness to release certain land, subject not to an unqualified right to cut the timber but instead to modified Forest Service rules. The Secretary complained the regulations were so "modified" they would be useless and declared he had little further interest in the proposed exchange.[19] Shortly thereafter, the director of the United States Geological Survey completed an examination of the reserve. He advocated enlarging it and excluding sheep from only the relatively small portion sloping toward the south, but pointed out that most of the damage to the irrigation canals came from silt originating elsewhere.[20]

The railroad and other landowners by this time were discouraged and were on the point of abandoning their efforts, when suddenly they achieved victory. First, certain friends of Perrin talked with Theodore Roosevelt. Then W. J. Murphy, of the southern Arizona irrigation interests, and others secured an interview with the President at which Hitchcock and his subordinate, Judge Vandevanter, were ordered to appear. Hitchcock, naturally resentful at the order to bring Vandevanter, offered various objections to the exchange, but one by one these were overruled. At the end of the long and somewhat bitter conference, Roosevelt declared the Secretary would probably see his way clear to enlarging the reserve to include the odd-numbered sections. The owners, realizing Hitchcock would feel humiliated at the outcome of the interview and would hardly wish to exert himself unduly to bring about the exchange, drafted a letter stating their position so clearly that if the Secretary had raised further objections, they could easily have proved to Roosevelt they had kept their part of the agreement. When the owners' representative first presented the letter to Hitchcock he promptly stated that it did not in any way represent the understanding reached at the conference, but upon reading it more closely he withdrew his accusation and promised to consider the matter further.[21]

With very minor alterations, he then accepted the proposal, and on April 12, 1902, the President signed the proclamation enlarging

---

[18] Hitchcock to A. B. Leach, July 2, 1901, NA L&R Div. Letter Book No. 442.

[19] Hitchcock to Kenna, November 7, 1901, TSW B-SF.

[20] Charles Walcott to the Secretary of the Interior, November 25, 1901, NA L&R Div. Letter Book No. 3239.

[21] B&G to Kenna, January 4, 1902, TSW B-SF.

the reserve. The agreement between the owners and the government enumerated how much acreage was to be exchanged, how much was still to be cut over, and how much of the lieu rights were to be of restricted type rather than good anywhere.[22] It was as follows:

Name of owner	Deeded to the United States, acres	Retained the right to log, acres	Accepted in restricted lieu, acres
Aztec Land and Cattle Co. . . .	132,000	—	28,600
Saginaw and Manistee Lumber Co.	40,720	31,960	—
William F. Baker	79,296	—	17,600
Perrin Brothers	134,000	48,500	32,120
Santa Fe Pacific	552,358	45,000	146,680
Total	938,374	125,460	225,000

The private owners had promised that as soon as the President issued his proclamation they would exclude all sheep from the forest area. When the sheepmen heard of this, consternation prevailed. They sent a two-man delegation from Coconino County to see Roosevelt, who pounded the desk with his fist to emphasize that no further sheep grazing would be allowed. A few days later Gifford Pinchot persuaded him to reverse his position. Ever since, sheep have been permitted in the reserve.[23]

While busy with other owners arranging the San Francisco Mountains transaction, the Santa Fe Pacific did not neglect the area where it was sole private owner, the Grand Canyon reserve. Since this was the region where Harrison in 1893 had proclaimed the forest over both the even- and odd-numbered sections, it regarded this exchange as virtually automatic. To its surprise, some people in Coconino County, probably as a flanking movement on the San Francisco Mountains proposal, protested the Grand Canyon project. Hitchcock, reconsidering in 1901, decided that since the greater part of the railroad property was not timbered, the unwooded parts should be eliminated from the reserve. Railroad officials, having paid over $50,000 in surveying fees to the government in the faith they could make the exchange, considered this stoppage of the transaction "most reprehensible."[24] The matter dragged until the following year. Although the company believed there was no more than 50,000 acres of mer-

[22] "San Francisco Mountains Forest Reserve," *loc. cit.*, pp. 8–12; "Contracts in Forest Reserve Timber Lands," *Senate Documents*, 61st Cong., 2d sess., No. 612, p. 22.
[23] Gosney, *loc. cit.*, p. 23.
[24] Kenna to Jones, December 9, 1901, TSW B-SF.

chantable timber standing in the reserve, the government apparently thought there was more and made no effort to have a timber cruiser actually appraise the situation. Hitchcock finally agreed to give the railroad for its 375,000 acres of Grand Canyon land 260,000 acres in the same kind of restricted rights previously given in the San Francisco Mountains reserve and 115,000 acres of unrestricted scrip.[25] If the railroad figures of 50,000 acres of merchantable timber were correct, then the Secretary of the Interior paid it handsomely when he gave 115,000 acres of unrestricted scrip good on wooded land anywhere in the public domain.

In relinquishing the land to the United States, the company first deposited with the government half the cost of surveying the area, since it claimed half the land. When this task was completed, the railroad could identify individual sections and for the first time since the passage of the 1866 granting act was in a position to make formal demand for full legal title to specifically described acreage. This it did and the United States conveyed title by a land patent to the Santa Fe Pacific. Once this was done, and in theory as an entirely different transaction, the railroad deeded title back to the government, submitting an abstract to show the property free of unpaid taxes or other lien. When these documents were accepted, the Santa Fe Pacific received in payment the right to select lieu land from the remaining public domain. It had to use the restricted rights in the designated area but could apply the unrestricted anywhere in the United States.

In exercising lieu rights the railroad sometimes took acreage for itself but generally sold the privilege to another. To enable the buyer to select the tract he wished, the company issued a document called "scrip." In this scrip the Santa Fe Pacific recited that it had previously surrendered to the United States a specifically described parcel of land and that it authorized the purchaser as the railroad's so-called attorney in fact to exercise its lieu right. It left the space for the name of the purchaser blank and as soon as the proper company official signed the scrip, anyone could use it. The railroad issued scrip in denominations of forty acres, which was the smallest legal subdivision of land, or in multiples thereof. Sometimes the attorney in fact made a selection which the local United States Land Office disallowed. He could then appeal the decision to the General Land Office in Washington, to the Secretary of the Interior, and finally to the courts. In making his protest, he acted under the name of the Santa Fe Pacific but had to bear the burden of proofs and the cost entirely himself. When a selection

[25] B&G to Jones, July 2, 1903, TSW 530.

was approved, the United States issued the railroad a land patent for the acreage and the company deeded the tract to the original purchaser of the scrip. Since lieu rights generally changed hands several times before being used, the corporation placed on those who had handled it the responsibility for seeing that title finally came to rest in the proper person. It hoped the deed would actually be transferred through each intermediary, thus protecting everybody and leaving a clear legal trail.

The first step in the routine of land exchange, obviously, was to have the land surveyed. Various difficulties made vexatious delays. Some of them were easily solved, such as those of the surveyor who ". . . bucked on [the] quality [of the] water the company furnish[ed him] from Williams Dam. Claims impossible for any white man to use it."[26] Others were more difficult, such as correlating this new work with earlier adjacent surveys either executed in careless fashion or fraudulently run while the surveyor was "seated on some hotel porch." There was generally little difficulty in gaining access to sections which the railroad wished surveyed, but W. O. Secor undertook work in especially difficult terrain and once reported as follows concerning it:

On July 31 [1902] we moved camp to a sec. . . . which is as far south as a wagon can go; then packed our bed and grub on horses . . . making a detour of about eight miles [en route and then camped]. After working for two days from that camp, we packed, each man, a single blanket and a little grub on our back [going] off the rim and down the can[y]on about four miles. This was necessary in order to do even four or five hours work a day.

There are but few places where it is possible for a good mountain climber to pass over the Rim, and it oftentimes requires three or four hours to reach our work which may be but a mile or two distant.

Our lines thus far have been composed of distances mostly vertical, and, in order to avoid the back-breaking walks to and from work we have spent two nights away from any camp, without even a blanket, and for food but a few hard tack and cans of corned beef. If the company wants its scenic artist to earn his salary he could accompany me a week down here.[27]

[26] Telegram, W. G. Navin to I. L. Hibbard, November 3, 1900, TSW A-GC.

[27] W. O. Secor to Jones, August 11, 1902, TSW B-SF. The Santa Fe Pacific aided all the surveying parties by giving them passes from their headquarters in New Mexico, Arizona, or California to the site of their work and return. During these years, of course, all railroads distributed such favors widely. A member of one of the parties, Sheridan Downey, planned to enter the law school at the University of Michigan but was hard pressed financially. Jones, as a special courtesy, arranged for him to travel over the Atchison on a pass and also gave him some free advice on how to be a successful lawyer. It is not clear from the railroad files whether the young man heeded Jones's injunctions but he did become a United States senator.

Impatient at these delays in surveying, the railroad took what steps it could to hasten the routine process of exchange and lieu land selection. In 1902 its Washington attorneys were insisting they had allowed nothing in the capital to follow the normal Department of the Interior routine, but had arranged for handling of everything "special." They even furnished some good cigars to clerks who performed the mechanical job of preparing land patents.[28]

Much more important was the possibility that the 1897 law authorizing lieu land exchanges might be repealed. In 1902 Railroad Land Commissioner Howel Jones was so alarmed that he wired three congressmen to watch closely all appropriation bills to which might be tacked an amendment curtailing the right to exchange lands. The crucial struggle started in 1904. Atchison President E. P. Ripley urged Jones to consult Henry E. Tainer, whom he described as potent in the Connecticut councils of the Republican party and probably able to put the landman in touch with Orville H. Platt, an influential senator from that state. Representative F. W. Mondell of Wyoming introduced the bill Jones most feared. Just exactly what happened is not clear, but by March 1904 it was understood that the Arizona forests would be exempted from the proposed repeal. Although passed by the House, the bill died in the Senate Committee on Public Lands.[29] The measure was debated again in 1905. Representative J. F. Lacey of Iowa defended lieu rights as the best solution to the troublesome problem of checkerboard land ownership. Representative John Lind of Minnesota pointed to the Santa Fe Pacific as especially benefited in the exchanges, explaining this as merely poor judgment. Congress finally decided to prohibit making any more exchanges unless the government had completed the arrangements prior to March 3, 1905.[30] Actually, this exempted only the San Francisco Mountains, Grand Canyon, and Santa Barbara, California, reserves. The Santa Fe Pacific was the chief beneficiary of this proviso, but it might not have been had it made no effort to protect its own interests.

The railroad at various times encountered lesser difficulties with the government. Some Department of the Interior officials asserted the 1905 repeal act revoked the Santa Fe Pacific's existing exchange rights, but the Secretary finally overruled their interpretation of the law. Another problem was whether the railroad must actually designate specific acreage with all its restricted lieu rights before it could

[28] B&G to Jones, August 6, 1902, TSW 107, and October 24, 1902, TSW 14.
[29] E. P. Ripley to Jones, March 1, 1904, TSW 385; *Congressional Record*, 58th Cong., 2d sess., pp. 4078, 5586, 5816.
[30] *Congressional Record*, 58th Cong., 3d sess., 3602, 3825, 3875, 4034-37.

make any selections with the unrestricted. After two months the government decided that if the Santa Fe Pacific merely surrendered to the United States all land to be paid for in restricted lieu, it might then make selections with both types of rights at its leisure. The company found itself in difficulty when the loggers, working on land it had surrendered subject to a right to cut the timber, failed to follow government regulations; the Santa Fe Pacific forced them to conform. The company and the United States quarreled for seven years over the retention of "Jack Smith" springs for railroad operating purposes; the railroad won.

Despite these disagreements, the Santa Fe Pacific relinquished its land as rapidly as possible to the government. It was faced with the problem of what to do with the lieu rights it had received for a total of 927,358 acres. Although retaining 16,150 acres for townsites, operating purposes, and a tie reserve, the railroad sold the great bulk of its scrip. Its first important sale was 205,001 acres of restricted rights at $1.50 an acre to J. J. Hagerman, a rancher who proceeded to select a solidified range near Roswell, New Mexico. The Santa Fe Pacific sold most of its other lieu rights to dealers. It thus disposed of the scrip quickly and avoided the creation of a retail organization. Once the initial sales were made, the company conducted most of this business by mail. Although anxious to market its rights, it did not hawk them about promiscuously but waited for purchasers to come to it. Most dealers, handling several varieties of scrip, advertised and built up a clientele; they created a demand in their particular region. Knowing what different kinds of rights were valid to select the type of land their customers wanted, they generally decided whether to purchase Santa Fe Pacific lieu or some other variety on the basis of comparative cost. The railroad, instead of employing a force of salesmen, attracted purchasers by carefully adjusting its prices. It sold to dealers almost always for cash. They, partly as a service and partly to avoid disagreeable complications, either supplied their customers with specific instructions how to use the scrip or else themselves attended to the mechanics of entering selections at the local land office.

By the end of 1904 the Santa Fe Pacific had disposed of all but thirty-five acres of its restricted lieu rights. Although a few lots commanded as much as $3.75 an acre, most of this scrip, aside from the Hagerman transaction, brought $2.50 to $2.75. Since existing federal laws were so ill-adapted to the arid West as to prevent stockmen from legally securing title to the large ranges they grazed, these lieu rights were generally used to select a strategic tract with the deliberate purpose of controlling the surrounding public domain.

The Santa Fe Pacific disposed of its first large block of unrestricted lieu rights, good anywhere in the United States, for $5.50 an acre. Demand declined, but the company hurried to unload the scrip for fear Congress might make it invalid. The railroad sold many acres at $4.00 and some for as little as $3.50. When Congress forbade any further lieu land exchange not arranged for prior to March 3, 1905, the Santa Fe Pacific became virtually the only source remaining for forest scrip. The company resisted the temptation to charge high prices which might have attracted criticism of its favorable position. It did not ask over $7.50 an acre in 1905 or $10.50 in 1906, thereafter allowing a steady upward rise until it secured $15.00 and $16.00 in 1917.[31] After 1907 the company had sold such a large part of its unrestricted lieu that nobody noticed unfavorably a higher price on the relatively small quantity remaining. While the company clearly profited from the favorable position Congress had placed it in, it could have made much more had it deemed such action expedient. The railroad did not care where these unrestricted lieu rights were used and kept no records on the subject. It is clear that some customers purchased the scrip because they themselves knew of a timbered tract they wanted, others consulted a professional timber cruiser for reports about suitable acreage, and still others obtained information from scrip dealers. It has been charged that some of the lieu rights were placed on more valuable timber lands than the railroad surrendered; this is almost certainly true but virtually impossible to document.[32]

The scrip transactions arising from the San Francisco Mountains and Grand Canyon reserves caused some criticism, aside from unfavorable comment made about the exchange policy in general. A private attorney had first called to the railroad's attention the 1899 law authorizing the deposit of money with the government for making surveys, which was an essential preliminary to a land exchange. He was amply rewarded at the time, but later tried to force the company to pay him an additional $200,000 for his alleged services. His three-year campaign of innuendo-filled letters to Atchison President Ripley resulted only in requests to produce real evidence of misconduct or else stop writing. In 1905 New Mexico politicians opposing the appointment of J. J. Hagerman's son Herbert as governor of New Mexico maintained that the father had used $1.50 scrip to select land with artesian wells on it worth $25 to $50 an acre; the result-

[31] Scrip Deed Book, LCA.
[32] "Contracts in Forest Reserve Timber Lands," *loc. cit.*, contains much information but in a form hopeless for practical use.

ing Department of the Interior investigation proved he had not.[33] In 1908 Secretary of the Interior James R. Garfield wrote Ripley demanding an explanation of the Grand Canyon exchange, charging that the company had released absolutely worthless land and selected very valuable acreage.[34] The railroad's attorneys believed the Secretary's real objective was to find something amiss about Hagerman's use of a portion of the lieu rights in order to help justify Roosevelt's hasty and probably unwarranted removal of the rancher's son from the governorship. Garfield subsequently characterized the exchange as unwise but officially exonerated the Santa Fe Pacific from any suspicion of fraud.[35] In 1912 and 1913 three congressmen made unpleasant remarks about the company's forest scrip transactions, but these were only incidental to the main subjects of their speeches. The private attorney, the New Mexico politicians, and Secretary Garfield all had strong motives for finding something improper about the Santa Fe Pacific's forest lieu exchanges. They could not dig up anything. It would seem unlikely that they overlooked any source of information.

An evaluation of these two transactions involves three important and sometimes interrelated matters: the creation of the reserves, the negotiations for the land exchanges, and the legislation authorizing lieu rights.

When the government established the Grand Canyon reserve in 1893, it showed no visible regard for the railroad's right to the odd-numbered sections but included them without mention of recompense. Passage of the lieu legislation in 1897 presented a solution, and railroad officials would have been remiss if they had not grasped it. The company thought it had 50,000 acres of merchantable timber within the reserve but Secretary Hitchcock gave it 115,000 acres of scrip good on any timber land in the remaining public domain. It would seem Hitchcock's judgment was faulty.

The government was more considerate but not wiser when it created the San Francisco Mountains reserve in 1898. It deliberately extended the reserve over only government-owned even-numbered sections, thus striving to prevent any possibility of a scrip transaction, but in so doing it created an almost impossible problem of administration. The Forest Service believed the timber worth saving but had no funds; a land exchange was the only available solution. Secretary Hitchcock rejected the idea of enlarging the reserve and of giving

[33] J. J. Hagerman to Jones, December 16, 1905, TSW 3148.
[34] James R. Garfield to Ripley, January 21, 1908, TSW A-GC.
[35] Frank Pierce to Ripley, June 4, 1908, TSW A-GC.

lieu rights, but Roosevelt overruled him. The President acted hastily; someone overimpressed him about the evils of sheep grazing in the region. Although his judgment was poor about sheep and there is no available evidence how much he considered Hitchcock's objections, the forest was worth saving.

The lieu rights in these two exchanges were authorized by the act of 1897. Congress failed to provide that the base land surrendered and the lieu selected must be of equal quality because almost certainly it did not recognize the unfortunate possibilities of the measure. Once the danger was evident, Congress was slow in repealing the law. Until this was done, any scrip owner who held back from picking the best timber area he could find was only inviting some other holder of lieu rights to acquire it. The Department of the Interior made the best of a bad situation in the two exchanges discussed when it insisted on issuing restricted scrip, good only on untimbered land, in return for the surrender of land of a similar nature. While in theory it might also have insisted that part of the lieu rights be used only in the railroad grant area, resulting in large solid blocks of grazing land and thus conferring most of the benefits of the Taylor Grazing Act upon the range thirty years sooner, actually the majority of ranchers would have made such vigorous protest they would have defeated such a proviso.[36]

There seems little ground for doubting that the preservation of the forest in the two regions benefited the nation. The crucial question is whether the United States had to give too much to secure the private land. There are good reasons to believe it did so. The fault lies at the doors of Congress, Hitchcock, and Roosevelt. The private owners would have been foolish to dispose of their land at less than the best bargain they could make.

[36] Had such an agreement been made, the government would have had to give more than an equal area of lieu rights for the actual timbered land, since the acreage selected in the grant area would have been of less value.

CHAPTER VI

THE SMALL HOLDERS AND SOME OTHER
EXCHANGES

THE Santa Fe Pacific, after its success with the forest lieu transaction, made other exchanges covering property that squatters claimed, the National Park Service desired, or the government Bureau of Indian Affairs wanted. It wisely extracted itself from difficult situations involving conflicting interests and obtained lieu rights whose immediate cash value was at least as great as that of the acreage relinquished. The railroad sold this scrip, directly or through dealers, to stockmen all over New Mexico and Arizona.

Stockmen used the rights in an attempt to solve the difficult problems posed by national land laws which were unrealistic for arid ranching country. They could not legally acquire from the national government nearly enough land for an average ranch nor could they purchase it from private sources. They bought as much scrip as they could afford and with it secured small, desirable, strategically located tracts selected to control the maximum adjacent public domain. Often they also arranged for the state of New Mexico or Arizona to select, as part of its gift from the federal government, strategic plots; these they then purchased. By these two methods the ranchers sought to limit the orgy of uncontrolled grazing and to secure certain publicly owned range exclusively for themselves. Since they could not or would not persuade Congress to amend the national land laws, they were to a considerable extent justified in their objective.

The buyers in using their railroad scrip had to comply with more formalities than had the purchasers of forest lieu. Especially they had to observe the fundamental rule that the base and the lieu be of equal quality. They furnished affidavits about the quality, posted notice of their selection on the desired acreage, and for a month advertised it in a neighboring newspaper. Their documents, with a variety of others, were mailed by the local land office in the monthly dispatch to Washington. Here the General Land Office took about five months to note the selection in various tract books, to card it, and to index it. Government inspectors, different ones usually because the base and lieu were seldom close together, inspected the two areas. They received, and the railroad urged, legitimate assistance from the ranchers. Their reports, occasionally buttressed by the advice of the Geological Survey, formed the basis for the decision to approve or reject the selection. During the years when these lieu transactions were quite active, railroad attorney Alexander Britton pressed the General Land Office for prompt action and by daily visits to its divisions kept the company's business moving "nicely."[1]

Of the three types of lieu transactions, two will be discussed in this chapter and the third in Chapters VII, VIII, and XII. The first transaction, the so-called small holders exchange, arose from squatters' claims to parts of the Santa Fe Pacific's land grant in New Mexico. Some interlopers mistakenly believed they held legal title derived from an old Mexican or Spanish grant, which actually had been adjudged spurious by the special Court of Private Land Claims. Others frankly pleaded the many years their ancestors had squatted on the acreage and their valuable improvements.[2] Their trespass upon the railroad's odd-numbered sections was legal justification for it to oust them, but Howel Jones thought this was cold-blooded and might cause serious repercussions. He considered relinquishing disputed land to the federal government, which would then give the settlers legal title, but objected to an acre-for-acre swap under the existing act of June 22, 1874. He declared that most squatters occupied less than

[1] Hugo Seaberg to Jones, August 27, 1925, LCA 821. Seaberg once reported that when a certain rancher had been discourteous to a federal inspector, his selection had been "roughly speaking blacklisted." The method which the railroad used in selecting lieu lands was described by Jones to Engel on February 18, 1916 (TSW 8113), in the following passage:

". . . [W]e, in order to avoid mistakes, make a thorough examination of the condition of each tract [in the records of the local United States Land Office] the day before the day that we are going to file our selection, and again we make another examination before nine o'clock on the day that the selection is made, and heretofore we have always been successful in getting in before anyone else on the morning the selection is made. The land offices open for public business at nine o'clock, and then all papers are filed and the fees in cash are filed. The Register and Receiver are not permitted to accept anything but cash, other than Postoffice [money] orders.

". . . The records of none of the land offices have been correct, consequently it is very difficult to know before hand what the result is going to be until you have checked and rechecked the lists that you have in connection with the plats on file.

". . . These land offices are conducted mostly by inexperienced men, and they at first believe that the railroad company is trying to take advantage of them. Consequently the greatest task that we have is to convince the Register and Receiver . . . that we are honest and that we want to do business fairly and the way that we have succeeded in getting along with those officials so well, is to do anything and everything that they desire to be done."

Seaberg declared that sometimes land would appear vacant on the tract books in the local United States Land Office and a year or two later it would develop that the land had already been patented to somebody else. He explained that sometimes clerks forgot to make the proper entries on the records and sometimes the local office was far behind in its work.

[2] "Relief of Certain Small-Holding Settlers," *House Reports*, 58th Cong., 2d sess., No. 1203, p. 1; Jones to B&G, June 22, 1903; Jones to Ripley, July 21, 1905; Manuel R. Otero to B. S. Rodey, April 21, 1901, LCA 821.

forty acres, but had located their plots so wisely that the rest of the
arid section was valueless. He persuaded Congress in 1904 to pass
a new law authorizing the railroad to surrender an entire section, when
interlopers had used part of it for at least twenty-five years, and to
pick any other section of equal value in the territory. This was usually interpreted as authorizing the selection of 640 acres in separate
tracts as small as forty acres. Thus the government, perhaps because
the company as owner of land which squatters wanted was in a superior bargaining position, allowed the railroad to surrender all of one
arid section and pick as lieu portions of many dry sections.[3]

The Santa Fe Pacific urged government officials to submit at least
one claim for every section possible. It pressed so vigorously that by
late in 1908 almost all squatters had filed their requests. It received
21,325.55 acres of lieu rights and sold them for more than the property relinquished was worth. It peddled 14,155.36 acres, good on
grazing land only, to the Raton scrip dealer Hugo Seaberg at $3.50
to $6.00 an acre, and 2,771.88 acres elsewhere. It sold 4,037.31
acres, valid on coal lands, to the Victor-American Fuel Company.[4] Its
customers had to observe the Department of the Interior rule that they
could not apply the scrip on unsurveyed land. The department used
the "Rule of Approximation," allowing a holder of rights for more
than twenty but less than forty acres to purchase enough land from it
to increase the size of the tract selected to the legal minimum subdivision of a section, forty acres. Government officials made numerous
decisions in special cases and even made unusual concessions in unique
problems. The Department, for example, received a protest from
Lorenzo P. Garcia of Magdalena, New Mexico, that he had used
forty acres of scrip to obtain title to what he thought was the land
where his house, well, windmill, and corrals were. Ignorantly he had
followed the original 1883 survey of his township and disregarded the
1920 correction. Actually he had obtained a worthless tract. His complaint prompted the Department to change his title to the area where
his improvements were.[5]

The Department and the Victor-American Fuel Company had so
serious a controversy over small holders' lieu selections of coal land
near Gallup that the case finally reached the United States Supreme
Court. The 4,037.31 acres of base lands, located in the same county

[3] *Statutes-at-Large*, XVIII, 194, and XXXIII, 556; *Congressional Record*, 58th
Cong., 2d sess., pp. 20, 2900–2901, 5818; *Land Decisions*, XXXIII, 157; Jones to
Ripley, July 21, 1905, LCA 821.
[4] Scrip Deed Book, LCA; Jones to Engel, November 10, 1911, LCA 821.
[5] George R. Wickham to Register and Receiver, Las Cruces, N.M., January 20,
1922, LCA 821.

as the lieu, had been occupied by various Navajo Indians, who were apparently ignorant of the fuel beneath their claims. They asked for title to their plots under the terms of the Small Holders Act, their request was granted, and the railroad relinquished the land. Later Jones somehow learned of coal underneath the base. He feared if the railroad used these particular lieu rights itself that McKinley County authorities would try to claim most of the grant there was similarly underlain. He sold the scrip to the Victor-American Fuel Company, well organized politically there, for $15.00 an acre. When it picked as lieu a number of contiguous forty-acre tracts, opposition nurtured by the many citizens of Gallup who bitterly disliked the Victor-American erupted. A written protest signed by Thomas Leaden, a miner it had dismissed for "agitating propensities," was sent to the General Land Office. The GLO, following an investigation, approved a few selections but rejected the majority, declaring that the base was farther from the railroad line than the lieu and asserting that the coal on the base was neither of as good quality nor as easily mined as that on the lieu. Its unfavorable decision was appealed by the fuel company to the Secretary of the Interior, who ordered a hearing at Gallup. This was held, but the stenographer soon confessed that the broken English of some witnesses and geological terminology of others prevented him from reading his own shorthand. Because of his incompetence, another complete hearing proved necessary.

Washington authorities, laying aside the transcript of the second Gallup meeting, inquired whether the original claims of the Navajos to the base were fraudulent. This question, Jones thought, had likely been raised by the Gallup enemies of the Victor-American. The answer hinged on the difference between a white man's conception of "occupancy" as that of genuine residence and a Navajo's as merely that some member of the family always stayed in the same general region. Investigation convinced the Department of the Interior that there had been no fraud by either the Indians or the railroad.[6] The government, however, rejected the entire exchange because of unequal value, citing in a typical forty-acre instance that the base was worth $20.00 to $56.00 an acre but the lieu was appraised at $119.00 an acre. This decision was appealed eventually by the Victor-American Fuel Company to the United States Supreme Court, where the company was victorious. The court pointed out that had the exchange actually been completed when first proposed, it would have been ap-

---

[6] Two unpublished land decisions, First Assistant Secretary of the Interior, April 18, 1916, LCA 821. For the Navajos' concept of occupancy, see Clyde Kluckhohn and Dorothea Leighton, *The Navaho* (Cambridge, Mass., 1946), pp. 7–8.

proved because at that time the base and lieu appeared to be of equal quality. The court ruled that more accurate information obtained during the long controversy could not be considered.[7] This decision actually settled only the dispute over one tract out of many selected. Did it apply to the rest? Yes, said the Victor-American, as there was a gentlemen's agreement that it should. No, said the government, as there was no such understanding. The fuel company went to law again and won in the circuit court of appeals. The government then capitulated.

This controversy affected selections of grazing land made with small holders' scrip. During an entire year of the struggle the Department of the Interior held in abeyance all ranchers' applications. When it finally considered them, railroad lawyers justly complained of the "remarkable refinement in attempted designation of the poor qualities" of both the base and the lieu. The government rejected about a third of the lieu selected as being slightly better than the base.[8] It withstood an eight months' campaign of persuasion by Britton and Gray before abandoning its differentiation between the various classes of grazing land. Later in a few instances the Department apparently again made unreasonable distinctions in such tracts.

[7] SFP RR Co. v. Payne, 259 US 197.

[8] B&G to Jones, July 15, 1916, LCA 821. In a typical forty-acre selection, one government inspector reported about the base as follows: "The land is 30 miles west of Albuquerque, New Mexico, the nearest railroad point of importance. The altitude is about 5300 feet and the estimated rainfall about 12 inches. The country is devoted exclusively to stock raising on the ranges because of the scant rainfall and no water is available for irrigation. The tract is situated south about 300 feet from a small canon which had an intermittent flow of water. The land slopes to the north and is rocky and rough with almost no soil cover at all. There is very little vegetation present and almost no grass at all. Scattering clumps of cedar and pinion brush lessen rather than enhance its value. The land is totally unfit for anything but grazing and for that purpose it is poor. I regard it as not better than poor 3d rate grazing land." He said there was a little gypsum, but of no commercial value, on the base.

Another inspector looked at the selected lieu tract and wrote as follows: "Lies on the prairie in the southwestern part of the State and was selected to cover a watering place for stock on the range. There is on the tract, a small earthen dam across a rough draw which catches flood waters during violent raises and forms a small reservoir. The surface of the tract that is not covered by the rough bottom of the draw is sidehill, rough, broken and very stony and grazing land of the 2nd rate only. No plow land exists on the tract except a few acres that are covered with water in the reservoir and the rainfall is so light (under 10") and variable that dry farming would be of no avail. The land is wash of sand and gravel over Rhyolite country flow and has a cover of 2nd rate grass only. It is non-mineral and non-timbered and grazing land of the above rate only."

The Commissioner of the General Land Office, because the lieu was reported to him by one man as second-rate grazing land and the base by another inspector as third-rate, rejected the selection. (The Commissioner to Register and Receiver, Las Cruces, N.M., July 13, 1916, LCA 821.)

The small holders' transaction solved the most pressing problem about interlopers in New Mexico, but other squatters also had occupied certain acreage so long they had a moral claim to it. These the Santa Fe Pacific aided under the act of 1874, which it had earlier considered unfair because it received lieu rights for only the exact acreage given up. One of the more unusual claims it considered was from a Mohave County man who explained how a man named Warren had first occupied a certain tract in 1868; how Shipp, having shot Warren, took possession in 1874; and how he himself was the direct successor of the two. How, reasonably inquired Howel Jones, did Shipp acquire legal title from the man he had killed? Despite this embarrassing question, Jones admitted there was a moral claim because of long, continuous occupancy and agreed to relinquish the land.

The railroad under the act of 1874 surrendered 5,396.66 acres, mostly in Arizona. It sold the lieu rights to various dealers and ranchers for $6.00 to $8.00 an acre.[9] Its largest customer was Hugo Seaberg, the Raton scrip dealer, who bought in all 1,200 acres. Once when he purchased 520 acres, he frankly announced he was going to attempt the selection of coal land as lieu, even though the railroad had turned in only grazing land as base, because the original 1866 granting act allowed the company to pick coal and iron tracts. His legal reasoning did not impress the railroad, which willingly sold him scrip for this speculation, or the General Land Office, which rejected his application, or the Secretary of the Interior, who upon appeal refused approval, or the United States Supreme Court, which hardly deigned to discuss Seaberg's arguments. He attempted to secure approval through special legislation introduced by Senator A. A. Jones of New Mexico, but the measure died in the committee room. The plan to surrender scrip for base worth $1.25 to $3.00 an acre and secure lieu worth $133 to $135 an acre was a failure.[10]

Exchanges under the act of 1874 did not cover quite all the remaining squatters on Santa Fe Pacific land. About thirty of them had located along the banks of the Big Sandy River in Mohave County, Arizona. They picked off all the choice spots in three townships, making the remainder so valueless that the railroad did not want to exchange less than all its acreage there. It allowed the matter to drift until 1921, when Chief Clerk Taliaferro urged W. F. Neal of Mohave County to take action. ". . . I told Neal that I wanted him to get all the credit, and he fell for it," circulating a petition which

[9] Scrip Deed Book, LCA; *Statutes-at-Large*, XVIII, 194.
[10] *Land Decisions*, XLIX, 180; SFP RR Co. v. Work, 267 US 511; A. A. Jones to Seaberg, March 12, 1926, LCA 8720.

led Congress to authorize the surrender of all railroad property in the three townships and the selection of lieu of an equal value of vacant, surveyed, nonmineral, nontimbered public land in Mohave County. The company sold the 28,136.73 acres of so-called Sandy scrip to a variety of purchasers at prices from $3.00 to $6.00 an acre.[11] In 1931 the railroad secured a law benefiting a number of Mexicans who had settled about 1883 around the hamlet of Riley, New Mexico, and sold the resulting 3,720 acres of lieu rights, good only in that state, to scrip dealer Charles B. Barker and two landowners.[12]

The Santa Fe Pacific, in addition to lieu transactions to benefit settlers, also made exchanges at the request of the National Park Service. It held acreage within the Petrified Forest, a national monument set aside in 1907 without the formality of removing the intermixed, privately owned land. It was asked by the National Park Service in 1929 to accept scrip not only for its own property but also for that which it must purchase from a man named Wade. Land Commissioner Collinson did not relish the suggestion, but Passenger Traffic Manager W. J. Black urged approval because the enlarged Petrified Forest might develop into an added tourist attraction offsetting the work of the Union Pacific Railroad in the Utah national parks, "as their sole purpose is diversion of long-distance California traffic," and because he thought the National Park Service, if irritated at failure to co-operate, might not continue so friendly at Grand Canyon. The railroad accepted the government's proposal, purchased Wade's land, and received three acres of lieu rights, good only in Apache and Navajo counties, Arizona, for each one acre of land relinquished. It used the 9,581.70 acres of resultant scrip plus 30,760.20 additional acres of Petrified Forest rights, obtained as settlement of an old, unpaid debt of $53,298.75 from the New Mexico and Arizona Land Company, to solidify some of its best grazing lands in Apache County. During a joint examination of the base and lieu the railroad's Art Saunders silenced the joshing of the federal agent by telling him ". . . we had no idea of trying to justify the exchange on grazing values, but . . . the lands which we were relinquishing . . . were valuable primarily for their 'gazing' value."[13] The National Park Service shortly suggested an even exchange of land in connection with the Chaco Canyon National Monument, and the railroad sold this 6,362.68 acres of scrip to Charles B. Barker.[14]

---

[11] LCA 10282, *passim*; *Statutes-at-Large*, XLII, 829.
[12] W. B. Collinson to Engel, November 3, 1932, LCA 8192.
[13] Art Saunders to Collinson, August 31, 1934, LCA 11575.
[14] A. E. Demaray to Collinson, November 15, 1929, LCA 11699.

Barker and other scrip dealers were important to the railroad's lieu transactions because they purchased the rights wholesale and relieved it of building up a retail sales force. Barker, an attorney, sold lieu as a side line during the late 1920's and the 1930's. Leroy O. Moore left an estate of $296,922.32, earned mostly by energetic sales of railroad rights in the four years before his death in 1918.[15] Theo. N. Espe, first as administrator of Moore's affairs and later on his own, was active until the middle 1930's. All three lived in Santa Fe and, at various times, had been employed in the United States Land Office there. Fen S. Hildreth of Prescott and Phoenix retailed much scrip during the 1910's. So did John H. Page and Company, formerly M. E. Leverich and Company, active in various Phoenix land matters down to the present day. Smaller dealers were Ben B. Wetmore of Roswell and B. H. Gibbs of Phoenix.

Most important to the Santa Fe Pacific was Hugo Seaberg of Raton, who purchased directly from it a total of 119,796.24 acres.[16] In 1939 he estimated he had made a net profit of about half a million dollars from handling Santa Fe Pacific and other kinds of scrip. Trained as an attorney, he paid only slight attention to building up a practice and threw himself energetically into various money-making ventures. His headquarters after 1902 were Raton, a New Mexico mining and railroad division point, which by 1930 had grown to about 6,100; but he used the small town merely as a base of operations and traveled extensively on business outside the Rocky Mountain area.

Seaberg purchased lieu rights from the railroad between 1903 and 1918. He was a pioneer in handling scrip, doing much to educate New Mexicans to its advantages.[17] He gave purchasers careful instructions about the mechanics of its use. At first he took greater chances than he realized by guaranteeing that the government would accept as lieu a specific tract which a rancher desired and, when difficulties arose

---

[15] *Albuquerque Morning Journal*, September 6, 1918.

[16] TSW 377, LCA 821, *passim*. These 119,796.24 acres consisted of 39,389.69 acres of forest lieu restricted; 19,471.91 of forest lieu unrestricted; 14,515.36 of small holders; 1,200.00 of act of 1874; and 45,220.18 of Navajo Exchange in New Mexico.

[17] Seaberg commented to Jones (December 13, 1918, LCA 377) as follows:

"I remember vividly one incident: I had made a large sale to an old German, a Mr. Roth of [I]ndian exchange, made in advance of and in anticipation of, purchases I intended to close with you. . . . The purchaser's contract being good, financially, I in turn agreed to pay him $1,000 if I failed to make selections before a certain date. My dealings with you were so delayed that I could not make the time, and on the day my contract [calling for] delivery expired, my customer called at my office saying: (neither more nor less) 'I want my thousand dollars.' There being no way out of it, I merely wrote him out a check for it. It is true I afterwards closed the same deal with him, at the same price, but he was ahead the $1,000.00."

over the Small Holders, had to work desperately in preventing rejections which would have destroyed all his profits. He was venturesome and Howel Jones was conservative, the two thus forming a good team for mutual advantage. He was very friendly to the railroad, paying it higher prices than it otherwise would have obtained; the Atchison made him its attorney in Raton, which included pass privileges valuable to a man who traveled extensively. Once when he had so serious a difference with Britton and Gray, his Washington attorneys, that he severed relationship with them, it was Howel Jones who wrote to each such a kindly and understanding appreciation of the other that the breach was healed.

Seaberg was an optimist. He was overenthusiastic, as is clear from what actually happened, but it would be a serious mistake to underestimate his genuine ability. In a 1921 speech, for example, he said that in ten years Raton would double in population and quintuple in business volume, that the mines would double or triple production, and that the surrounding land, then used only for grazing, would be farmed. He put his beliefs into practice, dealing in scrip, town lots, and grazing land as well as venturing into mining and oil development. About 1905 he built a theater seating two thousand, or about half the then population of Raton, upon the theory the town would soon grow; it didn't, and he lost heavily before the venture ended. He opened a twenty-four-room hotel, the Seaberg, in 1909. By 1929 he had expanded it to two hundred rooms and added an art gallery containing five hundred oil paintings as well as native *objets d'art*. At the height of its glory, this hotel, remote from tourist traffic, would have attracted favorable attention if located on Broadway in New York. In the depression of the 1930's, he went bankrupt and lost the hotel. Yet it was this same spirit of taking chances that enabled him to make about half a million net from the scrip business.[18]

Hugo Seaberg was certainly not an average businessman. "He is a philosopher and a thinker," Jones once wrote, "and a great reader of current literature." The two once exchanged half a dozen letters devoted to Irving Fisher's monetary theories. Seaberg, at another time, sent a religious book that interested him, and Jones's sole comment was an incredulous inquiry as to where he had obtained it.

[18] Was Seaberg ever conservative? On May 12, 1917, he wrote to Jones as follows (TSW 8821):

"This is not a new [type]writing machine I am using; but some fifteen years ago when the 'Caligraph' manufacturers quit building the machine I had learned to operate, I bought a half dozen second-hand machines of the make that I could operate, so that I would not have to learn over on some new make. This is one of them, taken from the warehouse. I have several more, enough to last me 20 years."

When Jones suggested that he use his service as a New Mexico delegate to the Republican national convention in 1912 as justification for political assistance in securing approval of some of his pending scrip selections, Seaberg declared, "I feel a little too sensitive to make a voluntary service or the voluntary aiding of a righteous cause the basis of a counter claim."[19] He once dabbled in the small money-to-loan business but withdrew because he did not feel a man with a conscience should engage in it. On the other hand, he once tried to use the railroad's grazing land scrip to claim coal land.

Howel Jones repeatedly testified by written word and by action that he regarded Seaberg's ability as a businessman highly. He also clearly liked him as a friend. Hugo Seaberg made a genuine contribution to the success of the railroad's scrip business and the company was fortunate to have such an ally.

[19] Seaberg to Jones, June 29, 1912, LCA 821.

CHAPTER VII

NEW MEXICO INDIAN LIEU RIGHTS

IN ADMINISTERING its land, the Santa Fe Pacific encountered Indian rights of occupancy as well as white. In 1872 the road filed a map of definite location with the Secretary of the Interior to establish its claim to all odd-numbered sections in the grant not yet appropriated. The company obviously sought no land within the already established Navajo reservation, then only a fifth as large as now, or the Laguna, also smaller than at present. Later the federal authorities established new reservations and enlarged others. The government assigned the Indians only the even-numbered sections, because previously it had granted the railroad the odd-numbered ones, and created a checkerboard of intermixed land as awkward as that in the San Francisco Mountains Forest Reserve. Subsequently it often, but not always, solved the difficulty by a lieu scrip transaction with the railroad.

The most perplexing situation was in the reservation of the Navajos, located north of the Atchison main line in the northwestern sixth of New Mexico, the northeastern quarter of Arizona, and the adjoining parts of Colorado and Utah. There the federal government in 1868 had placed ten thousand Indians on 3,500,000 acres of land; these grew by 1940 to forty-nine thousand people in an area of 15,000,000 acres. The expansion in land provoked the inevitable conflict between the best interests of white men and red. The arguments centered on the removal of so much acreage from the tax rolls, the development of additional water resources on the reservation, the practices causing range deterioration, and the methods to secure maximum utilization of Indian-controlled land. A related problem was the Navajos' use of the public domain outside the reservation in competition with white ranchers; all too often neither had any scruples about trespassing upon the other's range.

The strongest advocate of the Navajos was Father Anselm Weber, Father Superior of the Franciscan Friars at St. Michaels, Arizona, from 1897 to 1921. Of him Jones once wrote:

He has great influence with the Navajo Indians, with the various county officials, with the Indian Agent, and with everyone with whom he comes in contact. He is sincere, and he is devoted to the work of elevating the Indian. I have had a great deal to do with him for a number of years and my admiration for him grows. He knows every spring, every valley, and every bit of timber on the southern portion of the Navajo reserve. . . .[1]

[1] Jones to W. B. Jansen, July 21, 1906, TSW 28-110.

Weber concentrated on uplifting the red men morally and economically rather than on preaching the Gospel to unprepared and unwilling listeners. He vigorously advocated lieu land exchanges. He accomplished much, securing results sometimes immediately and other times after a lapse of as much as twenty-five years. Weber and Howel Jones co-operated since both favored lieu transactions. The railroad man greatly admired the padre personally. Jones's letters to the priest contain a warm note of friendliness and good will to be found in no other land department correspondence, not even that sent Hugo Sea-

Some New Mexico Indian Reservations

berg. Jones and Weber were both fortunate to have each other as allies in seeking to solve the problem of intermixed Navajo and railroad land.[2]

After this general consideration of the problems the railroad and the government encountered in the various Indian reservations, it is time to turn to the specific details.

In 1902 the Santa Fe Pacific abandoned the unrealistic dream that somehow it might solidify all its grant and turned to securing more scrip, which commanded an immediate market. Jones, guided by the orders of General Solicitor E. D. Kenna, took the initiative in Washington to secure a law authorizing lieu transactions to eliminate private land within Indian reservations. He convinced Secre-

---

[2] Many of the railroad's difficulties with the Navajos were solved by lieu exchanges, but it also sold the government 11,520 acres in Arizona for them at $1.25 an acre and leased a relatively small amount of land to individual red men or their economic advisers. (TSW 639, *passim.*)

tary of the Interior E. A. Hitchcock and Commissioner of Indian Affairs W. A. Jones, who persuaded Congress to pass an act providing:

That any private land over which an Indian reservation has been extended by Executive order, may be exchanged at the discretion of the Secretary of the Interior and at the expense of the owner thereof and under such rules and regulations as may be prescribed by the Secretary of the Interior, for vacant, nonmineral, nontimbered, surveyed public lands of equal area and value and situated in the Same State or Territory.[3]

Jones promptly offered to relinquish railroad holdings within the Zuñi reservation, located a few miles south of Gallup, New Mexico. He insisted on knowing the rules, since this might be the first of many exchanges. During the lengthy discussions, Jones once reported:

The rules have gone from one department to another in the General Land Office and they have finally lodged in the forest division which has been the most rigid and unyielding of all of the divisions in the Commissioner's office. Its head is one Mr. McPhaul, a Texan, who believes it to be his duty to prevent the government from giving up any of its lands. With the hue and cry sent up by all the newspapers in the land Mr. McPhaul is strengthened in his opposition to doing anything to facilitate any exchange, and on account of the attitude of the administration it is difficult to get the head of any department to take any stand against the attitude of the head of any division, providing that attitude is against making any exchange.[4]

After three years the railroad and the government finally agreed on the rules.[5] These allowed the Secretary of the Interior to reject any lieu selection merely by "exercising his discretion." They required the railroad to pay for a government appraisal of both base and lieu lands as well as for an affidavit by a "disinterested party" that the two were of equal quality. At first they forbade the company to select less than a full section as lieu, but in 1907 this minimum was lowered to 160 acres.

Jones, with the rules formulated, renewed his proposal to surrender the railroad's entire 121,000 acres within the Zuñi reservation and added 94,000 acres in the recent New Mexico addition to the Navajo reservation. He expected to select as lieu a solid block of 215,000 acres north of Clovis and adjacent to a projected, but never built, Atchison through line from Galveston to Denver. At the time

[3] *Statutes-at-Large*, XXXIII, 211; Kenna to Jones, December 2, 1902, TSW 383.
[4] Jones to Ripley, December 12, 1905, TSW 1964.
[5] Proposed draft of rules, *ca.* February 2, 1906; Jones to Jansen, June 9, 1906, TSW 1964.

he believed the tract contained little except grazing land and was worth $1.50 an acre.[6] He persuaded the Department of the Interior to "protract" the base surrendered rather than go to the expense of actually surveying it. He secured affidavits from veteran New Mexico landmen R. G. Marmon and George H. Pradt that the base and lieu were of equal quality. He had all the relevant papers filed in the United States Land Office at Clayton, New Mexico. When told they had gotten lost between Clayton and Washington, he made a special visit to the capital and, after considerable insistence, unearthed the missing documents. Jones was further delayed by the Department of the Interior's decision to examine the base and the lieu, although a year earlier it had rejected his proposal of a joint railroad-government inspection.

While awaiting the results of this examination, Department of the Interior officials in Washington made an unfortunate mistake that created another obstacle to the exchange. They had previously reserved the lieu land for the railroad, pending a final decision. Their clerks had marked this fact on the tract books at Clayton but had failed to make the same notation in Washington. When somebody telegraphed to the capital asking whether he could apply for a homestead on the land in the lieu tract, he received the incorrect reply that nothing hindered such an entry. This mistake precipitated a mad rush from Clovis to Clayton of speculators who decided the land must be valuable if the Santa Fe Pacific wanted it, especially since the Atchison had started building the Clovis-Belen track which was to form part of a second main line from Kansas to New Mexico. Urged by professional "locators" who would make an entry for anybody at a fee of $5.00 cash and $20.00 additional if the government disregarded the claim of the Santa Fe Pacific, they speedily tendered six hundred applications. They were informed by Assistant Commissioner of the General Land Office Fred Dennett, who had become "very much worked up" over the situation, that the land was not open for entry. Howel Jones, angry, blamed the "carelessness" on Dennett himself.[7]

When federal inspector Will M. Tipton, two months after this excitement, completed his examination and submitted his report, he opposed the exchange. He appraised the base at $7.50 an acre and the lieu, allegedly suitable for raising crops without irrigation, at $10.00 to $25.00.[8] His report naturally encountered opposition from

[6] Jones to Engel, June 9, 1913, TSW 5319.

[7] B&G to Jones, November 16, 1907; W. C. Reid to Jones, November 23 and 28, 1907; Jones to B&G, November 12, 1907; Jones to Jansen, November 22, 1907; Clovis Townsite Co. ("locators"), undated handbill, TSW 1964.

[8] Will M. Tipton to the Secretary of the Interior, January 25, 1908, TSW 1964.

the railroad, which emphasized the good qualities of the base and argued that the lieu was not unusually valuable because the state of New Mexico, picking land to fulfill a grant from the United States, had selected only 40,000 acres in the Clovis area despite pressure for more from local ranchers.

The dispute over the exchange assumed a political tinge when Governor Curry of New Mexico suggested that the railroad voluntarily withdraw its application. His plea was rejected by Howel Jones because the railroad had "a sort of agreement" with the Commissioner of Indian Affairs to solve their mutual land problems by making exchanges.[9] He then threatened to use this refusal as a political weapon against the railroad at the next session of the territorial legislature. He obtained several interviews with Secretary of the Interior James R. Garfield in which, as a former "Rough Rider," he praised President Roosevelt's policy of preserving the public domain for settlers and homemakers.[10] To counteract his influence, Atchison President Ripley apparently also saw Garfield. The pressure upon the Secretary grew so strong that he apparently hesitated to act on his own responsibility. He consulted President Theodore Roosevelt and then rejected the exchange. He said that he did so "for the best good of the three interests involved, namely—the government, the Indians on their reservation, and the would-be settlers in the lieu area proposed for exchange, because of the wide difference in conditions and character of the base and lieu lands."[11] He emphasized that there was nothing improper about the railroad's actions. He permitted the homesteaders to perfect their claims and, in the area where nobody had filed, said the land would still be reserved for the Santa Fe Pacific. He said he would consider a new application for an exchange if it covered at least the company's odd-numbered sections within the Zuñi reservation where the government had already built a $250,000 dam and $100,000 worth of irrigation ditches.

It is hard to believe that anything but politics dictated Garfield's decision. If he was interested in the "best good of the Indians," it is difficult to see why he had to insert an elaborate provision forcing the railroad to surrender first its land within the completed irrigation

[9] B&G to Jones, April 23 and 25, 1908, TSW 1964. *The McKinley County Republican* of February 15, 1908, contained an article attacking the exchange written by a Gallup attorney who was angry because the railroad refused to give him a position. (C. Selvy to I. L. Hibbard, March 3, 1908, TSW 1964.)

[10] Jones to Jansen, April 30, 1908, TSW 1964.

[11] James R. Garfield to Commissioner, General Land Office, May 30, 1908, TSW 1964.

project. If there was actually such "wide difference in conditions and character of the base and lieu lands," it is hard to understand why he suggested another exchange involving parts of the same selection. If his subordinates had not been so careless, clearly no "would-be settlers" could ever have filed homestead requests. He placed the railroad in a position to embarrass the government greatly by refusing an exchange of its land under the irrigation system, but perhaps he realized it could not afford to be disagreeable if it hoped to arrange other lieu transactions.

Following Garfield's suggestion, the Santa Fe Pacific filed a new application. It was supported by the Commissioner of Indian Affairs, who "made it quite clear" to the Secretary that he especially wished the railroad land eliminated from the Zuñi reservation. The company received title to 97,782.56 acres in the original region north of Clovis and the right to pick 23,000 acres elsewhere in New Mexico, which it did in the so-called Ranger Lake region about sixty miles east of Roswell.[12]

The railroad for a while simply held its Ranger Lake property, located on an Atchison branch line proposed but never built from Lubbock to Roswell. It did not sell the last of the acreage there until the 1940's. It at once sought a market for the tract north of Clovis. After a year of effort, it sold the property to the Arkansas Valley Town and Land Company, an organization with much experience in retailing land, for $5.00 an acre, about one-tenth down and the balance spread in payments over four and a half years. It encountered difficulty in securing this money because the purchaser, despite strenuous efforts, could not resell the land fast enough to small-scale buyers at $7.00 to $8.00 an acre. It finally in 1915 made a compromise settlement of $2.52 an acre, without collecting any interest.[13] The figures of $2.52 an acre actually received for the land wholesale and $7.00 to $8.00 retail are an interesting commentary on the railroad's original valuation of $1.50 an acre and the federal inspector's 1908 appraisal of $10.00 to $25.00 an acre.

Howel Jones meanwhile had been thinking of other possible lieu transactions. He believed that if the railroad itself used the rights to secure even-numbered sections in the grant area where it already owned the odd-numbered ones, he could not sell the solidified tract for over $1.50 an acre. He pointed out that if the company held these

[12] Garfield to Commissioner, General Land Office, March 3, 1909; Jones to B&G, August 15, 1910, TSW 1964.

[13] H. M. Bainer to Jones, October 13, 1915; Jones to Engel, December 27, 1915, TSW 5319.

lands for twenty years, it could get a higher price but meanwhile would pay taxes so out of proportion to value that they would more than offset future profit.[14] He and his superiors therefore decided to sell others the lieu rights, valid only in New Mexico or Arizona, for not less than $2.50 an acre. Between 1907 and 1919, under his guidance, the Santa Fe Pacific surrendered 294,258.15 acres of land in New Mexico and sold the scrip.

The railroad made several exchanges totaling 229,233.85 acres within the Navajo reservation. Between 1907 and 1915 it deeded 45,220.18 acres to the federal government in a series of transactions so little mentioned in the railroad files that negotiations must have been conducted orally in Washington. It sold all the lieu rights to Hugo Seaberg for $2.10 to $2.50 an acre.[15] He had some difficulties securing approval of certain exchanges, but nothing nearly as serious as his troubles with the small holders' transaction.

The Santa Fe Pacific's next Navajo exchange, much to the railroad's surprise, was launched by Leroy O. Moore, a scrip dealer in the city of Santa Fe. One day, encountering A. A. Jones, First Assistant Secretary of the Interior and a New Mexican, in Santa Fe, he urged on him additional lieu transactions. Moore, despite the company's refusal to allow him to represent it, had many New Mexicans write the Assistant Secretary advocating exchanges. He enlisted the aid of Thomas B. Catron, lawyer, very large landowner, master "practical" politician, and United States senator from New Mexico, whose methods once caused a newspaper editor to comment, "Tom has a record that would stink a Ute out of his tepee."[16] By February 1917 Moore had the promise of the Commissioner of the General Land Office that if the local Indian superintendent approved, the government would ask the railroad to relinquish all its New Mexico land within the Navajo reservation.[17] This request the government made, seeking even the tract previously offered in the Clovis transaction and rejected for political reasons. The railroad accepted; it sold

[14] Jones to Ripley, October 6, 1907, TSW 1964.

[15] Seaberg to Jones, July 22, 1907, TSW 377, enumerated the fees Seaberg would pay: (1) the fee for recording the deed relinquishing title to the United States; (2) the fee for making an abstract of title, when necessary, to the base; (3) the taxes which might accrue on the base after Seaberg had purchased the lieu rights and before the exchange was completed; (4) the fee of $2.00 for each quarter section or less when the lieu selection was filed with the United States Land Office; (5) the salary of a "disinterested person" who would make affidavit that the base and lieu were of equal quality; (6) the office and field expense of the government in surveying the lieu; (7) the cost of a federal inspection of the base and the lieu; and (8) the conveyancing fee charged against the selection when the patent was issued.

[16] William A. Keleher, *The Fabulous Frontier* (Santa Fe, 1945), pp. 97–118.

[17] Leroy O. Moore to Jones, February 3, 1917, LCA 8333.

127,912.80 acres of lieu rights immediately to Moore for $2.50 an acre and, next year, 56,100.87 acres additional for $4.00 an acre. He first made contracts to sell scrip to many small-scale ranchers; with this as evidence of a market, he borrowed from a bank enough money to pay the railroad. He announced that he would secure final approval of the proposed exchange by going with influential friends in Washington to the Secretary of the Interior; whether he actually did or not is a question.[18] Moore easily obtained some of the lieu selections his customers made, but with others there was so much trouble that in 1921 his estate sent a representative to Washington who procured many of them.

The railroad made lieu transactions in New Mexico covering land placed within reservations by President Wilson's executive orders of 1917. It surrendered 11,780.67 acres in the Lagunas' area and sold the scrip to Charles B. Barker for $3.55 an acre. It gave up land now in the Zuñi reservation, but not so at the time of the Clovis transaction, and sold the lieu rights to two dealers—6,888.92 acres to Theo. N. Espe of Santa Fe at $4.165 an acre and 30,354.71 acres to Ben B. Wetmore of Roswell at $4.25 an acre.[19]

The Santa Fe Pacific thus solved many problems of intermixed land within New Mexico reservations, but encountered further difficulties with the Navajos over certain acreage tribesmen had used for so long they believed they had a moral claim to it, even though they did not have a legal right. Neither the United States nor the railroad wished to herd these Navajos back to the reservation without regard for their long tenure. One possible solution lay in a congressional law of 1913 authorizing the Secretary of the Interior to ask private owners for land in New Mexico, Arizona, or California which an Indian had been occupying for at least five years and to offer in lieu other vacant, nonmineral, nontimbered, surveyed public tracts of equal value and area in the same state.[20] But Navajos seeking to use this law received no apparent assistance from federal authorities and had to pay for the necessary surveys themselves. They met strong opposition from Senator Albert B. Fall of New Mexico, Assistant Secretary of the Interior Jones, and Hauke of the Bureau of Indian Affairs. They were vigorously championed by Father Anselm Weber, who kept prodding the government until it finally investigated the Navajos' applications, approved most of them, and asked owners to surrender the desired

[18] Jones to Engel, May 6, 1917, LCA 8333.

[19] TSW 8293, 8935; LCA 9474, 9650, *passim*.

[20] *Statutes-at-Large*, XXXVII, 1007. This exchange was limited to 16,000 acres in New Mexico, 3,000 in Arizona, and 5,000 in California. The time limit for starting these exchanges, several times extended, finally expired on March 1, 1941.

land.[21] The Indians occupied land owned chiefly by the Santa Fe Pacific, which relinquished 16,000 acres in New Mexico and 2,667.31 acres in Arizona. The lieu rights valid in New Mexico it wholesaled for $3.50 an acre to Leroy O. Moore and those in Arizona it retailed to various stockmen for $5.00 an acre.

The railroad sought less successfully to cope with two particular areas containing so many Navajos that the government attempted to extend the limits to include the tracts. One area, used by the Indians since 1863, was immediately east of the present bounds in New Mexico. In 1907 the United States added the acreage into the reservation, but encountered such opposition from whites who had also been using the land that in 1908 and 1911 it gradually canceled the extension. The Bureau of Indian Affairs, reluctant to see the red men lose the land they had used so long, encouraged them to secure individual, private allotments on the even-numbered sections. It thus created a problem of intermixed landownership which was never effectively settled until the passage of the Taylor Grazing Act, to be explained in Chapter XIII. Another much used region was the so-called Butte Country, lying north of Winslow and Holbrook in Arizona, which was not included in the Navajo reservation until the 1930's. During the struggle between the Indians and the whites over these two areas, the Santa Fe Pacific at first refused to lease its acreage to any but red men. However, it found the Navajos so reluctant to lease that in the late 1910's it began renting to whites. There followed constant bickering between Indians and lessees, which in a few cases developed into physical fights, inconclusive and intermittent, between the two races.

The Santa Fe Pacific had surrendered 415,040.71 acres of land in New Mexico, located both inside and outside Indian reservations, for the benefit of red men. It would have been willing, apparently, to exchange additional land had this been included within the boundaries of the Navajo reservation. The railroad also relinquished land in Arizona reservations, and to those lieu transactions the next chapter will be devoted.

[21] An unusual and interesting case is that of Hastin Dil, who had lived all his life on the acreage he desired and had built there three hogans and a corral. Shortly after one local official of the Bureau of Indian Affairs told him he should stay on the land, a Bureau forester and a Mexican incorrectly informed him that the tract did not belong to him. The Mexican proceeded to destroy the corral and two of the hogans. Wishing to avoid trouble, Hastin Dil moved off the land. When the General Land Office inspector went over the acreage, he naturally could not find sufficient evidence of occupancy to justify a favorable report. When the whole situation was explained, the Department of the Interior agreed to recognize the Indian's rights, include the tract in the exchange, and grant him title. (Unpublished land decision, First Assistant Secretary of the Interior, June 15, 1918, TSW 6227.)

CHAPTER VIII

ARIZONA INDIAN LIEU RIGHTS

THE Santa Fe Pacific relinquished 1,225,755.59 acres within Arizona reservations between 1908 and 1920. Its general policy was the same there as in New Mexico, but its difficulties were greater.

The railroad's first Arizona exchange involved 344,689 acres within what is now known as the Hopi reservation, but was then called the Moqui. The Santa Fe Pacific apparently arranged to relinquish this land as a result of oral negotiations in Washington. It sold lieu rights to the promoters of two irrigation schemes and to dealers. The schemes became so involved we shall have to discuss them in some detail.

One of these irrigation projects, called the "Agua Fria," lay about twenty miles northwest of Phoenix on the Atchison line to Ash Fork. Its backer, W. H. Beardsley of Ohio, spent $200,000 erecting a concrete dam on sand rather than bedrock, only to see the structure washed out before completion. Deciding to take the project more seriously, he began steps to secure title to the land he would irrigate. After six years of negotiation he finally agreed in 1908 to purchase Moqui scrip. The other irrigation scheme, called the "Gila Bend," was located about fifty miles southwest of Phoenix on a main line of the Southern Pacific Railroad. After a wooden dam on top of sand and forty miles of canals had been built in 1894, an immense flood nearly annihilated the project. The enterprise eventually came into the hands of Charles F. Ainsworth of Phoenix, who arranged to buy Moqui scrip.

With these two sales negotiated, the Santa Fe Pacific sought to surrender its base in the western part of the Moqui reservation and select the lieu required for the irrigation projects. To make the necessary examination of the tracts involved, the Commissioner of the General Land Office had to pick a federal inspector. In his selection he followed these instructions from a Department of the Interior attorney: ". . . furnish a man . . . who is so trustworthy that you personally can have no doubt whether he is improperly influenced by Railroad officials."[1] He chose Raymond H. Satterwhite. The inspector, accompanied by railroadman Taliaferro, examined under difficult field conditions the base and the lieu. His behavior caused "Tally" to write ". . . chaperoning a government expert around[;]

[1] G. W. Woodruff to Commissioner, General Land Office, December 23, 1908, TSW 1964.

89

to stand his kicking and complaints—to smile and take it all, is not what it is cracked up to be."[2]

Satterwhite in his report disapproved the exchange. He declared that 65 percent of the western portion of the Moqui reservation was entirely valueless and the rest there was worth 35 to 50 cents an acre. He believed these Indians already had too much land but, despite this, recommended obtaining the railroad's holding in the eastern portion of the reserve. Turning to the lieu, Satterwhite said the present

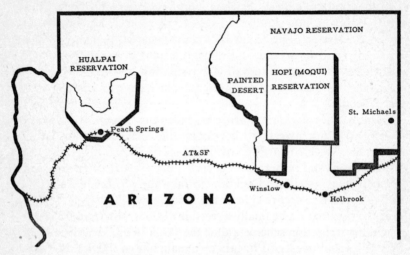

SOME ARIZONA INDIAN RESERVATIONS

worth of the desert waste at Agua Fria was 25 cents an acre, while at Gila Bend half was valueless and the rest he appraised at $2.50 an acre. But if the irrigation projects were completed, he thought almost all the land would then be worth $3.00 to $5.00 an acre. Since the base was worth less than the speculative value of the lieu, he opposed the exchange.[3]

Despite his adverse opinion, the Santa Fe Pacific resolved to secure the two tracts. It made formal selection, without difficulty, of the Gila Bend area. When it tried to file on the Agua Fria land, it failed at first. The United States Reclamation Service had earlier withdrawn the area because the site seemed suited to a possible federal project. The government afterward had abandoned its nebulous plans without restoring the tract to entry. After much negotiation, the United States

---

[2] Taliaferro to Jones, February 12, 1909, TSW 1964.

[3] R. H. Satterwhite to Commissioner, General Land Office, March 22, 1909, TSW 1964.

again threw the land open to entry by anybody, effective June 3, 1909. To secure the tract, the railroad sent Taliaferro to Phoenix. Perhaps he learned of competition, for on the evening of June 2 he and several others formed a line in front of the United States Land Office, remaining there all night. Next morning he saw officials post a notice that, because of veiled threats of violence and possible bloodshed, they would not receive an application for over 320 acres from any one person. When Taliaferro, third man in line out of a hundred, offered them Moqui scrip for 49,918.53 acres, they would not even touch it "as if it had been handled previously by a leper." They accepted applications totaling 25,000 acres for Agua Fria land from various individuals, many of whom were connected with "Melczer and the Southwestern Realty Company's crowd."[4] This unusual procedure elicited a vigorous protest from Howel Jones to Washington. His views were sustained by the Department of the Interior, which ruled that the railroad's selection would be weighed on its merits, and, since Taliaferro would have filed ahead of the other people had the Phoenix officials permitted, the company's application would be granted preference over those of others for the same acreage.

The government, upon further consideration, rejected the exchange because the base was not as valuable as the lieu. It indicated that, if the railroad wished to offer other base elsewhere, it would consider a new proposal without prejudice. In its decision it may have been influenced by Secretary of the Interior R. A. Ballinger, for shortly he was deploring to Atchison General Manager A. G. Wells the company's apparently "deliberate effort to 'get the better' of the Land Office."[5] He was soon interviewed by Howel Jones, who succeeded in correcting a few matters of fact but not in proving that it was improper to consider the speculative value of the lieu.

The railroad, eager to secure the Gila Bend and Agua Fria land, offered new base in the eastern portion of the Moqui reservation. It was examined by federal inspector F. C. Dezendorf, who reported it worth more than the unimproved Gila Bend acreage and about the same as the undeveloped Agua Fria tract; he did not consider speculative value. To supplement his favorable opinion, Ainsworth and Beardsley at Jones's suggestion brought political pressure through prominent Arizonans, the state governor, and eight congressmen.[6]

[4] Jones to B&G, June 1, 1909; affidavit, Taliaferro, June 3, 1909, TSW 1964; *Arizona Democrat* and *Arizona Gazette*, June 3, 1909; *Arizona Republican*, June 4, 1909.

[5] Wells to Jones, October 23, 1909, TSW 1964.

[6] Jones to Ainsworth, July 31, 1909, and Ainsworth to Jones, December 27, 1909, TSW 1007; Jones to Beardsley, September 16, 1909, and Beardsley to Jones,

Thus urged, the government approved the exchange and the formalities were shortly completed.

The Santa Fe Pacific now made the disagreeable discovery that neither Beardsley nor Ainsworth could pay cash, as promised, for their scrip. Since the undeveloped desert land was worth less than the value of the lieu rights used and since it did not wish itself to undertake the irrigation projects, the railroad resolved not to foreclose but rather to keep prodding the two. After one such interchange with Beardsley, Engel reported to Jones, "It got us just as far as usual, I am tired of the entire subject."[7] The company collected one-seventh of the $2.50 per acre purchase price in 1914 and, finally, the rest in 1920. Beardsley's successors then built Lake Pleasant Dam and the completed irrigation project proved fairly successful. The Santa Fe Pacific was unable to secure any money from Ainsworth and in 1916 reluctantly foreclosed. It eventually sold the 72,133.88 acres through an intermediary to F. A. Gillespie of Tulsa, who paid it $150,000. His successors later finished the undertaking, and at present there is considerable agricultural development there.

The Gila Bend and Agua Fria irrigation projects, which neither the state nor the federal government wished to sponsor, were thus finally completed. Although it is not clear whether any of the private promoters made "excessive profits," certainly the railroad did not. It sold the lieu rights in 1908, but received nothing until 1914 and the last of its money in 1920. It secured, by waiting, $2.08 an acre for seven-elevenths of the land and $2.50 for the rest; its standard price in 1910 for such scrip was $2.50.

The Santa Fe Pacific had relinquished about one-third of its land in the Moqui reservation for the lieu rights necessary for the irrigation projects. In 1910 it surrendered the rest to the Bureau of Indian Affairs, which was anxious to solidify the area because the Moqui refused to move elsewhere.[8] The company sold the resulting lieu rights for $2.50 an acre to Arizona scrip dealers: 57,954.94 acres to M. E. Leverich and Company, 22,529.33 to Fen S. Hildreth, and 54,252.40 directly or indirectly to others. They had no more difficulty in securing approval of their lieu selections than might be expected when their customers were usually trying to pick the most

December 28, 1909, TSW 22-50. Beardsley secured promises to speak personally to the Secretary of the Interior, favoring his exchange, from Senator Charles R. Dick and Representatives Thomas E. Burton, Nicholas Longworth, H. P. Goebel, R. D. Cole, Albert Douglass, E. L. Taylor, Paul Howland, and J. M. Cox.

[7] Engel to Jones, January 22, 1918, TSW 22-50.

[8] F. E. Leupp to the Secretary of the Interior, August 14, 1907, Bureau of Indian Affairs, Washington file 71294/07/371.

desirable tracts in a given region. In addition to these sales to dealers, the Santa Fe Pacific peddled a relatively small amount of Moqui scrip direct to those using it. The largest of these transactions was 14,240 acres to Senator James E. Watson of Indiana and associates. They built, merely as an exploitation, a small irrigation project a few miles northwest of Prescott. The Santa Fe Pacific refused to sell lieu rights to three different promoters, who wished to establish colonies along the Atchison's Wickenburg-Cadiz line in southern Arizona, because it feared they might exploit innocent purchasers unacquainted with the great difficulties of farming in a desert.

The railroad, having relinquished all its Moqui land, late in 1912 initiated discussions about the Navajo region of Arizona. It dealt with Acting Commissioner of Indian Affairs F. H. Abbott, who believed these red men needed every available acre within their reservation.[9] It offered him 327,404.44 acres in the Painted Desert around Canyon Diablo, which he especially wanted, and he accepted. The company sold the lieu rights at $2.50 an acre, mostly to the following:[10]

Name	Gross amount purchased, acres	Lieu selection rejected and money refunded, acres	Net retained, acres
Philip Contzen	5,268.00	3,508.00	1,176.00
M. E. Leverich and Co.	127,208.45	7,920.00	119,288.45
Fen S. Hildreth	132,698.64	8,394.67	124,303.97
J. C. Dobbins	5,000.00	—	5,000.00
Hampton & Arnold ..	3,760.00	160.00	3,600.00
Leroy O. Moore	7,480.00	1,280.00	6,200.00
Riggs & McCourt ...	31,854.64	560.00	31,294.64
N. R. Vail	22,795.40	1,480.00	21,315.40
New Mexico and Arizona Land Co.	7,077.88	—	7,077.88
J. W. Sullivan	6,000.00	560.00	5,440.00
Total	349,143.01	23,862.67	325,280.34

Clearly the first six buyers were dealers, generally retailing scrip for $3.00, and the last two themselves used the lieu rights.

The purchasers made their selections so quickly that in May 1913

[9] F. H. Abbott to the Secretary of the Interior (concurred in by the Commissioner, General Land Office, and the First Assistant Secretary), September 25, 1912, TSW 1964.

[10] TSW 3868, 4510, 4719, 5376, 5522, 6501, 6755, 6959, 7011, 10359, *passim*.

the government sent Benjamin H. Gibbs to find out whether, taken as a whole, the base and lieu were of equal quality. He was accompanied by railroadman Albert E. Lyon, who helped him see the land with the least hardship. He viewed this aid with suspicion, fearing it was an attempt to influence him. He was so careful that at the very start of the trip, when he ate on a train with two railroadmen and a scrip dealer, he refused to match to see who would pay for all the lunches.[11] He reported in October that 14 percent of the base was worthless for grazing, 38 percent poor, 34 percent fair, and 14 percent good; that of this grazing area 10,000 acres could also be cultivated; and that the total value was $599,287.75, or an average of $1.83 an acre.[12] He then began investigating the lieu.

Meanwhile a controversy arose over a Navajo transaction between the New Mexico and Arizona Land Company and the government. It grew to include also all the Santa Fe Pacific's exchange. The N. M. & A. L. Co. planned a $7,000,000 irrigation enterprise on its odd-numbered sections adjoining the Little Colorado River, near Winslow. It did not try to eliminate Navajo land from the project but did make a 21,095.77-acre swap so each party would have a solidified tract. To obtain additional even-numbered sections outside the reservation, it purchased from the Santa Fe Pacific 28,454.62 acres of Moqui scrip and 7,077.88 acres of the Navajo rights. It encountered rivalry from an organization headed by A. T. Cornish of Winslow. He wished to have considerable portions of the Navajo reservation restored to the public domain. He hoped then to have the government of Arizona, as part of the state's land gift from the United States, select acreage in the proposed irrigation area and co-operate with his company somehow in completing the project.[13]

Cornish's scheme appealed to Mulford Winsor, state land commissioner, who said he would like to secure those sections involved. He was much more concerned, however, about the general problem

---

[11] Jones commented to B&G, December 19, 1913, TSW 1964, as follows: ". . . if somebody extends to him a common courtesy, and he is not strong enough to accept it without feeling that the other person is trying to influence him, then he is not a suitable man to make an examination. The western people are generous people as you know, and if there is a crowd goes to lunch some one pays for it. . . . No one has ever tried to influence Mr. Gibbs. . . . [Because] these trips at best are fatiguing and carry with them a good deal of hardship . . . my instructions to everybody are to make the trip as comfortable as possible and to get Mr. Gibbs to the lands he is to examine [in] the best and easiest way, and all of these courtesies are in fulfillment of my instructions. No one tries to influence him, but he thinks they do because they suggest how he can get to a destination quicker and easier."

[12] B. H. Gibbs to Commissioner, General Land Office, October 29, 1913, TSW 1964.

[13] A. S. Greig to Jones, April 22, 1914, TSW 3868.

of Arizona's land policy. This question arose when Arizona became a state in 1912. Its legislature, organizing a three-man land commission in May 1912, soon ordered them to prepare their policy and to pick about two and a quarter million acres to which the state was entitled by various federal laws. These three appointed Winsor commissioner. They decided to favor the little settler, rather than the large rancher, and to make their selections in tracts that would be suitable for small-scale operations. When they began their activities, many individuals realized the danger in further delay about procuring legal title to coveted land and decided a convenient method was to use the Santa Fe Pacific's scrip. The commission at first knew nothing of these lieu exchanges, but soon became acutely conscious of them.

In September 1913 Winsor, for the state commission, protested to the Secretary of the Interior, chiefly about the New Mexico and Arizona Land Company's selections within the proposed irrigation project both by its own swap with the national government and its exercise of Santa Fe Pacific lieu rights. He also complained that the Moquis and Navajos had far more land already than they needed and that scrip was "a species of exploitation from which this State has grievously suffered."[14] The commissioner roused Arizona Senator Henry F. Ashurst, who previously had gone with the head of the N. M. & A. L. Co. to urge approval of its selections before Secretary of the Interior Franklin K. Lane. In a Senate speech, Ashurst distorted earlier forest lieu transactions and warned of the "unfair" Navajo exchange. He thus caused the Department of the Interior to stop action on all Navajo scrip selections of the Santa Fe Pacific's customers and on the special swap with the N. M. & A. L. Co. The suspension was shortly removed, probably through the efforts of A. S. Greig, head of the N. M. & A. L. Co. He may or may not have heeded the advice of Howel Jones to exert political pressure through Senator William J. Stone of Missouri. His success was short-lived, for less than a month later Ashurst made another speech in the Senate, and the Department of the Interior again suspended the transactions.[15]

Obviously a struggle was developing. Jones inspired the scrip dealers to have each customer make written protest in his own way to the Secretary of the Interior and to Ashurst. He urged as many as possible to see Senator Marcus A. Smith, who briefly returned to Arizona. Governor George W. P. Hunt was subjected by his constituents to considerable arguments, "political in tone and implication,

[14] Mulford Winsor to the Secretary of the Interior, September 8, 1913, reproduced in *Congressional Record*, 63d Cong., 1st sess., p. 5119.
[15] *Congressional Record*, 63d Cong., 2d sess., pp. 863–68.

that it would be to his interest to effect a change in the Commission's policy."[16] He remained steadfast; Ashurst again changed to approving the exchange; Smith consistently advocated it; and Representative Carl Hayden, while avoiding expression of an opinion, urged that the state commission present a fully prepared case to Washington authorities.

Even before this suggestion, the commission took action. It had W. A. Moody and assistants examine the base while Cy Byrne's group inspected the lieu. These men, Howel Jones complained at the time, carefully concealed their intent; these men, wrote Winsor in 1943, frankly stated their purpose.

The land commission, in a written report after the investigation, valued the Painted Desert base at less than 10 cents an acre and described it in the following "purple passage":

. . . it is only by a questionable assumption of practical values . . . and viewing the whole from the Indian rather than the white man's standpoint, that any value at all can be given to the [base]. . . . It has been seen how the tracts giving greatest promise to the eye have been proved, by analysis and actual experience, worthless for agriculture, because of their enormous content of mineral salts; . . . how great areas, closely classified for their sparse growths of mediocre grasses and abundant growths of worthless ones, and given the benefit of every doubt, would support so few head of stock as to render their use by stockmen impractical, and how wind and sand and the lack of water add to the hazard; how the best grazing lands, insignificant in quantity, are so dry and so covered with sharp rocks as to render them almost useless; how miles upon miles, comprising the widest area of all, stretch away hard, barren and shining, or rear great heads of brilliantly colored "bad lands" clay; how over it all the fierce winds sweep, the fine sand drift[s] and inevitable, unconquerable drouth reigns.[17]

The land commission declared that the lieu selections were the choicest of the remaining unappropriated public domain and valued them at $2.00 to $50.00 per acre. It said they had been made by desert land homesteaders too unenterprising to meet the government's "reasonable requirements," by stockmen and by speculators. It branded the Santa Fe Pacific as "committing a fraud" in the whole exchange. It attacked the N. M. & A. L. Co. swap, alleging there was a great difference between the two adjacent tracts. It declared that the "most fanciful hopes or fears of the most ardent Indian-protecting imagination can

---

[16] Mulford Winsor, "The Moqui and Navajo Scrip Case," MS study, 1943, deposited in the State Library of Arizona, Phoenix.

[17] Report to the state land commission, unsigned, May 25, 1914, TSW 1964.

hardly summon a need" for such a large quantity of land as that to be procured by these two transactions for the Navajos. It pointed out that the area involved was not within the official "legal boundaries" of the reservation but had merely been set aside from homestead entry by executive orders of November 14, 1901, and January 8, 1910.

After this report of the state reached the Department of the Interior and before federal inspector Gibbs submitted his own appraisal of the lieu, there was a two-day hearing in Washington before First Assistant Secretary of the Interior A. A. Jones. Present and favoring the exchange were many representatives of the railroad, the N. M. & A. L. Co., and the scrip dealers. As opposition there was Mulford Winsor. The inconclusive hearing, dealing in generalities, involved discussion of the unequal value of the base and lieu. During the session, Winsor admitted there had been no intentional misconduct by either railroad or government officials.[18] Shortly thereafter Father Anselm Weber published a pamphlet telling why he believed all the acreage within the reservation should belong to the Navajos.[19]

After a considerable delay, the government asked the railroad to substitute for the base in the Painted Desert, westernmost portion of the reservation, an equal quantity of land around St. Michaels in easternmost Arizona. This request was at once executed, for the company wished to lose neither the money involved in its sales nor the good will of the many retail purchasers. Federal authorities promptly assigned examination of all the base and lieu to Gibbs from Arizona and E. L. Culver and Rufus W. Pearson from Washington. Gibbs alone had completed a report on the lieu eight months previously. He was treated in very undiplomatic fashion by his two Washington associates, who, for example, commented in his hearing that his previous report was so voluminous a horse could hardly haul it and that his summary caused the Commissioner of the General Land Office to exclaim, "For God's sake, make a brief of this brief." The three were accompanied by the railroad's field examiner, Albert E. Lyon. In the midst of the trip, this arrangement aroused Governor Hunt. He did not charge the company with improperly influencing the inspectors but thought state representatives should also accompany them. His request was accepted in principle by Washington authorities, but it was too late to honor it. The tour was made entirely

[18] Transcript of hearing before the First Assistant Secretary of the Interior, June 9 and 10, 1914, TSW 1964. Sometimes when Winsor became confused by adroit answers of those he was cross-questioning, First Assistant Secretary A. A. Jones took over the examination for a moment and elicited what Winsor had been seeking.

[19] Anselm Weber, *The Navajo Indians: A Statement of Facts* (St. Michaels, Arizona, 1914).

by automobile, to the sorrow of Gibbs who wanted a horseback ride to cause Culver and Pearson "a little misery." The two Easterners gradually grew cool to each other and finally every one of the three was making Lyon his confidant. They indicated during the examination that they hoped to approve the exchange, Gibbs commenting that clearly Washington authorities so wished it.[20] Although Lyon did not learn their final opinion, he expressed to Jones his own that the base was "the best grazing proposition in Arizona."[21]

During the interval between the end of the examination and the government's final decision, Mulford Winsor was ousted as Arizona state land commissioner. His attack on lieu rights and his other policies which did not favor large cattlemen had angered them. He had also irritated those who leased state land around Phoenix in the 1870's and irrigated it, for he now wished to sell the acreage off to the highest bidder and have the purchaser pay a fair value for the improvements. These two opponents combined to bring so much pressure on the state legislature that it eliminated the old three-man land board and created a new five-man one. The new group at first seemed to favor Winsor but met such objections that at the last minute it voted to remove him.[22]

In August 1915 Commissioner of the General Land Office Clay Tallman, with the approval of Secretary of the Interior Franklin K. Lane, sanctioned most of the Santa Fe Pacific's exchange. He said 60 percent of the lieu was clearly grazing land, about 30 percent meadow land, and about 10 percent had once been claimed by desert land act or homestead entries. He accepted 303,351.04 acres of lieu and rejected 24,223.72 acres that contained a spring or were river bottom land or were of exceptional strategic value.[23] He shortly authorized the company to make other selections as replacement for those he had disapproved. The railroad, after refunding the money of the original purchasers, resold the scrip to the two chief Arizona dealers, Leverich and Hildreth. It had no difficulty in securing ap-

[20] A. E. Lyon to Jones, May 14, 1915, TSW 1964.

[21] In an interview with the author in the summer of 1949, Winsor conceded that the new base was valuable land, much better than the original, but would not commit himself whether it was of "equal value" to the lieu.

[22] Interview with Winsor, summer 1949. In the state elections of 1920, five years after Winsor's removal, it was charged that the state land commission had leased large areas of grazing land for long periods to large stockmen at rates much lower than the tracts were worth. (*Mohave County Miner*, October 2, 1920.)

[23] Clay Tallman to the Secretary of the Interior, August 27, 1915, TSW 1964. In this exchange, as in virtually every large land transaction the Santa Fe Pacific ever made, there was much confusion as to the exact acreage involved, and the author has used his best judgment in deciding what was the final figure used. In this case, for example, the various figures for the new base were 327,402.44, 330,000, 330,928.65, and 327,574.76, of which apparently the last is the accurate one.

proval of the new selections. It took no action about the original base in the Painted Desert and, as we shall see in Chapter XII, in 1934 finally received cash for it from the Bureau of Indian Affairs.

The government in 1915 rejected the New Mexico and Arizona Land Company's proposed swap. When combined with the bankruptcy of the corporation's parent, the Frisco railroad, this killed the irrigation project. The N. M. & A. L. Co., however, had picked 35,532.50 acres in the area with Santa Fe Pacific scrip, and the selection itself was approved by federal authorities. The land company actually received title from the railroad to 5,900 acres for which it had already paid, but did not at the time obtain the additional 29,635.50 acres for which it lacked money. Its debt was canceled by Howel Jones's superiors, over his violent protests. It ultimately secured the rest of the tract when it arranged a land swap with the railroad during the Petrified Forest lieu transaction described in Chapter VI. This was the final act in settling the complicated Navajo exchange.

Several interesting questions arise regarding the whole transaction. What was the real value of the first base in the Painted Desert? Less than 10 cents an acre, said the Arizona State Land Commission; $1.83, said federal inspector Gibbs; $1.00, said railroad landman Collinson in 1928, and that was the price the federal government eventually paid. Despite Howel Jones's admission that one-eleventh of the area was "very inferior land," $1.00 was likely a fair value. What was the worth of the second base around St. Michaels? Everybody thought it was much better than the Painted Desert region. Lyon told Jones that "it was the best grazing proposition in Arizona." Tallman valued the pasture at $1.50; considering farm land, timber, and coal, he appraised the whole base at $4.00 an acre. What was the value of the lieu? It was $2.00 to $50.00 an acre, declared the Arizona State Land Commission; at least $3.00, said almost all the purchasers when they paid that much retail for their scrip; $4.00, on the average, said Tallman.

Was the Painted Desert land actually within the Navajo reservation? No, said the state commission, because the executive orders had merely withdrawn the land from entry. Maybe, said the federal government. It disapproved the N. M. & A. L. Co. swap as unauthorized under the act of 1904, which applied to "any private land over which an Indian reservation has been extended by Executive order." It did not, however, at this time or later directly admit that the Painted Desert area was legally outside the reservation nor has it ever so treated the region.

What of Mulford Winsor? He believed that white men rather than red should have as much of Arizona as possible. He thought that his department should favor small-scale ranchers rather than large. He wished to secure for the state the best of the remaining public domain. His complaints about the principles of lieu rights in general were accurate as far as he went but were not a fully rounded picture of the situation. His protest that those executive orders as worded did not legally put the Painted Desert area within the reservation caused the railroad and the government considerable embarrassment. He correctly pointed out that the original base was not worth a great deal, but he should not have supported such a ridiculous valuation as 10 cents an acre. He ought not to have talked of the railroad's "committing a fraud," since he admitted there was no intentional misconduct. Since he did do these things, he could hardly justify his complaints that pressure brought on Washington to approve the exchange violated "the Marquis of Queensbury rules." All in all, he displayed a quality most praiseworthy in a public servant—the willingness to fight, almost alone against great odds and despite threats of dismissal, for a cause he sincerely believed in.

The railroad, in surrendering the Painted Desert land, gave the Bureau of Indian Affairs acreage its acting commissioner said was especially desired. Because this first base was not as valuable as the lieu selected, an exchange involving the new base around St. Michaels was more equitable. It is now clear that the Navajos really needed both areas and it is very doubtful whether Congress would ever have paid cash for all the land they required. During the struggle over the exchange, there was little discussion in the newspapers and apparently the majority of Arizonans were either not interested or not informed about the case. Political pressure was exerted by those on both sides of the dispute.[24]

The next lieu transaction was begun by the Navajos themselves, who conducted a two-year campaign of persuading Washington authorities to acquire 223,422.08 acres of Santa Fe Pacific land located south of the tract around St. Michaels, just discussed.[25] Their pleas were finally heeded by the government, which in 1918 asked the railroad to relinquish the land. The company did.

The Santa Fe Pacific sold all the lieu rights at $3.00 an acre to

[24] The only publications stating an opinion were the *Tucson Citizen* and *Dunbar's Weekly*; both opposed Winsor. The latter, he told the author, ceased its objections when he sent a one-hundred-word telegram from Washington containing such unpleasant truths about the weekly that the telegraph company made him rephrase the message.

[25] Chee Dodge to Cato Sells, May 28, 1918, TSW 8540.

Tom E. Pollock of Flagstaff, Arizona, who used them to pick about two-sevenths of the even-numbered sections within an area where he had previously purchased the company's odd-numbered ones.[26] His selections were appraised by federal inspector J. A. Ramsey, accompanied by the railroad's Taliaferro who discovered that the government man "surely likes bacon and good butter." His choices met strong opposition. Part of it stemmed from those stockmen whose free use of the public domain, intermixed with the land Pollock already owned, would stop if he secured title to the acreage. Part came from his chief rivals for the economic control of northern Arizona, the Babbitt family. These two groups formed the so-called Northern Arizona Protective Association, which proclaimed Pollock's selections as 1,173,241 acres rather than the actual 223,422.08 and trumpeted that all ranchers in northern Arizona would be driven out of business.[27] It could not persuade other stockmen's organizations, even in the immediate area, to join the protest. It forced the General Land Office to hold a hearing in Washington during which it attacked the selections and, without proof, federal inspector Ramsey's integrity. It failed and the government approved the lieu.

Pollock was the only owner in the Santa Fe Pacific grant area who ever undertook a large-scale solidification of his ranch by purchasing railroad scrip. He gained absolute ownership of all the odd-numbered sections and of two-sevenths of the even, which apparently gave him *de facto* control of his entire range. He could keep out interlopers, but did not secure much improvement in the capacity of the area to feed additional livestock. He and his successors gradually came to feel that $3.00 an acre, the then current price for railroad lieu rights, had been too expensive. Their opinion is supported by the observation of the railroad land commissioner in 1932 that the return from their enterprises would not justify an average price of over $1.00 to $1.25 an acre.[28]

[26] See Chapter IX. Pollock founded the Arizona Central Bank, the Apache Lumber Company, the Apache Railway, and the Arizona Lumber Company. He controlled coal mines in British Columbia and Utah as well as a steamship line. He overextended himself. Between 1922 and 1924 he surrendered control of everything to his creditors except three-sevenths of his livestock enterprises. During the great depression of the 1930's, the bank he formerly owned failed, and through his intervention depositors eventually received 51 percent of their money instead of 20 percent. (*Holbrook Tribune News*, March 11, 1938; LCA 9363, *passim*.)

[27] *Coconino Sun* and *Northern Arizona Leader*, December 26, 1919. The two newspapers each carried exactly the same article about the association. The *Mohave County Miner*, January 17, 1920, contained a more accurate account of the Pollock transaction.

[28] Collinson to Engel, May 26, 1932, LCA 9363.

The successful completion of Pollock's lieu transaction marked the end of the railroad's Indian exchanges in the period from 1897 to 1920. It had surrendered 1,640,796.30 acres in New Mexico and Arizona, receiving 1,313,393.86 acres in lieu rights but no compensation in this period for the 327,402.44 acres in the Painted Desert. After a long struggle with the government over rules, it had struck difficulties in the first Zuñi transaction because "boomers" had mistakenly been allowed to make homestead entries on its lieu. In the Moqui swap, it had trouble over selecting land for two irrigation projects. In the first Arizona-Navajo exchange it met opposition from the state land commission, especially Winsor, and in the second from those who wanted to continue grazing the public domain without hindrance. It had no problems with the Laguna, the New Mexico–Navajo, or the second Zuñi transactions. It ran into much politics in the first Zuñi and first Arizona-Navajo altercations; into a little in the Moqui. What further kinds of complications it could have encountered is difficult to imagine.

These lieu transactions solved a difficult problem of intermixed land. The railroad secured the right to pick a series of small tracts, at least as valuable as the land relinquished, in exchange for relatively large areas in the reservations. The government obtained land which the Indians, especially the Navajos, clearly needed since most of them refused to leave their reservation areas as established earlier. It is very doubtful, had there been no exchanges, whether Congress would ever have appropriated money to pay for this acreage. The lieu transactions were fought by white men who coveted the Indians' land, who opposed additional acreage for the red men on more legitimate grounds, or who objected to the lieu selected. On the whole, the basic principle of eliminating private land within reservations by exchange had considerable merit.

CHAPTER IX

LAUNCHING A LAND SALES POLICY

THE land activities of the Santa Fe Pacific between 1897 and 1920 embraced more than the lieu transactions. They included selling or leasing grazing tracts, vending irrigable areas, deeding a little dry-farming acreage, marketing coal land, disposing of timber, hawking town lots, arranging for surveys, obtaining title to land, paying taxes, considering claims arising from four Atlantic and Pacific contracts, and noting range deterioration. To these various matters this chapter and the next one will be devoted.

The Santa Fe Pacific never sought settlers for its grant. It knew that the area was too arid for farming without irrigation and that the land was too crowded with interloping ranchers for much space to be available for additional stockmen. It shunned unethical sales campaigns among the uninformed as well as avoided possible range conflicts between old-timers and newcomers. It tried to find customers among those already in the region.

When the Santa Fe Pacific first took over the grant in 1897, it relied on two part-time commission agents to secure customers and to determine whether prices the prospects offered were fair.[1] It received little business through the two. When demand quickened in 1912, it hired Albert E. Lyon as a full-time field examiner to appraise its land, to talk with prospects without committing the railroad, and to forward offers to Howel Jones. He resigned in 1917 and was not replaced until 1922, except for Charles L. Moore's eleven months of service starting July 1918.[2]

The Santa Fe Pacific at first knew only vaguely the nature of its

[1] The Arizona agent was John T. Hogue of St. Johns, who had fought in the Civil War, edited an Ohio country newspaper, served in the Arizona territorial legislature, appraised land for the Atlantic and Pacific, and managed a star route mail service. When President Garfield's administration uncovered wholesale star-route frauds in the West, Hogue hid in Arizona's Round Valley to avoid prosecution. Later he settled in St. Johns, although he was "decidedly too big a man" for the numerous county offices which he held concurrently to make a living. In 1910 Hogue left for the East. (*St. Johns Observer*, August 18, 1934.) The New Mexico agent was a veteran surveyor, R. C. Marmon of Laguna, who was ". . . a squaw-man but with all a pretty good kind of fellow and very influential with the Laguna [Indian] tribe." He attended to a few matters for the railroad until his death in the early 1920's. At no time did the Santa Fe Pacific have any other commission agents.

[2] Lyon shortly entered the United States Army and died while in service. Relatives purchased land from the railroad in his home town, Gallup, and established a municipal park in his honor.

property and had not informed itself in detail until the early 1930's, because it never felt the volume of sales warranted a grantwide appraisal. It had no price list, but asked a prospect to make an offer and then learned from its field examiner or commission agents if the proposal was fair. If it thought the bid was too low, it asked for more without saying how much; if it believed the price was too high, it hurried to accept. If two people wanted the same land, the railroad never disclosed the name of either party or the price offered but merely told each prospect whether his bid was the larger of the two. Its system of secrecy enabled it to obtain higher prices than it otherwise would have. If somebody wanted a tract which was rented to another, it gave the lessee an opportunity to bid but no other preference.

In deciding whether to accept an offer, the railroad tried to make the good land sell the less attractive by refusing, for example, to dispose of a spring without all the surrounding acreage dependent upon the water. It alleged it would never sell less than a township, but actually did so if clearly the transaction would not later interfere with marketing the remaining land. It considered unusual circumstances, such as those in a sale where it required the purchaser to pay a nearly bankrupt lessee for a valuable dam he had built on the property. If two ranchers were disputing over range rights, the company would sell to neither until they had settled their controversy. The entire correspondence about land sales reveals that in each instance the railroad treated everybody alike and did not "play favorites."[3]

The Santa Fe Pacific virtually never granted options. It nearly always sold its grazing land for one-fifth down and the rest in four equal annual payments with 6 percent interest. In order to avoid difficulties with foreclosures, it never took a mortgage. Before 1920 it had little trouble with delinquent installments and did not even need to consider repossessing any land. It generally accepted anticipated payments but refused a discount for them. Contrary to its standard practice, the railroad sometimes sold unsurveyed land and assumed each section contained 640 acres; but if later this was found not so, it made financial adjustments.

The Santa Fe Pacific used a standard land sales contract and refused to vary from it. It exempted from the transaction all acreage "now" or later to be used by the Atchison for railroad operating purposes, in earlier agreements merely reserving the land but by 1915 promising to repay the customer the average selling price per acre plus

---

[3] On several occasions Atchison traffic or operating officials tried to persuade Jones to sell to one person rather than another. He invariably replied with a rude letter telling them to mind their own business.

the value of any improvements made. If it could not deliver a valid deed to any portion of the area sold, it promised a proportionate refund plus 6 percent interest. If the purchaser failed to make the payment due at a specified time, it could repossess the land just as though the sales contract had never been made. In administering these agreements, the railroad adopted certain rules. It would not allow a notary to acknowledge any signature, because then the contract could be recorded in the county courthouse and cloud the company's title. When payments were completed, the agreement must be returned or a bond posted before the road would issue a deed.[4] It permitted a purchaser to transfer his contract to another if he would remain liable for the money yet due. It forbade a purchaser doing anything that lessened the value of the land until he had completed his payments. It told a third party nothing about a sales contract, unless the purchaser so requested.

After having considered these general principles, let us discuss specific sales. Through 1912 the company sold only 14,000 acres of grazing land in Arizona and 1,600 acres in New Mexico.[5] It attained little success in convincing ranchers already in the area they should purchase the company's acreage rather than trespass on it. The company encountered difficulties because many of its tracts were still unsurveyed. It concentrated on lieu right exchanges, which brought an immediate profit, while between 1902 and 1912 the value of its grant land more than doubled.[6] The company began in 1912 to receive for the first time a noticeable number of inquiries about its acreage. Becoming more aggressive, it hired Lyon as field examiner. In 1913 and 1914 the company disposed of 11,538 acres in Navajo and Apache counties, Arizona, and 1,280 acres in New Mexico.

While Howel Jones continued selling grazing land in his own

[4] On a rare occasion when violating this rule, Jones explained to the anxious railroad secretary, E. L. Copeland (May 28, 1912, TSW 4349) :

"Mr. [J. W.] Sullivan is an old time cow man. I think he got part of his education in Texas and finished it in Arizona, and the theory of the ordinary cow man is to give anything pertaining to letter writing and paying bills attention after everything else in a business way is completed; but if anything is to be neglected it is letter writing and bill paying. Now this gives you a picture of Mr. Sullivan; he is trustworthy, reliable and a great friend of the Santa Fe. We will get the contracts one of these days, providing he has not lost them."

[5] Various totals on grazing land sales in this chapter were obtained from ninety-one correspondence files concerning individual transactions. Where the letters referred to "sections" or "townships" without giving specific acreage, it is assumed these units were standard size although they were not in all cases. For example, there are several "sections" in Mohave County that actually contain over 1,000 acres each.

[6] Jones to Engel, July 6, 1912, LCA 3131.

conservative fashion, he allowed Hugo Seaberg to experiment with aggressive or promotional methods.[7] He granted the Raton scrip dealer an option on 40,767.16 acres in San Juan County, New Mexico, at $2.50 an acre. Seaberg believed the whole area was underlain with coal; the railroad that about 4 percent of it was. The dealer tried to hawk the tract at $4.25 an acre by publishing six thousand copies of an expensive prospectus in which he discussed oil possibilities, emphasized coal probabilities, suggested ranching, and recommended retailing the "wonderfully rich" area to small farmers. His booklet, unusually rosy even for Seaberg's optimistic outlook, failed to sell the land. He turned to less expensive letters, with lure but no details, then to extensive newspaper and magazine advertisements. He received many inquiries, but secured no purchasers, even though he reduced his price. In 1921, having bought seven sections for himself, he surrendered the option. He had conclusively demonstrated, without cost to the railroad and probably without mentioning its name, that high-pressure tactics would not sell the grant land.

Howel Jones, meanwhile, achieved considerable success using conservative methods. He followed Engel's instructions to sell every acre possible if offered a reasonable price. He sold a number of odd-numbered sections to ranchers who believed their purchase would enable them to control the intermixed even-numbered sections. In other words, they believed that for every acre of Santa Fe Pacific land purchased they virtually got an acre of government land free. Their decision to buy was influenced by the Stock Raising Homestead Act of 1916, which for the first time authorized selections as large as 640 acres and brought a number of newcomers into the grant region. An even more important influence on the old-timers was rising livestock prices during the First World War. To exploit conditions to the fullest, they sought to conserve the water normally wasted through runoff and to distribute their stock more evenly over an area by building many small earthen reservoirs. To protect these investments in improvements for increasing the carrying capacity of their range, the stockmen hoped to exclude all other persons from the tracts.

Jones became convinced that a number of ranchers around Flagstaff and Ash Fork, Arizona, would buy land if he could only persuade somebody to take the first step. Concentrating on Tom Pollock, he made his first sale to the Arizonan in 1915 and soon sold him a total of 718,242.40 acres in Coconino and Yavapai counties for an average price of slightly more than $1.00 an acre. Following Pollock's

[7] LCA 6141, *passim.*

lead, Babbitt Brothers bought 300,573.46 acres for $326,062.90, the Reid-Cashion Land and Cattle Company of Seligman, 179,037.58 acres, and twenty-eight other ranchers, 410,209.56 acres. In all, from 1915 through 1919, the railroad sold 1,608,063 acres in the central part of northern Arizona. It persuaded thirty-three ranchers elsewhere in the same state to buy 449,739.14 acres at prices from 75 cents to $3.00. This made a total for Arizona of 2,057,802.14 acres. In New Mexico, where for some obscure reason sales lagged, the company disposed of 138,577 acres to thirteen stockmen at from $1.02 to $2.50 an acre. To its three largest customers it sold about half of the entire 2,196,379.14 acres; to ten others, buying not less than 34,560 acres, one quarter; and to sixty-four others the remaining quarter.[8] Obviously it sold to medium or large operators, rather than small ones. It did not, however, have any policy favoring big ranchers over small ones, for even in refereeing range disputes between prospective purchasers it remained scrupulously fair. Almost all of its customers were already located in the grant area at the time they bought railroad land.

The Santa Fe Pacific's sales policy for arid grazing land compares favorably with those of others marketing similar acreage. Of the private companies, the Southern Pacific Railroad, whose curiosity prompted it in 1915 to have its own examiners appraise 34,620 acres in Arizona which Jones had sold for 93 cents an acre, reported it was obtaining $1.50 to $1.75 for similar land elsewhere.[9] In the grant area of New Mexico and Arizona, the Aztec Land and Cattle Company was selling property as fast as possible and hoped, overoptimistically, to dispose of everything before the boom in stock prices ended. The New Mexico and Arizona Land Company also sold some acreage but did not co-operate with the Santa Fe Pacific.

The states of New Mexico and Arizona, in selecting land which the federal government had given them, chose many tracts at the specific request of ranchers and picked others with an eye to controlling the adjacent public domain. These two states, Nevada, and the railroad all followed similar sales policies. None except possibly Nevada had an established price list, but all used a system of bidding. Arizona and New Mexico conducted public auctions while the railroad received secret, written offers in Topeka. Only the company considered special circumstances such as conflicting range right disputes. Arizona's min-

---

[8] In considering these figures, recall the generalization that it takes 40 acres to sustain a cow for a year in the grant area and that a township (23,040 acres) is the minimum amount of land a rancher there needs to earn a reasonable living.

[9] B. A. McAllister to Jones, April 1, 1915, TSW 1324.

imum price was $3.00 an acre, New Mexico's was $3.00 or $5.00 according to location, and the railroad generally charged $1.00 to $1.50. Arizona required 5 percent down, New Mexico at first 10 and later 5 percent, Nevada 20 percent, and the railroad 20 percent. Arizona collected 5 percent interest, New Mexico 4, Nevada 6, and the railroad 6. Arizona allowed thirty-eight years in which to pay, New Mexico thirty, Nevada first twenty-five and later fifty, but the railroad only four. The states, especially Arizona, had difficulties with speculative purchases, but the railroad did not. All four were lenient about delinquent payments, but only the railroad escaped serious problems during this period. The Santa Fe Pacific earned less money from its sales than the states will have if the terms of the contracts are fully carried out. One reason for the difference in prices was that the states could choose their land but the company had to take its odd-numbered sections where they lay. The sales policies of the railroad compare very favorably with those of the three states.[10]

Although sales of land for grazing were the most important, the Santa Fe Pacific marketed some of its grant for other purposes. It even considered one offer to purchase all its property and another to buy everything in New Mexico, but rejected both. It wondered whether to sell any land for agriculture, knowing that the soil was rich enough but that the scanty rainfall necessitated irrigation for successful crops. It decided to discourage any dry farmers, but yielded to six strong-minded individualists who between 1897 and 1920 purchased 10,683.87 acres at $2.00 to $3.00 an acre.[11]

The Santa Fe Pacific faced a special temptation in four large valleys adjacent to the Atchison's 150 miles of main line between Seligman, Arizona, and Needles, California. Each contains excellent soil and much level land but is entirely arid. The deficiency cannot be overcome by dry-farming methods, as at least seven attempts by private individuals have proved. It cannot be conquered by irrigation from the Colorado River, because a water lift of 1,500 or 2,500 feet to the level of the valleys is an economic impossibility. It might be remedied by wells, but none have been successful. This solution appealed to

[10] New Mexico State Land Office, *New Mexico: Its Resources . . . Its Attractions* (Santa Fe, 1916), pp. 10–13; Sanford A. Mosk, "Land Policy and Stock Raising in the Western United States," *Agricultural History*, XVII (1943), 20–24, 28. As late as the middle 1930's, neither New Mexico nor Arizona had appraised the state holdings.

[11] Jones asked one of the six an elaborate series of questions before consenting to make a sale and, in reply to his question why the applicant was so certain he could dry-farm successfully, received the answer, "The Bible tells us one Joseph and Pharaoh *et al.* made a stake out of a drought, so why can't we?"

Newton Evans, who dreamed of colonizing the railroad's land in thirteen townships. The company stipulated he must bore thirty-nine test wells as an essential preliminary, but he sank only three. All failed and, after ten years of scheming, Evans abandoned the enterprise. Edward M. Fowler, a Los Angeles real estate and insurance man, had similar ambitions. He drilled four of the wells required by the railroad, obtaining a small quantity of very salty water in one, and gave up.

The railroad would not permit anybody to settle farmers on its land in the four valleys unless he had obtained adequate water first. Jones believed an unsuccessful colonization project would disgrace both the Santa Fe Pacific and the Atchison. Between 1901 and 1920 he rejected schemes from fifty-two different promoters who merely wished to exploit ignorant outsiders. His successors have followed his example, even during the Boulder (Hoover) Dam excitement. This policy, based on ethical standards as well as enlightened self-interest, reflects real credit upon the railroad and upon the originator, Jones.

Outside the area of these four valleys, the company did own several tracts where irrigation was possible. It never sought promoters, but was approached by several. They reflected the general interest in western irrigation problems stimulated by the Carey Act of 1894, the Newlands Act of 1902, and the propaganda of George W. Maxwell. A Michigan promoter, D. M. Martin of Hillsdale, eyed a narrow shelf on the east bank of the Colorado River about opposite Needles and virtually level with the stream. He purchased 17,360.76 acres of railroad land there for $21,481.05. He and his associates threw out a "wing" to catch water rather than building a dam but met with little success in their project. Their successors laid out a townsite and offered farm tracts at $25 to $60 an acre, but uncontrolled spring floods on the Colorado River prevented the enterprise from ever prospering.[12] Another project was Lyman Dam on the Little Colorado River in Apache County, Arizona, south of St. Johns. It had originated with Desert Land Act entrymen. They eventually combined with two Denver attorneys, J. H. Sherman and Charles A. Stokes, who had purchased 44,258 acres of the railroad's land at $1.25 an acre. Three dams were built and washed out; a fourth, completed with state aid, held. The project was not an engineering success, since only 9,000 of the anticipated 15,000 acres could actually be irrigated; it was not a financial success, since the total cost of $70.33 an acre necessitated forgiving part of the debt; and it was not much of an eco-

[12] TSW 25-25 and 10917, *passim*. With the completion of Boulder (Hoover) and Davis dams on the river, it would now seem some of the land could be cultivated.

nomic success, since it was sixty-eight miles from the nearest rail shipping point, Holbrook.[13]

The Santa Fe Pacific owned land at two other irrigation sites. It discussed possible development just west of the Arizona–New Mexico line at Chambers, but none of its three prospects took action. It became involved in the Bluewater enterprise, a few miles west of Grants, New Mexico. Mormon settlers had built the first dam there, a failure, and then lost their water rights to the Bluewater Land and Irrigation Company, whose dam also washed away. The irrigation company sold out to Sidney M. Worthy of Chicago, whose dam was likewise destroyed. He then purchased 1,563.24 acres of railroad land at $3.00 each but it took him ten years to pay for it. He never completed his entire project, although, as we shall see in Chapter XIII, others did in 1929.[14]

In addition to grazing and irrigation areas, the Santa Fe Pacific owned more acreage underlain with coal than there would be demand for in the foreseeable future. It sold no land for coal mining except around Gallup, New Mexico, where development had begun in the early 1880's and where by the early 1900's the Victor-American Fuel Company, a subsidiary of the Colorado Fuel and Iron Company, had a monopoly of the field. The Victor-American in 1906 faced a suit from the Caledonian Coal and Mining Company charging that it had destroyed the small concern by use of its special secret rates over the Atchison, a concession allegedly granted it in a contract covering many matters between the railroad and the Colorado Fuel and Iron Company. The Atchison was ordered by the judge to produce a copy of the contract at the trial, but avoided compliance when the Victor-American purchased the Caledonian shortly before the court session.[15] Whatever the truth of these charges, the Santa Fe Pacific marketed its coal land only to the Victor-American prior to 1933. Between 1902 and 1917 it sold to the Victor-American 18,639.55 acres for $104,-051.67 as well as 4,037.31 acres of small holders' scrip.

The railroad also owned forest land. With the Arizona Lumber and Timber Company of Flagstaff it made a contract, shortly changed

[13] TSW 3866, *passim; St. Johns Observer*, March 12, 1927.

[14] TSW 2053, *passim.* During an extended controversy between local settlers and Worthy over water rights, the false rumor spread that Engel and Jones were secretly involved financially. Engel commented to Jones, June 8, 1921, TSW 9060: "The records of this office certainly are open and clear and you know fully the difficulties we have had here and the utter disgust with which I view the entire situation."

[15] *McKinley County Republican*, March 24, 1906; Rowland Thomas, "The Railroads and the Square Deal: The Story of the Santa Fe," *World's Work*, X (1905), 6616–28.

twice by complicated amendments, which authorized cutting on 264.5 acres. The early results of this transaction are not clear, although between 1902 and 1911 the railroad received $157,178.75 for timber on 39 sections. An interesting proviso in the contract forbade cutting within one mile of the main line, apparently to preserve attractive scenery for passengers.[16] The Santa Fe Pacific between 1905 and 1913 sold trees for fuel on 11.25 sections, generally at 25 cents a cord. It deeded 9,600 acres of tie timber, as well as the land itself, to an Atchison subsidiary for $50,000. It marketed, of course, most of its timber through the forest lieu exchanges described in Chapter V. For such miscellaneous purposes as excavating fire clay, quarrying building stone, and laying out a golf course, the railroad sold 9,077 acres of rural land. It gave away 80 acres to a missionary establishment and 12 to a cemetery.[17]

In addition to rural land the Santa Fe Pacific owned lots in the five towns laid out by the Atlantic and Pacific: Ash Fork, Williams, Flagstaff, Winslow, and Gallup. It used a banker at Winslow and Atchison station agents elsewhere as local sales representatives, paying them a 5 percent commission. It generally sold lots at $25 and $35, although a few ran as high as $100, always one-half down and the rest in six months. It placed no restrictions on its deeds, except that on certain lots near Fred Harvey's Ash Fork eating house it prohibited a saloon and use for "other questionable purposes."[18] The railroad sold its last lot in Ash Fork in the early 1910's; at Flagstaff it disposed of property remaining in 1911 to George Babbitt; at Williams, it wholesaled its unmarketed property to Babbitt in 1912; at Gallup, it retailed all its lots and then deeded 126.57 acres for $16.50 each to the local Atchison station agent for a new subdivision. At Winslow, Howel

[16] Contracts, Santa Fe Pacific RR with Arizona Lumber and Timber Company, November 1, 1897, April 16, 1898, and October 11, 1898, LCA A&P Document Box No. 1; TSW 1861, *passim.*

[17] Jones had much trouble in giving away the land, already long used as a cemetery, in what he considered proper fashion. He couldn't deed it to the village of Seligman, unincorporated, or to a cemetery association, which nobody would organize, or to Yavapai County, which flatly refused it. Finally, he persuaded one man to serve as a self-perpetuating trustee.

[18] When a mortgage company refused to lend any money to an Ash Fork garage owner until the clause was eliminated, the railroad at first refused to do so but later changed its mind at the request of several important ranchers. The mortgage company then complained that the actual location of the lot did not fit the spot shown on the official plat of the town. The railroad engineering department explained that the town as actually located on the ground was three degrees off from the paper location shown on the plat, that everybody had accepted the situation for years, and that to question it now would invalidate all titles in Ash Fork. The mortgage company yielded.

Jones was just ready to have a deed signed for all the remaining town lots when he received an Atchison "pink telegram," which must be given immediate priority by all who should handle it, warning him to hold the sale. The general manager of the Coast Lines blushingly confessed that the operating department had neglected to tell Jones when it had, at various times, placed on Santa Fe Pacific property part of the station grounds, some company houses, the "big Harvey bunk house," part of the Atchison's chief water main, a ditch to divert water from the switching yards, some sand fences, a ball park, and a grandstand. Jones then sold lots needed for railroad purposes to an Atchison subsidiary, the Santa Fe Land Improvement Company, and the rest to W. H. Burbage, a Winslow lawyer.[19]

The Santa Fe Pacific, between 1904 and 1922, made a gross revenue from town lot sales of $48,512.07. The company towns on its main line were much less numerous than those on some midwestern railroads because the region was so arid, because some villages predated construction, and because others were established by private individuals. Nor did the Santa Fe Pacific allow "insiders" to purchase townsites at bargain prices and then retail the lots at a substantial profit.

Between 1897 and 1920 the Santa Fe Pacific sold a considerable quantity of land. It established sound disposal methods for grazing land, comparing very favorably with those of the states of New Mexico, Arizona, and Nevada. It refused to allow promoters to colonize its arid desert in western Arizona. It sold timber, tracts underlain with coal, and acreage suitable for irrigation. In these transactions the railroad observed creditable standards of business ethics and established methods which, with some improvements, were used at least through World War II.

[19] In all the excitement, Jones overlooked five small fractional lots. He sold four easily, but on the fifth was a sidewalk in front of the home for the Catholic priest. Despite the fact that earlier he had donated lots free for various worthy causes, Jones for some reason determined he was going to get some money for that one and, after much effort, finally secured $5.00. He made out a deed on the grazing land form for .0103 acre and sent it without explanation to Engel for signature. He threw Engel into confusion, who asked if $5.00 was the real price or only a nominal one and inquired why the then customary oil, gas, and mineral reservation clause was omitted. Jones explained and it was signed.

CHAPTER X

LAND LEASE AND OTHER PROBLEMS

THE Santa Fe Pacific encountered as much resistance in persuading ranchers to lease land as to purchase it. Most of the difficulties arose from existing laws and customs which prevented the company from effectively stopping trespass. It refused to import outsiders into the already crowded ranges but instead sought stockmen as lessees. It wanted money, of course, but also hoped responsible renters would lessen destructive grazing and eventually purchase the land.

The railroad's first major achievement was in 1903. It persuaded ranchers in Socorro and Valencia counties, New Mexico, to lease its sections in thirty townships. From this arose an annual meeting of renters at Magdalena, New Mexico, late in August, during which Howel Jones transacted much business. He discontinued these assemblies in 1925, likely because he could handle everything by mail. Outside the Magdalena area Jones held no meetings but made slow and steady progress. At first he had more success with cattlemen than sheepmen, as was true throughout the West, but later this difference disappeared. He disregarded anguished complaints of ranchers who had refused to rent a tract, then regretted it when somebody else did.

The most important principle the railroad observed in its leasing program was tenure. If a rancher kept his promises and nobody wanted to buy the land, the company invariably gave him the right to renew on exactly the same terms, unless meanwhile it had changed its standard rental fee or altered its universal lease contract.[1] This policy, one of its most praiseworthy, was obviously fair and acted as an excellent inducement to attract the reluctant. The railroad would not lease white men any land actually within an Indian reservation, although it sometimes rented them adjoining acreage which red men coveted. It almost always allowed a rancher to transfer his agreement to another. When it rented unsurveyed tracts to which it could not yet officially secure land patent, it merely leased "all [of its] right, title and interest in and to" the area. It expected its customers to protect

---

[1] For example, Remijio Mirabel borrowed money from the Gallup State Bank for a herd of sheep and a railroad lease. When he went bankrupt, the bank demanded the right to lease the acreage at once, but Jones waited seven months, to be absolutely sure Mirabel would not renew, before complying with the request. (TSW 8172, *passim*.)

themselves from trespassers, as it could not afford to fence and under existing law it could not take effective legal action. The Santa Fe Pacific made no leases for longer than one year because it feared renters might install expensive improvements they would be loath to lose, because it wanted freedom if a sale offered and because in the early 1900's it dreamed of solidifying its sections.

The railroad refused to vary from its standard lease form. This agreement specified that the land could be used only for agriculture or grazing, reserved mineral rights to the company, absolved the railroad from any damage sustained while the acreage was used, forbade subleasing, stipulated that any improvements made would automatically become Santa Fe Pacific property at the expiration of the year, and provided that if the land were sold, the company after thirty days' termination notice would make a proportionate refund of rent.

The Santa Fe Pacific has not preserved systematic records about the rental it charged or the quantity of land it leased. The original annual rate was .5 cent an acre for large tracts, $25 for one ordinary section or $50 for three, and $50 for a section containing water. By 1917 its fee everywhere but in Magdalena was 2 cents an acre and in 1919 was increased there to that amount. In 1909 the company leased 995,385.17 acres in New Mexico and in 1917 1,645,069.78 acres but was relatively less successful in Arizona. Its gross income from rentals rose almost steadily from $4,189.25 in 1904 to $91,966.06 in 1919.[2] Railroad officials stated these fees did not pay all the taxes on the entire grant, leased and unleased. This forced the Santa Fe Pacific to sell part of its assets or operate at a loss.

The railroad owned some grazing land within national forests which it could not exchange because Congress had forbidden further forest lieu transactions. Portions of this the company leased in the usual fashion. As an experiment, in 1908 it arranged for the Forest Service to manage 113,817 acres of its odd-numbered sections intermixed with the government's even-numbered sections in the Mount Taylor section of the Cibola National Forest. Howel Jones thought federal authorities might demonstrate to neighboring stockmen the advantages of proper range management. The Forest Service followed its usual procedure, not leasing any specific tract to a rancher but instead giving him a permit to run so many head of stock in a designated general area. It gradually increased its fees, as elsewhere, here charging 30 cents a cow a year in 1909 and $1.00 in

---

[2] Complete figures are given in Appendix D. The railroad charged more than its usual rent for the land it had selected around Ranger Lake in Lea County, New Mexico, as part of the first Zuñi lieu transaction.

1919. It paid the railroad at first one-quarter and later one-half of the money collected.[3]

The lease practices of the Santa Fe Pacific compare favorably with those of others. The state of New Mexico in 1908 charged 2 or 3 cents an acre for grazing land if arid and 5 cents if watered; by 1916 the rate was a flat 3 cents. It leased for as long as five years. In 1909 it rented 2,000,000 acres and in 1916, 7,600,000 acres. The state of Arizona in 1916 had 68,715.49 acres leased and secured an average fee of 5.8 cents. The state of Wyoming, charging 2.5 cents for arid land and 5 cents for watered, received in 1902 an average return of 4.166 cents and leased for a five-year term. The state of Texas rented a considerable amount of land for not over five years and at not less than 3 cents. The New Mexico and Arizona Land Company, starting in 1912 to rent, apparently did not have very many customers during this period. Its lease form contained a ninety-day flat cancellation clause. The Northern Pacific, aided by an enforceable trespass law, began in the early 1890's to rent its land in eastern Washington for five years at 2 cents an acre. Its agreement forbade overgrazing. It was so successful that out of three hundred renters in 1897 only thirty-one still were leasing in 1901 and apparently the rest had purchased their land. The Southern Pacific in its grant area charged .5 cent to 10 cents an acre, subject to a ten-day cancellation notice if it sold the property. The Union Pacific also rented land, using a lease form almost identical with the Santa Fe Pacific's.[4]

Compared with other landlords, the Santa Fe Pacific offered good tenure and on the whole charged less. The only possible adverse comment is that it did not earn as much money as it might have, but conditions confronting it were perhaps enough different from those facing others to invalidate the criticism. Although most of its leases were for grazing, the railroad rented a little land for other purposes such as dry farming, operating a sand pit, and preventing any petty, long-established trespassers from securing legal title to its acreage.

The Santa Fe Pacific, in addition to lieu exchanges, sales, and leasing, faced other problems between 1897 and 1920. Howel Jones

[3] TSW and LCA 3664, *passim*.
[4] B. W. P. Greig to Jones, February 14, 1914, TSW 7230; E. O. Wooten, "The Range Problem in New Mexico," New Mexico Agricultural Experiment Station *Bulletin*, No. 66 (1908), p. 29; New Mexico State Land Office, *New Mexico: Its Resources . . . Its Attractions* (Santa Fe, 1916), pp. 13–14; Sanford A. Mosk, "Land Policy and Stock Raising in the Western United States," *Agricultural History*, XVII (1943), 25; *Annual Report of the State Land Commissioner of Arizona*, 1916, pp. 39–51, 70; A. F. Potter and F. V. Coville, "Grazing on the Public Lands," United States Department of Agriculture Forest Service *Bulletin*, No. 62 (1905), pp. 28–63; B. A. McAllister to Jones, April 1, 1915, TSW 1324.

early dreamed of solidifying considerable portions of the grant, since a single section was an economic absurdity. He hoped to swap grazing land with the government, giving each complete control of certain areas. He won support from Secretary of the Interior Hitchcock, perhaps by his promise to lease solidified townships to stockmen for twenty years with an option to buy, but could not persuade Congress, and finally in 1914 he abandoned the venture.[5] His failure is not surprising, for despite urging from some stockmen, Congress in this period would not adopt any suitable program for the arid grazing land yet remaining in the public domain.

Another matter confronting the railroad was the question of securing surveys, in order to identify individual sections, a necessary procedure before it could obtain legal title. Under the act of 1876 all land-grant railroads had to pay one-half the cost of surveying whenever the government decided to do the surveying; they could not, however, force action. After 1899, under a new law, they could deposit money in advance and specify the exact region where the work was to be done. The Santa Fe Pacific was in no hurry, but instead delayed because it escaped taxes on all unsurveyed land without affecting its ultimate title. Its attitude was exactly similar to that of the Northern Pacific.[6] To meet such dilatory tactics, practiced by many railroads, Congress in 1910 authorized the Secretary of the Interior to demand that all companies deposit within ninety days enough money to pay for surveying their entire grants. The government levied its charges, but in installments rather than a lump sum. By 1921 it had surveyed nearly all the grants and by 1924 all the Santa Fe Pacific's, except in the Hualpai Indian reservation. The only complication arose in 1913, when the government abruptly made a precedent-breaking demand for all rather than half the surveying expenses, claiming the unusual justification that it needed to identify only the odd-numbered sections and did not care where the even-numbered ones lay. The Santa Fe Pacific resisted, pointing out that any survey by its very nature applied to all land in an area. With this view, eventually, the United States Supreme Court agreed.[7]

When the act of 1910 made obvious that soon the grant would

[5] E. A. Hitchcock to the Chairman of the [House] Committee on Public Lands, May 29, 1902, TSW 27-15.

[6] Jones to Ripley, July 31, 1907, TSW 1342; Ray E. Appleman, "Timber Empire from the Public Domain," *Mississippi Valley Historical Review*, XXVI (1939–40), 201.

[7] A. A. Jones to B&G, August 8, 1914, TSW 6000; SFP RR Co. v. Lane, 244 US 492. Under the act of 1910, the railroad deposited $203,260.02; $191,488.22 was actually spent, the rest refunded.

be surveyed, the railroad pressed for final title by land patents to its sections, especially those listed on twenty requests originally filed by the Atlantic and Pacific between 1885 and 1897. Typical was New Mexico Indemnity List No. 3, first submitted to the government in 1887 and amended in 1913 and 1917. Howel Jones became impatient of delays. In 1918 he complained to his Washington lawyers, Britton and Gray, that after several times reporting to him that Mr. Pillow of the General Land Office was considering the list, they had discovered instead that a report from the Geological Survey was lacking and a month later it still had not been made. Jones proffered some free advice on methods:

If I were in Washington I would go to the Geological Survey every day until the promised report was sent to the Commissioner [of the General Land Office], and after the report reached the Commissioner, I would go to the Commissioner every day to see whether they were working on list 3.

Britton and Gray replied:

We . . . are greatly indebted to you for your kindly suggestion as to how, if you were in Washington, you would manage this matter so as to bring about the desired results.

. . . In your absence . . . we will, with our more limited ability and energy, do what we can. . . . Of course we know that you will be disappointed at the results of our efforts, but will nevertheless do what we can.[8]

In 1919 the railroad received title to much of the land on List No. 3 but did not secure all of it until 1927. In general, the Santa Fe Pacific by 1920 held title to most of its grant and had presented requests for all remaining land except a little in Mohave County.

If the railroad asked for land within six miles of a mining claim, it had to furnish a nonmineral affidavit and advertise its selection in a local newspaper. In 1911 it faced stricter regulations from federal authorities aroused by the Southern Pacific's successful securing of allegedly nonmineral land when actually there was active mining on it. The government required for land wherever located a nonmineral affidavit, an inspection by General Land Office men, and an examination by Geological Survey experts. For a time it also inserted in all land patents to railroads a clause reserving minerals "now known or hereafter discovered," despite the protests of the Santa Fe Pacific and the Northern Pacific. Promptly the United States Supreme Court ruled the stipulation void.[9]

[8] Jones to B&G, September 14, 1918, and B&G to Jones, September 17, 1918, TSW 1214.
[9] Burke v. SP RR Co., 234 US 669.

Another problem for the railroad was the claims arising from four Atlantic and Pacific contracts. The A&P, plagued by government reluctance to survey land or issue any patents, sold some acreage for which it had not yet obtained title but supposedly would later. Its customers clearly understood the situation. After the A&P went bankrupt and was liquidated, Congress in 1899 authorized the deposit of money for surveys in specific areas. Obviously the four purchasers, with their original sales contracts, could secure legal title to their areas as soon as somebody paid the surveying and patenting fees. Would the Santa Fe Pacific? No, because legally it was not the successor of the Atlantic and Pacific but merely had bought all the assets at the foreclosure sale.[10] This decision displeased the four. In 1905 S. G. Little requested the Santa Fe Pacific to pay the surveying fees, but was refused; he himself paid them ten years later. In 1915 the Cibola Cattle Company attempted to extract the cost of patenting from the railroad, but could not.

The claim of the Aztec Land and Cattle Company was more involved. It had purchased and paid for 1,000,000 acres of land, but received a sales contract covering by actual description 1,058,060 acres. The Aztec had bought land both in the place limits of the grant, where the A&P was supposed to receive all nonmineral odd-numbered sections not previously appropriated, and in the indemnity strip, where the railroad might select alternates for acreage it proved was unavailable within the place limits. About 1900 the cattle company began paying fees for the surveying and patenting of 429,438 acres to which it had not yet received title. To reinforce its right, it secured a quitclaim deed from the Santa Fe Pacific to the 429,438 acres, but, despite its urging, not to the 58,060 extra acres included in the original sales contract.[11] Presumably the Aztec did not receive any patent to 84,397 acres, out of the 429,438, which were located in the indemnity strip because the Atlantic and Pacific had not yet proved itself entitled to them when it expired. The cattle company promised that the deed settled all controversy. Despite this understanding, in 1924 it demanded replacement for 165,467.86 acres it could not secure because they now lay within the Black Mesa Forest Reserve; the railroad refused.

Dr. E. B. Perrin, the fourth claimant, had an interminable and disagreeable argument with the Santa Fe Pacific.[12] He had purchased

[10] E. D. Kenna to Seligman & Seligman, November 18, 1903, TSW 1109.

[11] TSW 1109, *passim*. The quitclaim deed transferred whatever interest the Santa Fe Pacific had, presumably nothing, in the 429,438 acres to the Aztec.

[12] LCA 304, *passim*.

258,873.08 acres from the Atlantic and Pacific, of which 23,000 were in the indemnity strip. In 1897, after the Santa Fe Pacific refused to pay his surveying and patenting fees, he borrowed $3,568.83 from the railroad for them but refused to repay the debt. When the San Francisco Mountains forest lieu exchange was negotiated, he balked at signing the contract with the government until Howel Jones reluctantly agreed never to collect this money. Jones regarded the promise as extortion and probably never forgave him. In 1911 Perrin, suggesting a half-million-dollar damage suit, again asked the company to pay his fees but it refused. In 1913 he demanded that the railroad obtain title for him to the 23,000 acres in the indemnity strip. If it would not, he threatened to promote a congressional inquiry into the land affairs of the Santa Fe Pacific which "would probably be more interesting than beneficial." Atchison President Ripley refused, challenging him to prove his "scurrilous intimations that there are things in our relations with the Departments in Washington that will not bear the light of day." His complaints about his particular grievances against the company were brushed aside by the Department of the Interior as none of its affair. In 1918 Perrin again tried to recover some surveying fees from the railroad, but his persistent efforts met with the usual rebuff.

Perrin in 1920 finally commenced legal action against the company. For some obscure reason his attorneys thought legal papers could be served on the Santa Fe Pacific only in New Mexico and Arizona; to avoid them Jones and Taliaferro deliberately stayed out of the region. In 1925 Perrin dropped the suit, although he lived until 1932. It was about him that Land Commissioner Williamson wrote in 1887, "This man is too troublesome to have any more dealings with." The last letter in the railroad's file on Perrin is from a company lawyer and reads as follows:

Yes, he is gone. Wherever he has gone, they kept him away as long as they could. He probably appeared with a mandatory injunction in his hand to let him in.[13]

---

[13] Chambers, Fennemore & Narin to Collinson, April 9, 1932, LCA 304. Perrin had controversies with his neighbors in Coconino County. ("San Francisco Mountains Forest Reserve," *House Documents*, 59th Cong., 1st sess., No. 613, pp. 55–56.) He had arguments with the officials of the Atchison's operating department in 1902, 1903, and 1911. About 1920 he threatened legal action to prevent the sale of a certain section belonging to the state of Arizona, and the state land commissioner told him the injunction would get about as far as a snowball in hell. The doctor rose indignantly, vowing to report the insult to the governor, whereupon the commissioner advised him also to see the rest of the members of the land board. (*Arizona Republican*, May 18, 1920.)

Three of the claimants under the Atlantic and Pacific contracts had to pay all their own patenting and surveying fees, varying between 3 cents and 10 cents an acre; Perrin was aided by the $3,568.83 "loan." Two secured title to all their purchase; Perrin to all but 23,000 acres in the indemnity strip; and the Aztec to everything it had paid for except 165,467.86 acres in the Black Mesa Forest Reserve and probably 84,397 acres in the indemnity. Perrin's claim had no more merits than those of the other three; he very disagreeably complained and threatened rather than going promptly to law. No doubt the Santa Fe Pacific's position was justified legally and by business custom of the day. However, the company without too much loss could have been more generous about the indemnity land. There the purchasers by their own action could not repair the Atlantic and Pacific's earlier failure to prove that a deficiency elsewhere entitled it to indemnity acreage.

Another problem facing the Santa Fe Pacific was taxes.[14] The officials at first avoided many levies by simply doing nothing to hasten surveys or patents. When Congress in 1910 required the surveying of all railroad grants, the company decided to pay taxes on all odd-numbered sections in the place limits, as soon as they had been mapped by the government crews, because eventually it would probably obtain title to them. It sent the counties nothing for acreage in the indemnity strip, because it was always uncertain whether or not federal authorities would honor its requests for particular tracts. The railroad continued its refusal to remit taxes on unsurveyed lands, holding to the theory they could not be "legally identified" even if the company had been leasing them to stockmen. Partly to meet this situation, the Arizona State Tax Commission in 1915 brought suits to collect on the "possessory rights" of stockmen who had bought unsurveyed land from the company. The actions threatened the Santa Fe Pacific itself, which had purchased the grant from the Atlantic and Pacific. The suits were not pressed vigorously and were finally dropped in 1921, when almost all the grant had been surveyed.

From time to time the railroad had to deal with more detailed tax problems. In 1905 Coconino County increased the valuation on the company's timberland from $3.00 to $5.00 an acre, but after vigorous protest reduced it to $4.50. In 1906 all the counties in Arizona tried to appraise the Santa Fe Pacific's grazing land at 40 cents an acre, but when opposed cut the figure to 20 cents and 25 cents. In 1911 Navajo County raised the amount from 25 to 35 cents, and the county Board of Equalization at a hearing refused even to listen to the com-

[14] TSW 1061, *passim.*

pany's representatives, whereupon the railroad paid no taxes whatever for six months until the county compromised at 30 cents. In 1912 and 1913 all Arizona changed from appraising every taxpayer's possessions at one-third actual value to assessing them at full price.[15] The railroad's lands in Yavapai County under the new system were valued at $1.46 an acre; in Coconino at 40 cents to $1.25; and in Apache, Navajo, and Mohave at 75 cents. The railroad actually paid under the new method slightly less than it would have under the old. In New Mexico in the later 1910's San Juan County attempted to value the company's grazing land at $3.00 and that underlain with coal at $15.00. It lost a court battle to the railroad and had to reduce its figure to $1.25 for all company land, because the entire county was underlain with coal but only 3,000 acres had been so assessed.

The Santa Fe Pacific gave passes over parts of the Atchison to those connected with taxation—assessors, commissioners, and county supervisors—until Congress illegalized this nation-wide practice in 1906.[16]

Another problem facing the railroad and all Westerners was range deterioration from overgrazing and other bad methods of handling livestock. West of the twenty-inch rainfall line, the carrying capacity on the public domain in 1936 had probably been depleted 67 percent when compared with its virgin condition; private tracts, state land, and acreage within Indian reservations had been cut 51 percent, and areas inside national forests were down 30 percent. This deterioration in the ranges of the West arose from early trial-and-error methods necessary before there was any fund of experience to draw upon, from

---

[15] The account in the *Prescott Journal-Miner* (July 11, 1912) of a tax hearing conducted in Yavapai County contained the following comment:

"The main reliance of the company, however, was Assistant Land Agent Taliaferro, than whom no better single-handed talker, bar no one, has appeared before the board. He was, or at least seems conversant with every detail of the company's land affairs, and that too, without the aid of data of any kind. At repartee he more than held his own and the man who had the temperity [*sic*] to cross verbal swords with him, had to be quick witted or suffer defeat in the encounter."

[16] TSW 1076, *passim*. In 1913 Jones informed Ripley that Secretary of the Interior Lane was touring the West on departmental business, and the Northern Pacific, over its route, was giving him the use of a business car. Ripley commented on May 12, 1913 (TSW 6742):

"The Secretary of the Interior has been changed about every two years since I have been with the Santa Fe and almost every year we have given the incumbent of that office a car to make a trip through the West, ostensibly to look at the reclamation projects. So far as I know it has never done us any good because the Secretary of the Interior[,] in addition to not holding office for any considerable length of time, has generally ruled against us in almost everything. We have taken around in our official cars Messrs. Hitchcock, Garfield, Ballinger and Fisher, and I suppose we shall have to take Mr. Lane, a gentleman who never did us anything but damage. Consequently I have written him today. . . ."

unfortunate conditions of land tenure, and from willful exploitation. In northern New Mexico and Arizona, ranchers in the 1880's placed about four times as many cattle on the grasslands as these would support without damage. The stockmen met disaster in the late 1890's and evacuated most of their animals. In 1904–8 a wet cycle so revived the depleted ranges that the ranchers again put too many animals in the area. As a result, between 1907 and 1927 they cut the carrying capacity in half. Their overgrazing left behind erosion, which was dramatically illustrated by the channel of the Rio Puerco around Holbrook, almost nonexistent in the 1880's and in 1927 a quarter of a mile wide in many places.[17]

The Santa Fe Pacific, like all the states owning land in the arid West, made almost no effort to control range deterioration and probably could not have taken any effective steps because it held only the odd-numbered sections. In 1903 it arranged for a government expert to advise it about restoring grasses in the grant area, with no apparent results. In 1918 it persuaded the Department of Agriculture to have E. O. Wooten investigate New Mexico–Arizona range conditions, which resulted in a published report.

The railroad donated $3,000 toward government agricultural experiments in the grant area. In Mohave County it sanctioned an unsuccessful attempt to grow spineless cactus as an allegedly excellent cattle forage and approved an economically unsound venture into making binder twine from yucca fiber.

If in 1920 the officials of the Santa Fe Pacific had sat down and reviewed what had been accomplished since they bought the grant from the bankrupt Atlantic and Pacific, they would have been pleased. They had arranged lieu transactions which solved difficult problems of intermixed land in national forests and Indian reservations as well as satisfied the claims of long-established squatters. They had sold considerable grazing land, especially in the central part of northern Arizona. They had vended irrigable areas, deeded a little dry-farming acreage, resisted promoters' attempts to colonize arid tracts, marketed coal land, disposed of timber, and hawked town lots. They had arranged for surveys, obtained patents to land, paid taxes, considered claims arising from four Atlantic and Pacific contracts, and noted range deterioration. They had earned a net profit of $7,869,-123.66. With the possible exceptions of the A&P claims and the relationships with the Victor-American, they had conducted themselves with due regard for ethical standards.

[17] Arthur Saunders to W. G. McGinnies, March 16, 1927, LCA 11256; "The Western Range," *Senate Documents*, 74th Cong., 2d sess., No. 199, *passim*.

CHAPTER XI

THE TWENTIES

THE Santa Fe Pacific during the 1920's continued its earlier sales and lease policies. It met special problems about Indian and oil acreage. It selected some land on which to seek patents.

There were various changes in the company's personnel during the 1920's. The first of these was in 1922 when it filled the vacancy of field examiner with Arthur Saunders, who served until his death in 1934. In 1924 it hired as another field examiner C. B. McClelland, who held the post until his appointment in 1950 as land commissioner.[1] The two were expected "to be acquainted with everybody," to know the scope of each rancher's operations, to give stockmen advice when asked, to avoid involvement in any controversies, to urge the lease or purchase of railroad land, to appraise company acreage, to locate suitable sites for small earthen reservoirs, to cruise timber, to help in securing land patents, to collect money, and to maintain friendly relations with tax officials. Their value was cumulative, making them increasingly useful to the Santa Fe Pacific. It would have been better had Howel Jones handled these two conscientious workers in conciliatory fashion rather than making consistently unreasonable demands and often finding fault but very seldom praising.[2]

In 1926 Chief Clerk Taliaferro died. He had a lifetime's knowledge of procedure and reportedly remembered everything of importance since the days of Land Commissioner Williamson.

Jones obviously could not find an exact replacement for Taliaferro, but as a substitute he selected William B. Collinson, chief clerk in the

[1] LCA 10616 and 10973, *passim*. Saunders, an Arizonan, had been in the livestock business since 1904. The railroad at first assigned him to Mohave County but in 1928 transferred him to the eastern part of the grant. McClelland, a graduate of Knox College, left the employ of an Illinois automobile dealer to work for the Santa Fe Pacific. His first headquarters was at Kingman, Mohave County, but in 1934 he was moved to Albuquerque. The salary of the two was increased in 1926 from $165 a month, plus expenses away from home, to $200. They put in long hours, under difficult field conditions, and often returned home only on week ends.

[2] Previously Jones through his niggardliness lost the services of Field Examiner Lyon, who "filled the place so well and so satisfactorily that we will never get a successor who will be as acceptable" and through his nagging caused Examiner Moore to resign. Once, runs an office tradition, Jones was rebuking a typist and emphasizing his points by pounding a small lead elephant on a glass covering a map. Suddenly the glass shattered; Jones looked abashed and quietly "promised to behave" if the typist would get another cover. While Jones showed these less agreeable traits in handling employees, he did not in dealing with outsiders.

123

Atchison operating department at Topeka. Collinson, made assistant land commissioner, set out to learn his new job by reading books and by gaining field experience. When informed he was coming west, Art Saunders commented:

We will not be able to extend to Mr. Collinson the royal range welcome of giving him the best pitching horse on the ranch to "top off" but in lieu thereof we will substitute our mountain climbing Ford which has no mean record.[3]

Once during the trip Jones instructed Collinson:

While at Los Lunas [New Mexico] see Ed Otero and Fred D. Huning and anyone else for you want to get acquainted with everybody. In seeing everybody you want to remember Polonius' advice to his son Laertes. That advise [*sic*] is as follows:

"Give every man thy ear but few thy voice."

The above quotation is from *Hamlet* and it applies now as well as it did in Shakespeare's day and it applies to the Land Department as well as every other department.[4]

In April 1928, almost two years after Collinson had joined the staff, Howel Jones one evening left the office apparently in good health. Early the next morning he died of a heart attack. In his honor the flags on the large Atchison office building at Topeka hung at half-mast and all business there was suspended the afternoon of his funeral. He had administered the grant for twenty-seven years wisely and public-spiritedly, as Chapters V through XII fully demonstrate. His successor was Collinson; Victoria C. Scott, a typist since 1905, became chief clerk.

During all the 1920's, despite the general prosperity during much of the decade, Jones and Collinson faced a nation-wide agricultural depression. The fundamental difficulty arose because agriculturists had greatly increased their production to meet unusual international demands of the war period and had gone heavily into debt. When peace returned, they did not reduce their output despite a sharp decline in purchasing power from abroad. No remedies actually adopted by the government, and likely none proposed, offered an enduring solution to the problem. What happened to stockmen is illustrated by the average price per one hundred pounds for good beef steers on the Chicago market, which was $9.33 in 1916, $15.45 in 1919, and $9.50 in 1923. During the same period, the cost of ranchers' supplies in-

[3] Saunders to Jones, April 6, 1926, LCA 1061.
[4] Jones to Collinson, October 28, 1926, TSW 1061.

creased sharply and stayed up. This maladjustment created serious financial difficulties, especially in repaying bank loans. To avoid the disaster of wholesale foreclosure and to obtain essential cash, bankers needed to rediscount the loans. Only gradually in the 1920's did private and government initiative provide adequate rediscounting facilities. The general agrarian distress was sharply felt in New Mexico and Arizona, where many banks had done more business than their capital warranted and now found they must loan what money was still available not to stockmen offering the best security, but to those who were on the brink of foreclosure and bankruptcy.

These adverse conditions confronted the Santa Fe Pacific with new problems. Jones in the early 1920's wrote numerous letters of encouragement to ranchers which, although unimpressive in the light of cold logic, were perhaps not closely analyzed. In the many cases of delinquent payments which arose, Jones sought only the company's fair share of any money a rancher might have to pay his various debts. Clearly he tried to be reasonable, not too harsh or too lenient. He repeatedly wrote that a rancher must not cripple his future operations by sacrificing livestock to pay his railroad debt. In general, when a person first sought more time in making a payment due, Jones would suggest sending half promptly and the rest later; if the stockman replied he couldn't, Jones would try to collect just the interest. Sometimes he grew peevish when embarrassed ranchers were slow in answering his letters. He seemingly never fully understood the stockmen's reluctance to give him the complete statement of their assets and prospects he occasionally requested. His broad policy was similar to that used earlier by other land-grant railroads selling farming land but was apparently more lenient. It enhanced the general reputation of the Santa Fe Pacific and avoided wholesale foreclosures which would have made further sales much more difficult. The company eventually received almost all the money owed it, plus 6 percent interest, but suffered the inconvenience of not getting funds when expected. During the 1920's the railroad repossessed only 12,861.36 acres, all of which had been sold to one person.[5]

Land sales in the early 1920's fell off to almost nothing and later increased only a little. This problem gave much concern to Howel

[5] A Mohave County purchaser of 69,120 acres paid off all he owed the railroad by mortgaging his land to a mortgage company and his livestock to a bank. He lost everything because the bank would not let him use any money from livestock sales to pay off the land mortgage. He charged the two financial institutions had conspired to cheat him out of his "life's work" and brought a million-and-a-half-dollar damage suit. It failed, perhaps in part because he had purchased his land for 50 cents an acre but mortgaged it for $1.00 an acre.

Jones. He wrote in 1921 that the railroad owned 1,400,000 acres in Mohave County but almost all the stockmen there were bankrupt. What did Engel think of trying to sell most of this area at the reduced price of 50 cents an acre, with ten years rather than six to pay and interest cut from 6 to 5 percent? Engel vetoed the suggestion on the grounds that the financial situation of most ranchers was gradually improving, that reduction in the railroad's already comparatively low interest rate would not attract reluctant prospects, and that perhaps Mohave County might someday be irrigated from the Colorado River. In 1923 Jones discouragedly asked for suggestions how to stimulate the marketing of any grant acreage and Engel admitted he hadn't any. The land commissioner unsuccessfully resisted, as a further handicap to sales, the addition of a contract clause reserving oil, gas, and mineral rights to the railroad. Engel assured him that careful investigation revealed it was almost a universal practice among companies selling large amounts of land. During the 1920's the Santa Fe Pacific sold 50,610.20 acres of grazing land—12,894.17 acres in New Mexico and 37,716.03 in Arizona—for which it obtained 50 cents to $3.00 an acre.[6] This seems small when compared with 2,214,787 acres sold in the 1910's, but probably was as much as possible.

Jones continued his opposition to promoters eager to colonize the railroad's desert land without first securing water. Besides many vague proposals, Jones considered four definite offers for specific tracts but rejected them as too visionary or too susceptible of fraud. To a suggestion for a religious colony, Jones commented privately:

Many of these church promoters think and act on the theory that God will take care of the colony. No matter how zealous and religious the colony may be they can only get commodities to grow by following the same rule that other people do, and that is to wisely plant, watch and water.[7]

In 1928 the government ordered construction started on the long-discussed Boulder (Hoover) Dam, a Colorado River flood control and power project in northwest Mohave County. Jones knew this would not enhance water prospects on the railroad's land because the great lift required from the level of the dam would doom such a project economically. Despite almost daily inquiries by small investors at the Atchison's Los Angeles office for "irrigation" tracts, he refused to market any Mohave County acreage because ". . . we would sell our lands and probably get the first payment and no more, and always

    [6] LCA 7489, TSW 10852, and twenty other files about land sales.
    [7] Jones to C. B. McClelland, June 19, 1926, TSW 11281.

get the adverse criticism." He and McClelland brushed off many promoters. Clearly the Santa Fe Pacific could have unloaded a large amount of its Mohave acreage at a high price had its officials not been restrained by ethical standards.

Promoters repeatedly attempted to purchase land in the county owned by the government of Arizona. The state's refusal of all offers was buttressed by the vigorous support of local stockmen who found in the railroad's position one of their strongest arguments. Promoters did obtain some tracts from other owners and also helped stimulate a boom in town real estate in Kingman; the results were what Howel Jones had always feared.[8]

Although opposing fake development in Mohave County, the railroad approved two proposed sales of land for large, genuine irrigation enterprises elsewhere, but neither deal materialized. It sold six isolated tracts totaling 2,145.60 acres to people who planned small private irrigation projects and 2,077.60 acres to one who petitioned for water from the Middle Rio Grande Conservancy. The Santa Fe Pacific played a passive role in the long-delayed completion of the Bluewater development, discussed earlier in Chapter IX, but another Atchison subsidiary, the Chanslor-Canfield Midway Oil Company, purchased $167,000 of the bonds issued. The railroad owned 3,000 acres of the 10,627 to be irrigated from the project.

The Santa Fe Pacific during the decade made a few miscellaneous sales. It disposed of 17,100.91 acres to insistent dry farmers. It marketed 11,058.90 acres for such assorted purposes as Indian trading posts, filling stations, motor courts, gravel pits, and airports.[9] It

---

[8] The Beverly Hills Development Company, issuing circulars which created a false impression, sold ten-acre tracts for $200, $50 down and $15 a month for ten months. The Kingman Locating Company offered to obtain government homesteads for alleged settlers at a service fee of $1.00 an acre, part in advance and part when federal officials approved the application. The *Mohave County Miner* of January 11, 1929, a typical issue, contained six large advertisements of five real estate dealers, one offering "suburban estates" at Wallapi Farms for $15 an acre, one peddling business lots at $150 which within six months should return 300 to 500 percent profit, one publicizing the Golden Gate addition to Kingman, one announcing a forthcoming subdivision, one proclaiming that the town was on the boom, and one warning rosy purchasers to "stay away from knockers."

[9] On February 24, 1924 (TSW 6446), Art Saunders, in discussing with Jones the owners of one Indian trading post which bought from the railroad, added a bit of gossip: "The latter is a doctor in Boston. He has a son who is an artist and well educated and the doctor sent him out here several years ago to paint. He did and married a Navajo squaw besides. The doctor is reported to be very well off and perhaps wealthy. Of course the son's marriage startled the father but the son's paint[ing]s have not been such as to startle the world and since the doctor did not see fit to take the son back to Boston he has tried to make it possible for him to make a living in this country."

sold a little timber, in one case procuring a tie contract from the Atchison for the purchaser.

The railroad continued its successful grazing lease policy. In 1921, 80 percent of its property was under lease. In 1925 the company rented 2,599,885.34 acres out of 4,232,800.88 owned, and received $59,636.19 in revenue but paid in taxes on all the land $79,721.99, of which $52,844.81 covered the sections leased.[10] Obviously the company did not earn enough to reimburse it for taxes on all its land, rented or not. It leased only by the year, except that late in the 1920's it made as an experiment six contracts running for ten years. When ranchers met hard times, it did not reduce its rental but followed the same lenient collection policy it used toward purchasers. It continued to leave its lessees to fight their own trespass battles, since the state laws were ineffectual.

Its two field examiners, alert for small-scale trespassers who had placed improvements on railroad property, prevented by a lease these interlopers from impairing the company's legal title. In one of these small, troublesome transactions McClelland drove miles to collect a $5.00 annual fee, got stuck in quicksand just short of his destination, and the lessee refused to assist him till paid in advance with a rent receipt. Once when Howel Jones arbitrarily ordered Saunders to confront immediately a squatter who used sheep as a blind for his bootlegging, the field examiner reported an unsuccessful interview because of

. . . what County [Farm] Agent H. P. Powers had told me. He said that the forepart of the week . . . [the wife] came to him in a terrible rage and swearing like a trooper (and believe me she can do just that) and wanted him to go with her out to the ranch right away. She said her fool husband had fed a batch of mash to the sheep and that over 100 head of them were already dead. They lost about 150 head all told.[11]

McClelland and Saunders were active in searching for larger-scale ranchers to rent company land. The two encountered especial difficulty in persuading anybody to lease in Mohave County, where a very large proportion of the company's property was vacant. What hindered them was the great drought there during much of the 1920's. This reduced the total number of cattle from 76,588 head in 1922 to 5,000 in 1929. It had a much less serious effect on sheep, which used the desert range only during the winter months. The two men faced another obstacle in the poor quality of much railroad land, as illus-

[10] Memorandum, March 24, 1926, TSW 1061.
[11] Saunders to Jones, February 4, 1928, LCA 11775.

trated by the fact that in 1925 it had about 500,000 acres under lease, had 100,000 more unrented which grew a fair stand of feed but were too far from water for really effective use, had 400,000 more which were capable of use only thirty to ninety days a year, and had 500,000 more which were practically worthless. To make the property more attractive, the examiners suggested selecting with scrip some even-numbered sections in railroad townships under lease, but abandoned the idea when stockmen showed no interest in the accompanying increase in rental charges proposed.

McClelland conceived the idea of stimulating goat raising in Mohave County both to utilize land unsuitable for other livestock and to persuade reluctant old-time cattle or sheep ranchers to lease. The railroad acted on his suggestion with such vigor that while there were only 7,000 head of goats in the county in 1924, there were 28,100 head in 1926. Between 1924 and 1930 the Santa Fe Pacific grossed $12,000 in lease money from goatmen and the Atchison grossed $8,000 in freight charges. When the price of mohair fell from 50 cents a pound in 1930 to three cents in 1932, the bankrupt goatmen had no choice but to ship out their animals as chicken feed; since then, there have been only a few goats in the region. It is not clear whether any cattlemen or sheepmen decided to lease upon the advent of goatmen; certainly there was no spectacular increase in the railroad's Mohave County rent rolls. The old-timers did resent the newcomers enough, however, to dynamite a thirty-one-year-old small earthen reservoir on a section which a goatman leased and to attempt generally unsuccessful legal harassment of all goatmen.[12]

The Santa Fe Pacific encountered a few miscellaneous lease problems during the 1920's. It decided to continue having the United States Forest Service manage its acreage within the Cibola National Forest. Its example was never followed by the Aztec Land and Cattle Company, which in the Sitgreaves National Forest fenced each odd-numbered section and leased it to a small-scale stockman.[13] The railroad rented a right of way for a high-voltage transmission line, granted a license for the first advertising sign authorized on its property, and leased for minerals one tract which proved unproductive.

Although the Santa Fe Pacific had selected prior to 1920 the great bulk of the land it had earned, it secured during the decade some additional acreage. It encountered several changes in federal procedure; the most important of these was an addition in 1927 to the land

[12] LCA 11155 and 11684, *passim.*
[13] Sanford A. Mosk, *Land Tenure Problems in the Santa Fe Railroad Grant Area* (Berkeley, 1934), p. 28.

patent form which reserved to the government all phosphate, nitrate, potash, oil, gas, and asphaltic minerals. The railroad faced a serious problem within the grant's place limits located in Mohave County. It disputed the federal contention that 171,219.35 acres it sought there were mineral and hence not patentable to the company. After a joint examination and after compromises about areas over which the two inspectors could not agree, the railroad lost 118,685.60 acres, clearly received title to 50,369.37 acres, and may also have secured an additional 2,164.38 acres. This outcome, Jones thought, was slightly more advantageous to the company than to the government.[14]

The Santa Fe Pacific met difficulties in securing replacements for mineral land it had lost in its entire grant, 150,000 acres in all, because Congress in 1866 had given as substitute the odd-numbered sections within twenty miles on either side of the line. Since it had already allotted the odd-numbered sections within forty miles as the place limits of the grant, actually it was giving only such acreage as was considered appropriated in 1872 but subsequently was returned to the public domain. This provision Collinson thought must have been an error, and he sought to remedy it by having Congress change the clause to read even-numbered sections. He aroused the opposition of the Department of the Interior, which pointed out that the stipulation was in all railroad land-grant acts containing a mineral proviso and which opposed the amendment as enlarging the original agreement; Collinson dropped the idea.[15] The company found only 38,949.40 acres of odd-numbered sections to replace the 150,000 acres lost.

Besides substitutes for mineral lands, the railroad selected ordinary acreage to which it was entitled. Jones became concerned for the first time about Mohave County land lying north of the Colorado River, isolated from the rest of the grant and economically linked to Utah. He dispatched McClelland and Collinson there in 1926; their inspection resulted in the railroad securing 82,886.11 acres in the place limits and 34,914.69 acres in the indemnity.[16]

The railroad showed occasional interest during the decade in

[14] TSW 1214, *passim*.

[15] Memorandum, William Spry to First Assistant Secretary of the Interior, January 22, 1929, LCA 1214.

[16] Collinson reported to Jones on August 16, 1926 (LCA 11150), that after a morning examining a township they heard a pounding noise in the car and found the universal joint broken in two. Fortunately they located a man in that isolated region who drove McClelland seventy-five miles to the nearest town for a new part, which the two installed themselves.

agricultural development and range improvement.[17] In 1920 Howel Jones commissioned a professor of agriculture at the University of California to appraise the farming possibilities of the grant, but nothing of practical value resulted. Collinson tried to reseed the company's grasslands artificially, rather than allow natural revival through nonuse. This he undertook despite the opinion of Dean J. J. Thornbeer of the University of Arizona that it was impossible. The dean was right.

During the decade the Santa Fe Pacific encountered adverse economic conditions and in Mohave County a prolonged drought. Its net income declined from $5,013,790.38 in the 1910's to only $1,781,942.05 in the 1920's. The railroad sold little of its grazing land but had considerable amounts under lease. It refused to aid "land sharks" eager to colonize arid lands, especially during the Boulder (Hoover) Dam excitement. It almost finished selecting land to which it was entitled. It met certain special problems about Indian land and about oil acreage, to be treated in the next chapter. Under the circumstances, Jones and his successor, Collinson, accomplished as much as anybody could have.

[17] TSW 9460, 11256, and LCA 9915, *passim.*

CHAPTER XII

INDIANS AND OIL

DURING the 1920's, the 1930's, and the 1940's, the railroad dealt with difficult situations arising out of Indians' desire for more land. It also carried out a profitable oil lease policy.

Many of the problems over Indian land centered in the area of the Navajos. Their reservation had been expanded during the 1910's, but not so much as experts like Father Anselm Weber deemed necessary. The Santa Fe Pacific had relinquished during the decade 788,898 acres that the Navajos wished and had secured lieu rights as payment. It also had deeded to the government 327,404.44 acres additional in the Painted Desert in the so-called Leupp extension area, but because of objections to the exchange it had proffered new base. By the end of the decade it had not yet received compensation for the original 327,404.44 acres.

The problem of land for these Indians was far from solved, but during the early 1920's nothing further was attempted. Federal authorities took an important step forward when in 1923 they appointed Herbert Hagerman, Republican ex-governor of New Mexico, to a new general supervisory position entitled Commissioner of the Navajo Tribe. Hagerman, having inherited wealth, probably accepted the responsibility because of *noblesse oblige*; he was sincerely devoted to his charges. Moreover he had ability; in Howel Jones's opinion he was "the best informed man on land matters in New Mexico" and had demonstrated on his own ranch how proper methods increased the carrying capacity of the range.[1] As commissioner he attempted much and accomplished considerable. But, apparently because he lacked talent for co-operating with others, especially those hostile to his program, he alienated more people than was necessary. In handling many complex matters involving the Navajos, he inevitably made some mistakes. His enemies seized upon these, emphasized the sharp difference in his basic philosophy about Indians from that of the important reformer John Collier, and at the outset of the New Deal drove him from office.

---

[1] Jones to B&G, July 30, 1923, TSW 1964; "Survey of Conditions of the Indians of the United States," *Hearings* before the Subcommittee of the Senate Committee on Indian Affairs, 71st Cong., 3d sess.; "Survey of Condition of Indians," *Senate Reports*, 72d Cong., 1st sess., No. 25; "Navajo Indian Reservation," *Senate Documents*, 72d Cong., 1st sess., No. 64, *passim*.

The particulars of his land work as commissioner should be traced. Upon taking office he set to work vigorously on the Navajo land problem. In this he received only passive and uninterested co-operation from Howel Jones. The railroadman by this time thought that the Indians were a nonprogressive hindrance to the best development of the region, that they did not use effectively what land they had already, and that they should be discouraged from securing more acreage. Also, his knowledge that there was almost no demand for railroad scrip removed one of his strong incentives for action. Jones's policy was later reversed by Collinson, who wanted to use lieu rights in solidifying company holdings.

Hagerman in 1923 made a general proposal to solve serious range conflicts between red men and white in the area just east of the present boundary of the Navajo reservation in New Mexico. He recommended a series of land exchanges and purchases, to cost the government about $200,000, but opposition from New Mexicans forced him to abandon the scheme. His superior, the Secretary of the Interior, then suggested merely swapping land within the outside limits of the reservation so that private owners and the government would have solidified areas. Although Congress passed an act authorizing this in 1925, nothing was done because Hagerman believed the Indians needed all the acreage in the reservation and more besides.

While Hagerman and his successors were seeking a permanent solution to Navajo land problems, they employed temporary expedients. For a number of years they arranged for the Bureau of Indian Affairs and certain Indians to lease railroad land at the usual fee charged white ranchers; for example, in 1936 the Bureau rented 231,516.66 acres. They also used the allotment system, long authorized for all Indians, to give some individuals 160 acres outside the reservation. They picked strategic tracts, with the obvious hope of keeping white stockmen out of the adjacent areas. Their practice at first caused no alarm, but in the fall of 1929 ranchers and the railroad protested three hundred allotments, some distance from the reservation, which had been made in the past eighteen months. Federal authorities, with the approval of the Navajo tribe, at first curtailed further allotting and in 1933 stopped it. These officials vetoed the plan of a subordinate to have four and a half million acres of public domain withdrawn from any entry except by red men, and then to allot as much as possible to Navajo tribesmen.[2]

Hagerman, his successors, and leading Navajos such as Chee

2 Herbert Hagerman to Collinson, June 29, 1931, LCA 11512.

Dodge were anxious to use tribal funds earned by royalties from oil to purchase railroad and other privately owned land. When first announced, the plan encountered opposition from neighboring whites who disliked any idea of more land for the Indians or their tax-exempt reservation. This dissatisfaction the railroad and federal officials assuaged. The two, between 1929 and 1934, gradually arranged for Navajo purchase of 388,161.25 acres at $1.00 each in New Mexico and Arizona, including the entire 327,404.44 acres on the Painted Desert in the so-called Leupp extension area.[3]

The Bureau of Indian Affairs also wished to swap acreage with the railroad. The Indian Appropriation Act of March 3, 1921, authorized exchanges limited to the New Mexico counties of San Juan, McKinley, and Valencia. At first the government and the Santa Fe Pacific took no action. In 1929 they made their first exchange and by 1935 had completed four additional ones. They traded 245,898.73 acres, the government securing much desired land and the railroad selecting even-numbered sections in good grazing areas where it already owned the odd-numbered sections. They encountered some opposition from Indians holding allotments in regions the government evacuated; only under pressure did these Indians return to the reservation. Federal authorities and the Santa Fe Pacific easily warded off an attack from the ephemeral *Oil News*, which complained that now wildcatters would have to lease some lands they wanted to drill on. The government overruled objections from the New Mexico and Arizona Land Company, which in also making exchanges sought some of the same lieu as the railroad.[4]

The Bureau of Indian Affairs was anxious to have Congress include officially within the boundaries of the Navajo reservation the land it hoped somehow to acquire. It first requested this in 1932. In 1934 it secured an extension act for Arizona. It never got one for New Mexico, probably because it sought to include so many sections of the public domain that white ranchers habitually used.

The Bureau was authorized by the Arizona extension act to exchange land in Navajo, Apache, and Coconino counties. It arranged to swap 185,015.45 acres with the Santa Fe Pacific and traded other sections with various private owners. It encountered unsuccessful resistance from Indians holding allotments outside the reservation. They did not want to trade their 160 acres for plots inside the boundary that were inferior to those surrendered. They complained because at first they received no recompense for the improvements previously

[3] LCA 11512, *passim.*

[4] LCA 12248, 12520, and 12551, *passim*; *Oil News*, September 19, 1932.

placed on their allotments. The railroad protested to United States Senator Hayden that this was unfair. In 1937 Congress appropriated funds to reimburse these Navajos. The Santa Fe Pacific and the government also met opposition over the exchange from local Arizona ranchers who did not want the Indians to have more land, did not wish to have the railroad select lieu outside their county to the detriment of local tax rolls, or did not relish the prospect of leasing solidified ranches. Representatives of the Bureau of Indian Affairs and of the railroad discussed these objections in each county, persuading the majority that the proposed solution to white men and red intermingling in the same area was the best obtainable. The government probably promised to pay for improvements which white lessees had placed on Santa Fe Pacific land surrendered. Later it denied this and recompensed only some of the stockmen. It agreed that Indians would not ranch south of a definite line, roughly forming a division between red men and white in the three counties, but later attempted without success to lease railroad land on the "wrong side." These various altercations and objections interested only a few people in the region; most were indifferent.[5]

The Santa Fe Pacific during the 1920's exchanged 430,914.18 acres for the Navajos in New Mexico and Arizona and sold them 388,161.25 acres. Previously it had swapped 788,898 acres and sold 11,520 acres. In all, it enlarged the Navajos' holdings by 1,619,493.43 acres.

The railroad encountered a variety of problems within the reservation of the Hualpais, located about thirty-five miles northeast of Kingman, Arizona.[6] These Indians had lived in the general region since prehistoric times. They numbered about 1,500 in 1869 and 440 in 1923. In 1870 they were herded onto a reservation at the Colorado River but the next year, without army restraint, they forsook it for their old haunts. The Hualpais petitioned for a new reservation, and in 1883 the government granted their request, giving them only even-numbered sections because previously it had authorized the railroad to take the odd-numbered sections. In 1900, when a tiny portion of their domain was surveyed, questions arose about the accuracy of the work done, and Howel Jones resolved to remain quiet for fear the

[5] LCA 12520, *passim*; *Holbrook Tribune-News* and *Winslow Mail*, February 1933 through July 1934, *passim*. When the Bureau of Indian Affairs tried to force back on the reservation Little Silversmith, a long-established railroad lessee well liked by his white neighbors, the company and the neighbors made such vigorous protest that the plan was dropped.

[6] TSW 4390 and LCA 6100, *passim*; "Walapai Papers," *Senate Documents*, 74th Cong., 2d sess., No. 273, pp. 19–257.

government might abandon the whole reservation. He apparently dreamed of some day arranging a lieu transaction.

The government about 1900 began leasing much of the area to white cattlemen. When in 1912 Jones asked for half the rent collected, on the theory the railroad owned half the land, federal officials refused because the area was not surveyed. When surveying did begin in 1919, the Bureau of Indian Affairs claimed the railroad had no legal right to any of the area, but the Secretary of the Interior overruled it. In 1925 Jones again requested half of the rental but did not get it. The next year Mohave County demanded taxes from the Santa Fe Pacific on all the odd-numbered sections within the reservation, but after discussion compromised on half; in 1928 the company began to pay at the full rate and continued to do so until it relinquished its rights in 1940.

As early as 1920 federal and railroad officials discussed a land swap. Since both believed the reservation contained more acreage than the Hualpais needed, they thought each should choose one or more solidified tracts within the outer boundaries of the area. This was authorized by Congress in 1925. To furnish information needed to swap intelligently, Jones dispatched Saunders and McClelland to examine the reservation. Saunders during the trip replied to a letter from his boss as follows:

Note in the second paragraph of your letter that you say, "Our understanding is that you were to report and keep us advised of your every movement." From this and the general tone of your letter it may be that you feel that we have been "soldiering" on the job although our reports on the lands examined should speak for themselves, but in case there is any doubt in your mind as to our "every moment" [*sic*] while in the field will say I get up every morning as soon as it is light enough to see to lace my shoes and proceed to get breakfast. By six fifteen we are generally saddling our horses with our lunch put up in our slicker pockets, and by six thirty we are on our way. We try to get back to camp at a reasonable hour in the evening about six o'clock but there are some rides that have to be made over rough country that makes it impossible to get back until long after dark. The latest we have been so far has been eleven o'clock at night. The only way I can see to increase these hours is to trade our beds for lanterns.[7]

Jones hastened to assuage the two inspectors. They reported, after three months of work, that the area had "very limited possibilities"

[7] Saunders to Jones, September 6, 1925, LCA 6100. When the two examiners had to hire an Indian guide to a limestone cave, much bargaining finally got the fee reduced to $1.55. In revenge, he made them scale with ropes a cliff fifteen hundred feet high, but when returning pointed out an easy way down.

except for grazing and suggested three alternate methods of solidifying the reservation. None of their proposals was selected by Jones; the whole matter drifted until 1930.

A vigorous controversy, meanwhile, broke out over the Peach Springs. These belonged to the Hualpais, said the government, as Indian title had never been extinguished. These belonged to the railroad, said the company, because the year before the reservation was established it had, as authorized in the 1866 granting act, purchased from two squatters this "additional land for operating purposes." The question finally reached the United States District Court, which said the springs were the property of the railroad but that the company must continue its long-established practice of selling to the Indians at the town of Peach Springs all the water they needed.

In 1930 Collinson and Hagerman took vigorous action to complete the proposed exchange. They agreed that each party should have an equal value of land. Furthermore the railroad was to surrender thirty-six sections additional in return for a clear title to the Peach Springs. A representative of the government and of the railroad spent two weeks jointly examining the reservation. The two recommended the details of a trade, which their superiors shortly endorsed. The government was to receive a total of 461,752 acres in the western end and the railroad 336,195 acres in the eastern end. Apparently the Indian authorities were securing considerably more than they gave. Actually, according to the more careful railroad valuation of 1925, the government would be surrendering $234,350 worth of land plus its vague claim to the Peach Springs and would be receiving $207,763 worth of acreage. It had simply been outtraded.

Objection arose, not on the question of inequality, but on the right of the railroad to the odd-numbered sections. The Senate Committee on Indian Affairs expressed doubts about the company's grant applying within the reservation. The Department of the Interior asked its solicitor, E. C. Finney, his opinion. Concerning him, Britton and Gray wrote:

. . . as I had been associated with him for so many years . . . I called on him today and put the direct question to him, preceding it with the statement that I supposed nothing was ever really settled in the Department no matter how many times the matter had been the subject of decision or opinion. He said he had been asked for an opinion but that he thought the matter had heretofore been decided, and rightly, and that as they wanted his opinion he would give it. He left me in no doubt that his opinion would sustain the [railroad's] right under the grant.[8]

[8] B&G to E. E. McInnis, September 10, 1931, LCA 6100.

When issued, it did. The Department then asked Assistant Attorney General Seth W. Richards what he thought; he agreed very strongly with Finney. Their views were attacked by the Indian Rights Association and, with especial vigor, by the Indian Defense Association. These two humanitarian organizations insisted that the matter was of such fundamental importance to the Hualpais that only the courts should decide the question.[9]

John Collier, head of the Indian Defense Association, was in 1933 appointed Commissioner of Indian Affairs. He had the vigorous support of Franklin Roosevelt and of Secretary of the Interior Harold Ickes. He believed red men should develop their ancient civilizations and tribal unity rather than seek in all things to ape the white man. He thought if there was any question of Indians' rights being infringed upon, that these should be strongly protected. He made many fundamental changes in our national policy toward the red men. Although final judgment is not yet possible, it appears that much of what he did was wise.

Collier, who had attacked his predecessor so vigorously over the proposed Hualpai exchange, could hardly have done less upon his appointment than continue to contest the railroad's right to the odd-numbered sections. He had suit brought. While the case was going through various courts, Congress in the Transportation Act of 1940 repealed portions of the reduced rates for government traffic charged by all land-grant railroads. To qualify, a carrier must surrender whatever unsettled claims for acreage it still had outstanding. This the Santa Fe Pacific did, for the value to it of the Hualpais' land was much less than the loss to the Atchison through reduced rates. Subsequently the United States Supreme Court ruled that the Hualpais' right of occupancy to northern Arizona had never been extinguished. It could not determine on the evidence presented whether or not the present reservation was actually their ancestral home, but, since the railroad had already surrendered its claim, the tribunal decided that the area should be given them rather than returned to the public domain.

In 1943 the government filed another suit against the Santa Fe Pacific. It alleged it had just discovered, despite all previous discussions, that the Hualpai reservation actually was larger than had been supposed. It claimed that the Indians' domain included 113,330 acres

---

[9] Concerning these complaints, Hagerman commented to Collinson on June 7, 1932 (LCA 12520): "I was not aware before this that I had proposed to divest the Walapai Tribe of Arizona or that it was claimed that the Walapai Tribe owned Arizona. My impression was that their friends only asked about a million acres of Arizona for this handful of Indians."

of railroad land, just west of the so-called boundary line, which surrounded the very valuable Clay Springs. It asserted that the army had, as an old map indicated, set aside this land in 1874 when making a reservation for the Hualpais, but that the military's action had been completely forgotten. When the reservation was established in 1883, for a second time, the area was omitted. The government, pointing to the Supreme Court's statement that the Hualpais' right of occupancy to all northern Arizona had never been extinguished, demanded title to the disputed property. The company refused. It was never shown the map and did not believe it existed. The resulting suit was still in the courts in 1946.

The odd-numbered sections in the Hualpai reservation, established in 1874 or 1883, belonged to the railroad just as much as did those in other reservations—the Navajo, the Moqui, the Laguna, and the Zuñi—established or enlarged after the company filed its map of definite location in 1872. Either the Indians of New Mexico and Arizona held title to most of the land in the two states, which must be legally extinguished by some means, or else the red men owned no acreage until the United States specifically appropriated it to them. The second theory was used from the 1870's until 1941, when the Supreme Court handed down its decision in the first Hualpai case. It cast vague doubts on all titles held by white men in northern Arizona when it declared the Hualpais' rights there had never been extinguished, but perhaps it intended only to make clear that these red men should have all their reservation rather than return any of it to the public domain. The court dodged the question of the railroad's rights to the odd-numbered sections in the reservation, apparently because the claim had been surrendered and the matter supposedly no longer needed decision. This omission made possible the second suit, based on the assumption that the company's rights were invalid in the area assertedly set aside in 1874.

The Bureau of Indian Affairs, in bringing the two suits, appears to have had different motives. In the first suit it advanced a new theory of Indian land rights contrary to that so long practiced in New Mexico and Arizona. The same theory was later used in a number of suits brought by tribes themselves throughout the United States against the federal government, demanding large sums of money for land titles assertedly never extinguished legally but merely seized. These suits by the Indians questioned the rights of those who had obtained the land from the United States but did not seek damages from the innocent landholders; they asked money from the federal treasury. In the first Hualpai suit the Bureau of Indian Affairs used the theory not against the national government but against the railroad. The

Bureau's first suit resulted in the loss to the Santa Fe Pacific of 486,564 acres of land, of the taxes paid Mohave County, and of $21,000 in special legal costs beyond the salaries of various regular employees. In defending the Hualpais' rights, federal authorities appear to have been so overzealous that they were unfair to the railroad. In the second suit the Bureau of Indian Affairs sought title to valuable springs it had been renting for some time and to additional land. It based its claim on an army map, but did not display the map. Until it does, there is good grounds for the belief that it is being more than overzealous.

The railroad faced a problem less complicated and more profitable in deciding what to do about oil development. Its first tentative request for a petroleum lease came in 1905, but actually it made no oil leases until 1917. Initially, following Engel's advice, it tried to earn a good income by renting only in townships and to ensure development by stiff drilling requirements reinforced with penalty clauses. It made only the relatively few leases necessary to obtain the testing of a particular area, rather than renting the whole of it. If anything valuable actually were discovered, Engel preferred to have considerable acreage available for lease upon more advantageous terms. In 1923 Howel Jones seriously questioned this policy, declaring the company could easily have earned twenty-five thousand dollars more over the past four years in the so-called Seven Lakes district had it rented every acre possible. He persuaded Engel to change his mind; thereafter the railroad leased as much land as it could. Its customers discovered only a little oil but paid it considerable rent.

The Santa Fe Pacific at first charged 25 cents an acre annually and later 50 cents. In 1927 the company revised its lease form. It adopted a sliding scale of 50 cents the first year, 60 the second, 70 the third, 80 the fourth, and $1.00 thereafter. It specified royalties of 12.5 to 30 percent, according to the type of petroleum products refined. It required the lessee to drill at least one well every twelve months until there were as many producing wells in the area as there were twenty-acre lots.[10] It refused to vary from its lease form. In the early 1940's it reduced rentals but imposed stiffer drilling requirements.

The company's land grant was all wildcat territory, distant from any proved field. Every lease was a speculation. Sometimes leases were undertaken by promoters who retailed a small portion of their rented area to a large number of small-scale investors, often ignorant and credulous but eager to "get rich quick." Two of these promoters

---

[10] Engel to Jones, March 8, 1927, LCA 10939.

in their sales methods violated the law and went to prison.[11] Another group of lessees were local businessmen in the grant area who seldom intended themselves to drill but hoped to sell their rights to another investor at a profit or else to persuade somebody else to put down a well under a share-profits agreement. A related type of speculator was the semi-expert who followed the wildcat developments described in oil newspapers and, where he believed prospects were good, rented acreage in the immediate vicinity. One of these held for twenty years, with no apparent profit to himself, a variety of small leases in many parts of the grant. He finally turned to a variation of the oil business—running a motel.

Besides renting to individuals, the Santa Fe Pacific leased to associations or companies. Sometimes these were rather informal, such as "an association of Santa Fe Boys on this [railroad operating] division." More often they were incorporated companies, strong in rosy anticipations but faced with a constant struggle for sufficient funds to pay the rent and to drill a few wells. These generally were honestly run, but "rich in hope as a prospector." A few of the companies were more intent upon making stock sales and then calling for additional support from the shareholders than in undertaking bona fide development. Such a company was the Great Basin Oil Company, which leased 60,016.43 acres around Holbrook from the railroad, 147,783.66 acres from the Aztec Land and Cattle Company, and additional land from others. It sold about $750,000 worth of stock in five years, largely through churches, until its improper methods caused the state of New York to secure a permanent injunction preventing further sales.[12] The Santa Fe Pacific made almost no leases to any of the large, well-known oil companies. It made none to the Atchison's oil subsidiaries, which had undertaken profitable developments in other areas served by the railroad.[13]

Between 1921 and 1927 the Santa Fe Pacific profited by the enthusiasm of speculators. During the period it made leases totaling about 237,526 acres, some of which were covered by an annual agreement which lapsed and later were included in another contract. In

[11] *Albuquerque Journal*, December 22, 1929; *Los Angeles Times*, December 18, 1933. One fledgling promoter sold half his lease in a clearly unpromising section to a professor at the College of the City of New York. He sold the same half again to a New Mexican. The professor charged fraud and the promoter went to the penitentiary.

[12] LCA 10261, *passim*; *New York Times*, May 5, 1926; *New York Tribune*, June 11, 1926.

[13] Hope for oil discoveries on the property of the New Mexico and Arizona Land Company, coupled with other alleged possibilities of large profits, caused considerable speculation in the stock of that organization during the early 1920's. The Frisco railroad, its parent, played no part in this. The speculation was en-

some years about half of its New Mexico property was rented for oil development. The average size of a new lease declined from 2,104 acres in 1922 to 916.5 acres in 1927, reflecting the increase of speculation by small-scale investors. After 1927 there was relatively little demand for new leases, but a few were made each year. In 1944 the Santa Fe Pacific had a total of 20,868.12 acres rented for oil.[14]

At several spots in the grant there was oil excitement at one time or another. Between 1919 and 1934 in the Seven Lakes district, about thirty-five miles north of Bluewater, New Mexico, there were six lessees strongly interested; they sank ten unsuccessful wells. In the vicinity of Magdalena, New Mexico, between 1919 and 1927, there were four renters especially enthusiastic, but their two wells yielded no oil. Around Holbrook, Arizona, the publicity of activities reported between 1921 and 1926 by the Great Basin Oil Company created interest. There was excitement around Gallup in the early 1920's and, more important, in 1927.

Oil in commercial quantities was discovered in only two places on the grant lands, where small pools promised to yield only a relatively small quantity of petroleum.[15] One was at the so-called Hospah field, about thirty-five miles north of Grants, New Mexico. It was found by the Midwest Refining Company, but most of the development came after 1938 when the Petroleum Products Corporation took over the field. The railroad's royalty in 1943 from this area was averaging $1,200 to $1,400 monthly. Another oil strike was made a dozen miles north of the Hospah at the so-called Red Mountain field. Although discovery was made in the early 1930's, there was little development until the 1940's, and by 1946 it was not clear how successful this small area would prove to be.

During the 1920's and after, the Santa Fe Pacific faced problems about Indian land. It exchanged and sold acreage to benefit the Navajos. It failed to secure the odd-numbered sections apparently granted it in the Hualpai reservation. With regard to oil lands it met another type of special situation during the period. It obtained considerable rental from those interested in wildcat speculation. Its lessees discovered little petroleum. The railroad, besides these unusual situations, faced the more routine problems discussed in Chapter XI for the 1920's and covered in Chapter XIII for more recent times.

---

couraged by a New York brokerage house which had obtained a considerable block of the stock on the open market. Although the par value was $1.00, the stock sold on the New York Curb Exchange as high as $8.00, which was clearly unrealistic. (Engel to Jones, March 21, 1924, TSW 11002.)

[14] E. O. Hemenway to R. G. Rydin, November 28, 1944, LCA 12181.
[15] TSW and LCA 10268 and LCA 12494, *passim.*

CHAPTER XIII

RECENT DEVELOPMENTS

THE Santa Fe Pacific after 1929 faced the great depression, the wartime boom, and the postwar readjustment. Its policies, slightly altered to meet new conditions, followed the precedents laid down earlier. In 1946 it launched a vigorous drive to sell what remained of its land grant.

In personnel there were various changes. Field Examiner Art Saunders died in 1934 and was not replaced. In June 1936 Land Commissioner Collinson was killed during a Sunday afternoon pleasure drive. His successor was E. O. Hemenway, whose long employment with Atchison engineering services had often taken him into Arizona and New Mexico.[1] When Victoria C. Scott retired as chief clerk in 1937, her post was taken first by Richard O. Bates and then by Mildred H. Balch. In 1939 Engel became president of the Atchison and surrendered general executive supervision of the grant to Rudolph G. Rydin.[2] The land commissioner's headquarters were moved in 1937 from Topeka to Albuquerque at almost the eastern edge of the grant. Many advantages came from having the office so close to the land supervised. There were also minor annoyances; for example, one day a lessee, visiting Albuquerque, arose as usual with the sun and phoned Hemenway at 5:15 A.M. for an appointment.

The economic situation confronting the railroad and the nation during the great depression was serious. Conditions grew progressively worse until the spring of 1933, then very slowly improved until the wartime boom. Agriculture, which had not shared the prosperity of the 1920's, faced disaster in the 1930's, and the government tried various expedients to assist it. Ranchers were hard hit, as illustrated by the fact that the average national price per one hundred pounds for beef cattle was $9.15 in 1929, but only $3.63 in 1933. In New Mexico and Arizona the sheepmen by late in 1931 were near bankruptcy and the cattlemen soon were in the same predicament.

Faced with these conditions, Collinson adopted the same lenient policy Jones had followed earlier about delinquent payments. He was

---

[1] Hemenway served until his sudden death in 1950. He was a public-spirited and enlightened administrator. His successor was McClelland, whose long experience as field examiner qualified him thoroughly for the post.

[2] In 1948 Rydin became an Atchison Vice President, but continued to supervise the grant.

143

cautioned by Engel that because many debtors asked extensions from the Atchison or its various subsidiaries while paying other creditors, he must make sure he was receiving fair treatment as well as giving it. He encountered serious difficulties in making collections during 1930, 1931, and 1932. In 1933 his problems grew much easier because most ranchers received loans from the Regional Agricultural Credit Corporation, a subsidiary of the Federal Farm Credit Administration. The stockmen, as additional collateral on their chattel mortgages, assigned their railroad leases or sales contracts to the credit corporation. This agency made the payments as they fell due. Had the Santa Fe Pacific not built up over the years such an excellent reputation for its tenure rules toward renters, its leases might not have been accepted so readily as collateral. The railroad, on its sales contracts, repossessed only 640 acres. In the boom 1940's, it had almost no difficulties with delinquent payments.

Next to the depression and the wartime prosperity, the most important force affecting the grant was passage in 1934 of the Taylor Grazing Act.[3] It placed virtually all the remaining unappropriated public domain in the eleven far western states under the control of a new bureau, the United States Grazing Service. It established a system of permits and fees which for the first time controlled grazing on the public domain. It stipulated that in granting grazing rights a preference must be shown first to those who owned or leased land in the immediate vicinity and then to those who had long used an area. It authorized swaps between the government and other owners to eliminate private land within grazing districts. It provided that the exchanges were to be for land of equal value; the lieu was to be located in the same state as the base or, if not over fifty miles from the land relinquished, in an adjoining state. The act said nothing about homesteading, but President Roosevelt shortly withdrew all land from entry.

The effects of the Taylor Grazing Act were not felt in the railroad area until 1936, when first steps were taken to organize the necessary grazing districts and to issue permits. Since the size and location of these grazing privileges depended first upon the amount of private land an applicant owned or leased, some ranchers who had never before rented railroad acreage now hurried to secure what was still available—the less desirable tracts. Sometimes range rights controversies arose. These the company and the Grazing Service strove to solve equitably. In making adjustments, the two and the state land

[3] One of the most useful discussions of the Taylor Grazing Act is E. Louise Peffer, *The Closing of the Public Domain* (Stanford, Calif., 1951), *passim.*

commissioners occasionally arranged for various ranchers to trade leases.

The Santa Fe Pacific in the late 1930's began land exchanges under the Taylor Grazing Act. It undertook no new ones after 1940 because experience taught that action on them was slow and annoyances were frequent. The company filed its initial request for a typical exchange in January 1937; later at government suggestion or on its own initiative it made amendments in July 1937, July 1939, June 1940, April 1943, and September 1943; and in July 1946 it still did not know whether its application would be honored. The Santa Fe Pacific up to June 1946 relinquished under the act 98,613.76 acres and received as lieu 112,390.35 acres of even-numbered sections where it already owned the odd-numbered ones. It had pending additional transactions involving 109,618.20 acres of base and 91,464.82 acres of lieu.[4]

The railroad, in executing these exchanges, successfully resisted the Department of the Interior's demand for a fee to accompany its application. It yielded to the Department's insistence it must surrender the mineral rights on 8,500 acres of base and at the same time allow the government to retain similar rights on the lieu. When an exchange was completed, the company gave former holders of government permits on the lieu the first chance to rent from it, and the Grazing Service extended to former company lessees on the base as much preference as its standard rules would allow. In addition to these swaps for itself, the company after 1940 sold 166,306.96 acres, mostly at 25 cents each, to those who announced they would use the land as base to make exchanges with the government. The railroad made no guaranties about successful completion of the proposed swaps.

The company considered whether it should take any action under a 1938 amendment to the Taylor Act which authorized the United States Grazing Service to lease state, county, or privately owned land within a grazing district. It knew the Southern Pacific in the fall of 1939 had placed over ten million acres in Utah and Nevada under the federal service. The Santa Fe Pacific, unimpressed, decided to retain complete control of its property.

The workings of the Taylor Grazing Act strengthened Collinson in his conviction that the railroad should solidify as much of its grant as possible. He thought ranchers would prefer to buy lands where they could operate without interference from the United States Grazing Service. Collinson and Hemenway relinquished 430,914.18 acres

[4] LCA 11761, 13430, 13513, 13553, 13752, 14107, *passim.*

in the Navajo reservation for even-numbered sections elsewhere; they used 40,341.90 acres obtained directly or indirectly through the Petrified Forest exchange for solidification purposes; they swapped 6,413.23 acres with two private owners; and they traded land under the Taylor Grazing Act. In all, by June 1946 they secured 583,646.43 acres of even-numbered sections where the company already held title to the odd-numbered ones and filed application for 91,464.82 acres more, which may bring the total to 675,111.25 acres.

The Santa Fe Pacific between 1930 and 1945 continued its traditional land sales procedures. In 1939 it decided to inform a lessee of the exact amount in any acceptable offer made by others for the land he used, because Hemenway felt it was only fair to give the renter preference at the price bid.[5] In exceptional cases the railroad began to permit the extension of payments over more than five years and in one instance allowed over twenty years. It sometimes compromised on mineral rights, retaining them on only half the acreage involved. Its yearly sales varied with economic conditions, but were somewhat stimulated by the Taylor Grazing Act. From 1930 through 1934 the company marketed 20,973 acres of grazing land; from 1935 through 1939, 30,967 acres; and from 1940 through 1945, 763,906 acres; or a total of 815,846 acres.[6] Its prices ranged from 50 cents to $2.10 an acre; most were $1.00 to $1.25. Its customers were almost all medium or small ranchers. It encountered much more success in making sales than did the states of New Mexico and Arizona, whose high prices repelled purchasers.

In 1945 the railroad received an offer of three million dollars from Thomas B. Scott, Jr., for the remaining grant lands. Hemenway strongly opposed its acceptance because he thought the company could make more money out of many sales to various people; because he believed marketing everything to one man would alienate many within the trade area served by the Atchison; because he knew the reputation of the existing lease tenure and sales policies was an asset to the Atchison; and because he feared a private owner might not stimulate maximum mineral and oil exploration.[7] Scott's offer was rejected. Two similar proposals were received later but were not much discussed.

Scott's offer and a quickening demand for grazing land caused Hemenway and McClelland in 1946 to launch a vigorous campaign to sell the remaining grant. Familiar with the tracts the railroad

---

[5] Hemenway to Floyd W. Lee, August 21, 1935, LCA 12678.
[6] Ninety-six files regarding land sales, *passim*. It sold land in Lea County, outside the grant area and obtained in the first Zuñi lieu transaction, for $4.50 an acre.
[7] Hemenway to Rydin, April 7, 1945, LCA 14734.

still owned, they fixed a price on each lessee's area as a complete, indivisible unit. They asked 25 cents to $2.00 an acre; this was generally 25 to 50 cents less than the maximum which could be secured for comparable land on the boom market. The company saw no point in charging so much that ranchers would encounter financial difficulties in the normal times everybody assumed would soon return. Also, it knew that a large portion of the higher sum would go to the federal government in taxes. The railroad, in addition to reasonable prices, reduced its interest rate from 6 to 5 percent. It sent out a personal letter to each lessee giving him the first opportunity to buy his tract at the appraised price. It presented him with the alternatives of purchasing the land or of losing it forever as soon as another customer appeared. The company's lessees hastened to buy; for most of them the tracts were absolutely necessary. From January to the end of July, 1946, the company sold 836,366.15 acres for a total price of $801,203.95, which was paid $68,455.89 in cash and the rest in installments.[8] Apparently the Santa Fe Pacific will shortly have placed all its land holdings under sales contract, and the disposition of the grant, except for mineral rights, will be completed.

The decision in 1946 to sell the grant was one of the most important the company ever made. It had been able to find few purchasers for grazing land except during World War I and was wise to capitalize on a repetition of the earlier boom. The policy of uninflated prices, requiring keen insight into the best interest of the Atchison, reflected credit especially upon Hemenway and McClelland.

The railroad owned other property besides grazing land. At the Bluewater acreage, the irrigation district faced a shortage and sometimes a complete absence of water. Between 1930 and 1940 its members averaged about three thousand acres under cultivation instead of the ten thousand originally planned. It met such monetary difficulties that it had to be aided by the Reconstruction Finance Corporation, which forced the bondholders to accept 30 percent of the money due them as complete payment and which reduced the size of the district to 5,700 acres.[9] In 1941 and 1942 the Bluewater project had

[8] Memorandum, LCA 12286. From August 1, 1946, through December 1952 gross sales of all types of land were approximately two million acres.

[9] Many owners could not pay the district's assessments and had to forfeit their land to it. One of these was Sidney M. Worthy, who had been in the early days the project's most vital force. Just before he lost his property, it seemed for a brief moment that he could sell it. Engel, hearing of this, instructed Hemenway as follows on September 4, 1937 (LCA 10151):

"Notwithstanding the fact that Mr. Worthy has taken up a good deal of our time for many years, I feel considerable sympathy for him. He did invest very large amounts in the Bluewater country in the early days and I suspect that such investment

ample water, then faced another period of shortage. It drilled wells, which were satisfactory as a temporary solution but not as a permanent one because the pumping will eventually deplete the underground sources. Within the district, as reduced, the Santa Fe Pacific owned 1,590 acres. The company by 1944 marketed 1,248.30 acres at $30 to $40 each to various vegetable growers. In negotiating, one of them unsuccessfully appealed to Hemenway's superiors for a lower price.

Outside the Bluewater area, the railroad sold 2,009 acres along the Colorado and Williams rivers, suitable for small-scale irrigation projects. It disposed of 5,027 acres to dry farmers. It continued to oppose promoters' schemes of colonizing land without water. About one of them Saunders wrote, "This fellow . . . must be an ignoramus or just a plain wrong end of a horse."[10] The Santa Fe Pacific sold 14,632.01 acres needed for the building of Parker and Davis dams on the Colorado River. At the latter, one of the cafés for construction workers was christened "The Damsite Cooler." The railroad marketed 8,887.32 acres for miscellaneous uses. The most unusual of these transactions was with magazine publisher Thomas H. Beck, who purchased a section of the cheapest and poorest land available to distribute, as a kind of Christmas card, to 640 friends. The company sold 680 acres of coal land and 278.71 acres for pumice stone. It donated 7,275.32 acres of archeological ruins to the National Park Service and 8.4 acres for recreational purposes to Mohave County.

The Santa Fe Pacific after 1929 disposed of virtually all its remaining timber. It sold the trees on 3,599 acres within the Cibola National Forest to the Big Chief Lumber Company at $2.00 a thousand board feet. It marketed the rest of its woods there in 1940 to the New Mexico Timber Company. The railroad peddled about

---

has been quite largely the cause of his financial difficulties in recent years. I have never felt that we are called on to assist him directly but if we could be of some help to him in disposing of such equity as he [has] left so that he can receive a few thousand dollars at least, I should like it and I believe it would be of intangible benefit to us."

[10] Saunders to Collinson, December 9, 1931, LCA 12682. In the early 1940's Hemenway's superiors granted an option to one promoter, over the land commissioner's vigorous protest, but fortunately no sale resulted. This is the one exception to the company's excellent record of opposing colonization schemes. The dreams of promoters about agricultural development of the arid areas in the region of the company's grant are still alive. In 1951 there was much serious discussion about a federally financed project which would carry the waters of the Colorado River through a twenty-five-mile tunnel to the Peach Springs, there to be distributed to the level valleys in Mohave County. Whether this billion-dollar project will ever be built is a question, but it is the latest manifestation of the urge many have felt to develop the region.

10,000 acres of isolated timber to small-scale operators, who marketed their output to the Atchison.[11]

The Santa Fe Pacific continued to lease its lands. In 1939 it rented about 80 percent of its holdings and in 1943 leased everything but a few desert tracts in Mohave and Yuma counties.[12] On its annual agreements the company in 1941 charged 2.5 cents an acre rental in nine counties and from 1.5 to 5 cents in the five others. Its net return, after paying taxes on the acreage rented, varied from .6 cent loss in Yuma County to 1 cent profit in Sandoval and McKinley counties.[13]

In 1935 Collinson began to encourage the use of a long-term lease. He persuaded many to sign a five-year contract, cancelable in case of sale, and later added an option to renew for five more years at a slightly higher figure. In all but three counties, under this long-term agreement, he charged 1 cent an acre plus the taxes the first five years and 1.25 cents the second five. In 1939 Hemenway introduced a modified five-year form which was noncancelable and contained no renewal clause. In 1944 the railroad began to eliminate the various existing forms of lease as they expired and substituted a new so-called five-year agreement. This allowed the company to cancel the contract for any reason upon ninety days' notice and authorized the rancher to do so on any anniversary date. Fees under the new agreement varied from .4 to 1 cent an acre plus the taxes.

The Santa Fe Pacific made only very moderate profits from its grazing land leases. Assuming its property was worth on an average $1.00 an acre, it secured less than 1 percent net on the valuation. It did not earn enough rental to pay the taxes on the grant, leased and unleased, until 1942. In comparison, the states of New Mexico and Arizona after 1929 collected 3 cents an acre, except that the latter for two years in the middle of the depression cut its rate to 1.5 cents. In 1943 the New Mexico and Arizona Land Company received 1 to 2

[11] The railroad occasionally had wood stolen and generally could do little about it. Saunders, however, reported to Collinson on March 9, 1932 (LCA 11197), that he had confronted a thief while en route to St. Johns on other business. ". . . [The thief] tried to be indignant and asked me if I meant to insinuate that he had stolen the [fence] posts. I told him I was making no insinuations but just stating the plain fact to him, and that he most certainly had stolen the posts. I told him I was not there to argue the matter with him, but was on my way to St. Johns, but before going, I wanted his answer. I suppose he thought we were going to send the sheriff after him, and he wilted and admitted he cut the posts, and said he was willing to pay whatever charge we thought right. I told him our charge was 4¢ each. . . ."

[12] One interesting lease in effect during much of this period was to the "Abeytas Community Allotment," a group of seventeen Mexicans who each owned a few head of livestock; they jointly leased 9,229.91 acres. They had a good set of written rules covering the use of the area.

[13] Hemenway to Rydin, December 14, 1942, LCA 13988.

cents plus the taxes. The United States Grazing Service, which did not secure enough to cover operating expenses, charged the equivalent of about 1 cent an acre.

Collinson in the early 1930's discreetly mentioned to lessees the desirability of shipping by railroad rather than truck, but apparently accomplished almost nothing. A freight traffic solicitor in 1938 hinted to a lessee that he might lose the use of 113,739.75 railroad acres unless he used the Atchison's service; instead the solicitor, on order from his superiors, had to apologize. Another type of problem faced Collinson when a rancher sold his lease and livestock to another sheepman, then had a fight with his new wife, was put in jail, and hanged himself. The sheepman asked for the lease, displaying the bill of sale. The wife also demanded it, showing a will leaving it to her. Collinson hardly knew what to do. His problem was solved when the county attorney proved the will was forged.

In the Cibola National Forest, the Santa Fe Pacific continued to entrust management of its land to the Forest Service. It was constantly dissatisfied because of the service's nation-wide policy of reducing the number of head grazed in any particular region. Between 1938 and 1940 the railroad complained vigorously because it wanted an increase in the number of animals authorized a large-scale rancher, who also leased adjoining railroad land. Its request was refused by the Forest Service, which said he had no moral right to more at the expense of small-scale operators. It finally in 1940 sold the rancher 25,050.08 acres he wanted and shortly marketed its remaining 80,034.20 acres in the forest to the New Mexico Timber Company, which exchanged the land for timber of an equal value elsewhere. Thus it resolved a conflict between large- and small-scale stockmen with one man securing about a quarter of the disputed area and many others the use of the remainder. The railroad was well out of a difficult situation never foreseen when Howel Jones made the joint management agreement thirty-five years previously.

The Santa Fe Pacific after 1929 became actively interested in making mineral leases. It adopted a standard lease providing a 10 percent royalty on placer operations; on lode mining the fee was 10 percent of ore worth $40.00 a ton or less and 20 percent of that valued more highly. If nothing was found, it charged a low rent for the land. It leased to thirty-two parties between 1930 and 1945, mostly in Mohave County, but little mineral was discovered.[14] Its most suc-

14 It would be disappointing indeed if there were not at least one "lost mine" story connected with the grant area. Art Saunders on May 31, 1930 (LCA 12384), told Collinson a yarn about Navajo County. In the late 1860's an old prospector

cessful agreement covered a bentonite deposit in Apache County, which yielded the Santa Fe Pacific only 10 cents a ton but gave the Atchison a haul of about 650 miles of a material almost impossible to damage.[15]

During World War II the company granted the army permission to maneuver over 26,318.80 acres in Yuma County. It sold Mohave County 1,896.52 acres upon which the air corps erected a $3,000,000 aerial gunnery school. For an adjoining gunnery range, it fought off a threatened condemnation proceeding and arranged for the army to subrent a large area from its lessees at the standard railroad fee for grazing land. To preserve the stockmen's tenure as renters, the individual ranchers, the railroad, and the army signed "all of these fancy forms" in eleven copies each.

The company after 1929 encouraged little experimental work. It showed no enthusiasm for the United States Soil Conservation Service, organized in 1935. It allowed those holding long-term leases to sign contracts for the service to improve and restore their range, but warned of the possible danger in governmental control of the number of animals to be grazed. All these contracts had expired by 1941. It placed none of its land in the soil conservation districts the service later decided to foster instead of individual ranch units. During World War II the railroad granted a license for removing yucca leaves to make fiber, but the project did not succeed.

Regarding taxes, the company faced routine problems. In Mohave

---

discovered some placer gold, which daily he dug out, took to Cottonwood Wash, and "panned." He soon learned Indians were watching him and grew alarmed. He cut a limb off a tree to point at a near-by spot where he set two cedar posts in the ground, halfway between which he buried a third post pointing to the diggings. He went to Prescott, where he became acquainted with a man named French. The two planned to come back, but the old prospector died. French, with two other companions, returned and finally managed to locate the pointer. Since they did not know the distance from there to the diggings and since Indians had destroyed evidence of the prospector's workings, they could not find the placer. French continued looking for it till he died, although the other two gave up earlier. In 1930 "two young Mexican sprouts" leased a section from the railroad, thinking they had rediscovered the old mine, but of course they had not. Saunders discouraged them but finally decided it was proper for the company to rent them the land "as I am sure they have gotten more thrills out of this than they have ever gotten before for $12.50 each."

[15] In 1950 the Santa Fe Pacific announced the discovery by a Navajo named Paddy Martinez of considerable uranium ore near Grants, New Mexico, on land which it had sold but where it still retained the mineral rights. By July 1951 it had spent about a quarter of a million dollars in further exploring and prospecting work. The company has not made any specific announcement of the size of this deposit. If it proves to be the "huge lode" some newspaper accounts have stated, the Santa Fe Pacific may be entering into an important phase of its history quite different from anything that has been told in this book.

County its tax rate was less than that charged individual owners of grazing land. Actually it paid too little on some areas and too much on others, this resulting in what railway officials believed was an average tax fair to everybody.

The Atchison was much more concerned than the Santa Fe Pacific over land-grant rates. These arose from a clause to be found in the act granting land to most railroads; later it was made applicable to the others. As interpreted by the courts, it required a railroad to carry government freight and passengers for half the rate charged others over that portion of the line adjacent to the acreage received; for mail, the fee was 80 percent of the ordinary rate. In order to secure a share of federal traffic, the railroads, which themselves received no land, had to meet these reductions. The carriers complained in the 1930's because the New Deal activities expanded government enterprise into fields never before covered and, naturally, increased the volume of federal traffic. Their pleas produced the Transportation Act of 1940, which abolished land-grant rates on all but military and naval traffic. After the government had secured huge savings during World War II, the remaining land-grant rates were eliminated late in 1946.

Atchison officials have estimated their road lost about $215,000,-000 by these reductions to the government between 1879 and 1946. Of this, part arose from meeting competition and the rest came one-third from the Atchison's Kansas grant and two-thirds from the Santa Fe Pacific property. The railroad naturally was anxious to take advantage of the Transportation Act of 1940. It relinquished its unsatisfied land claims in order to qualify. Nobody has determined the exact amount it surrendered.[16] In relinquishing its claims, the company thought it was omitting the still unused lieu rights scrip it had sold to others long ago. Unfortunately it did not mention this in the formal release. Its supposed exemption was ruled invalid first by the General Land Office and later by the United States Supreme Court. Apparently there was little scrip still unused that would be affected by this decision.

The Santa Fe Pacific after 1929 adjusted itself to varied economic conditions. It weathered the depression with little financial loss, thanks to mortgage holders who paid the ranchers' rent and installments on purchase contracts. From 1930 through 1945 it earned a net profit of $3,214,980.67.[17] It benefited by the Taylor Grazing Act. It continued its leases to stockmen, increasingly on a long-term basis. In

16 See Appendix G.
17 From 1946 through 1952 the net profit was $2,904,258.34.

1942, for the first time, its rental income paid the taxes on the entire grant, leased and unleased. It decided after World War II to sell its remaining property. Also it and the Atchison surrendered all unsatisfied land claims to the federal government. The Santa Fe Pacific, having placed most of its property under sales contract, apparently in the future will find its chief problem to be the development of its new uranium deposits.

CHAPTER XIV

SUMMARY AND CONCLUSION

In 1866 Congress chartered the Atlantic and Pacific Railroad to reach from Springfield, Missouri, to the Pacific Ocean. This the company interpreted as authorizing it to touch the coast at Ventura and then build north to San Francisco. To help cover the cost of construction, it was offered the right to earn from the federal government a land grant. The Atlantic and Pacific obtained little acreage in Missouri, already well populated, secured no tracts in Indian Territory, where the United States refused to extinguish the red men's title, and received no grant in Texas, where the national government owned no land. In New Mexico, Arizona, and California it would secure acreage when it reached these areas, but to early financiers this prospect was too much of a gamble to be attractive. The Atlantic and Pacific built as far west as Vinita, I.T., before plunging into bankruptcy in 1876. It was reorganized as the St. Louis and San Francisco Railroad, generally called the Frisco.

The Atchison, entirely independent of the old A&P, was meanwhile pressing westward. When it reached Albuquerque in 1880, it joined with the Frisco to form a new Atlantic and Pacific. They constructed the new road from Isleta, thirteen miles south of Albuquerque, to Needles and would have built farther west had not C. P. Huntington met them with an unwelcome branch of the Southern Pacific. In 1884 the A&P secured the route from Needles to Barstow and Mojave; later it purchased the line. In 1885 another subsidiary of the Atchison opened a railroad from Barstow to San Diego to complete a through route, independent of Huntington, to the Pacific.

Getting definite geographical areas as grants and administering them were also tasks beset with difficulties and uncertainties. The new Atlantic and Pacific could not obtain legal title to most of the acreage in its New Mexico and Arizona grant because the federal government would not survey the area. Its troubles were increased by the multitude of Mexican or Spanish grants in New Mexico, some fraudulent and some not, which, once proved genuine, had a prior right over the railroad to many odd-numbered sections. It never had anything but the most general knowledge about the nature of the land it claimed. In 1886 it forfeited through congressional action its unearned land east of Isleta and west of Needles. The next year its indemnity strip, where it could choose land to replace the odd-numbered sections un-

154

available within the place limits, was thrown open to entry by anybody, but few sought holdings there.

Disposing of the grant presented problems. Ostensibly the railroad sold 5,004,318.15 acres of grazing land. Actually it marketed voluntarily about a tenth of that amount, had to deed the Aztec Land and Cattle Company a million acres for 50 cents each, and turned over 3,492,684.90 acres to its two parents in payment of debts owed. It entered into no colonization schemes, but did try to interest outsiders in purchasing the grazing land old-timers preferred to trespass on. Its lands were much used by interlopers, who swelled the revenues of the railroad's traffic department but not those of the land department. It sold some timber, but accomplished nothing in fostering irrigation development. In 1896 the A&P went bankrupt.

Looking back over the whole history of the railroad and its land grant, how much did Congress aid in promoting a road to the Pacific by passing the granting act of 1866? It offered too little land in Missouri and actually none in Indian Territory or Texas; beyond, in New Mexico, Arizona, and California, it promised considerable acreage. During the 1860's and 1870's no capitalists thought the inducements sufficient to push the A&P through to the West. In 1880 the Atchison, expanding in a region where there was no bar to white settlement similar to that in the Indian Territory, reached Albuquerque. Undoubtedly it or somebody else would eventually have built through northern New Mexico and Arizona to the coast without a grant. The crucial question is when, and nobody can supply the answer. Between 1881 and 1896 the Atlantic and Pacific's net profit from the land, including the forced transactions with its parents, was $3,853,336.17. It preserved no records of what it spent to build from Isleta to Needles, but in 1896 the expense of reproducing the line was estimated at $13,068,142.49. Apparently the A&P earned from its acreage about 30 percent of the cost of construction. The real profit from the grant came after 1896.

In 1897 the Atchison purchased the bankrupt Atlantic and Pacific. To the management of the Santa Fe Pacific Railroad it turned over the A&P's remaining land and the so-called Frost acreage previously obtained as settlement of A&P debts owed the parent road. From this area of about 10,239,128 acres, according to the company's figures, the net profit between 1897 and 1919 was $7,869,123.66; in the 1920's, $1,781,942.05; from 1930 through 1945, $3,214,980.67; and from 1946 through 1952, $2,904,258.34. The total net profit between 1897 and 1952 was $15,770,304.72. Actually this figure is too high because it does not reflect what the Atchison itself paid for the land. It does not show the sums the railroad lost through land-grant rates which it had to allow the government on traffic moving between Isleta and Needles. However, these reductions would have applied to that stretch of track even if an outsider, rather than the Atchison, had purchased the grant. Whether the acreage was really profitable to the Atchison after 1897 is an involved, debatable question, incapable of definite proof.

Turning to a more detailed account of the railroad's land administration policies after 1897, the first important act of the Santa Fe Pacific was to commence a series of land exchanges intended to solve difficult land problems. It owned odd-numbered sections within the boundaries of two national forests and relinquished them, receiving in payment lieu rights to 927,538 acres. Between 1904 and 1932 it made four swaps for the benefit of squatters located in the grant area: the small holders, 21,325.55 acres; the act of June 22, 1874, 5,396.66 acres; the Sandy, 28,136.73 acres; and the act of March 4, 1931, 3,720 acres. It made two exchanges of land the National Park Service wanted: the Petrified Forest, 9,581.70 acres; and the Chaco Canyon, 6,362.68 acres. The railroad owned odd-numbered sections within parts of the Navajo, Moqui (or Hopi), Zuñi, and Laguna Indian reservations. Between 1897 and 1934 it surrendered 2,071,-710.48 acres and received lieu rights elsewhere. Under the Taylor Grazing Act it received, up to June 1946, 112,390.35 acres of lieu and had applications pending for 91,464.82 more. In all these exchanges the railroad actually received, by the middle of 1946, 3,186,162.15 acres. It used 552,886.23 acres of lieu rights to obtain even-numbered sections where it already owned the odd-numbered ones. It sold almost all the rest to a variety of purchasers. For the lieu rights it obtained a higher average price than it could have obtained for the base lands had it marketed them at the date the scrip was sold.

In making the exchanges, the Santa Fe Pacific became engaged in controversies. In those involving national forest land, it met opposition from ranchers in the immediate area and from farmers in southern Arizona; it also had to overcome the skepticism of the Secretary of the Interior. Those to whom it sold forest lieu rights selected wooded areas often more valuable than the timber surrendered. In the first Zuñi transaction, the railroad became involved in politics when a government mistake allowed "boomers" to homestead on land the company wished, and it eventually received at that location only part of its lieu. In the Moqui exchange, it with difficulty secured for its customers land that was inferior to the base while undeveloped but more valuable than that surrendered if used for irrigation. In the first Navajo swap in Arizona, the railroad, by changing the base surrendered, fought off strong opposition from State Land Commissioner Mulford Winsor. In the second Navajo trade in Arizona, it tangled with Coconino County ranchers who opposed lieu selections from the public domain which would prevent their free use of portions of the range. To the Navajo exchanges of the 1920's and the 1930's, there were less serious objections. To the railroad's other swaps, there were none. In almost all cases it secured the right to select lieu in smaller tracts than the base relinquished.

Selling land for grazing, the Santa Fe Pacific made no attempt to interest stockmen outside the grant area but concentrated on persuading ranchers already there that they should buy. It asked prospective purchasers to make a bid, sometimes competitive, and did not draw up a price list until 1946. Its terms were generally 20 percent down and the rest in five annual payments with interest at 6 percent. Its price, to make rough average, was $1.00 an acre. It made most of its sales during the booms engendered by the two World Wars. Its disposal policies about grazing land compare very favorably with those of the states of New Mexico, Arizona, and Nevada.

Selling land for other purposes than grazing, the company marketed acreage for use within irrigation districts and tracts its customers insisted could be dry-farmed. It refused, to its real credit, many opportunities to market acreage at high prices to promoters who wished to colonize arid land without bothering to provide any water.

In its sales to individuals and private organizations, the work of the Santa Fe Pacific is summarized in the following table:

Period	For grazing, acres	For irrigation or dry-farming, acres	For other purposes, acres	Totals, acres
1900–19	2,214,787	73,866	37,317	2,325,970
1920–29	50,610	20,324	11,059	81,993
1930–July 1946. . . .	1,652,050	3,257	21,479	1,676,786
Grand total	3,917,447	97,447	69,885	4,084,749

It sold 416,209.78 acres to governmental bodies. The Santa Fe Pacific's total sales of land between 1897 and the middle of 1946 were 4,500,957.78 acres and its lieu right sales were 2,633,275.92 acres, making a grand total of 7,134,233.70 acres. From August 1, 1946, through the end of 1952 it made additional sales of approximately two million acres gross of all types of land. It also marketed town lots in Ash Fork, Gallup, Williams, Flagstaff, and Winslow.

In leasing grazing land the Santa Fe Pacific gave lessees virtually permanent tenure until the acreage was sold. Its rental was so low that the income did not pay the taxes on the grant, leased and unleased, until 1946. It at first could persuade only a few stockmen to rent from it, but during World War II it had almost all its acreage under lease. It followed a lenient collection policy on delinquent payments of all kinds during the depressions of the early 1920's and the 1930's. Its grazing lease policies compare favorably with those of the Northern Pacific, Southern Pacific, and Union Pacific railways, the New Mexico and Arizona Land Company, and the states of Arizona, New Mexico, Wyoming, and Texas.

The railroad made its first oil lease in 1917 and experienced a brisk demand for such leases during the early 1920's. It obtained considerable income from rent although little petroleum was discovered. It began making mineral leases in 1928, but almost nothing of commercial value was found except some bentonite. It began exploring deposits of uranium in 1950. It had previously sold its various tracts of timber.

The history of land grants to other railroads farther east, some of which have already been studied by scholars, is almost entirely different from that of the grant in New Mexico and Arizona.[1] In regions suitable for agriculture, the railroads conducted large-scale colonization campaigns which marketed company land and provided settlers. The profits from these sales and from traffic generated by the growth of population apparently were considerably larger, proportionately, than the Santa Fe Pacific obtained. The more easterly lines encountered some difficulties with trespassers, soon evicted. They had relatively few controversies over their lands; their most common difficulties were with swampland grants made earlier to the states. They encountered no conditions similar to the forest and Indian acreage problems of New Mexico and Arizona. The Santa Fe Pacific, with an arid grant, had to handle its property in a very different way from railroads to the east. It encountered a surprising variety of problems and gradually evolved solutions to them.

This study reveals that, with a few minor exceptions, the Santa Fe Pacific conducted its business with strict honesty, showing due consideration for the welfare of the public in general. Railroad Land Commissioners Jones, Collinson, and Hemenway managed the grant well, securing a good profit for the company. They also made a real contribution to the economic development of New Mexico and Arizona.

[1] William S. Greever, "A Comparison of Railroad Land-Grant Policies," *Agricultural History*, XXV (1951), 83–90.

APPENDIXES
BIBLIOGRAPHY
AND INDEX

APPENDIX A

ESTIMATED COST OF REPRODUCING THE ISLETA-NEEDLES LINE, 1896

The Atlantic and Pacific earned its land grant in Arizona and New Mexico by constructing a line from Isleta, which is thirteen miles south of Albuquerque, to the Colorado River at Needles. There are no records now known to exist which show what the A&P spent in building this line. In 1896, however, an appraisal was made to decide what "would be the reasonable cost of reproducing at the present time, the now existing railroad."* It excluded anything connected with the A&P's line west of Needles, except it included all locomotives and cars because this equipment was constantly being used both east and west of Needles. It placed the total cost at $13,068,142.49. It went into considerable detail, but the only figures of interest for this study are the various classifications of expense:

Right of way ....$	77,485.48
Grading	2,733,790.35
Grading, sidetrack	32,181.71
Ditching	76,056.99
Riprapping	353,024.00
Ballast	88,222.00
Track ties	1,002,266.50
Switch ties	32,845.90
Steel and iron rails	1,955,013.85
Rail fastenings	280,677.64
Switches and fixtures	25,035.19
Cattle guards	546.00
Highway crossing planks	264.00
Tracklaying and surfacing	257,074.80
Train service	68,550.00
Maintaining water stations while tracklaying....	21,128.94
Maintenance of way during construction period..	175,909.22
Telegraph line	53,570.99
Wooden bridges	353,106.99
Iron bridges	729,285.61
Buildings and water service	808,712.31
Fencing	27,194.91
Station and roadway signs	1,848.97
Office and station furniture, law library, tools and supplies on locomotives	22,728.51
Temporary line across Colorado River	79,120.00
Track material in stock	92,285.66
Track tools, Road Department	13,079.22
Water service supplies and tools	2,635.28
Bridge and building tools	2,578.39

* Louis Kingman to E. P. Ripley and C. W. Smith, December 22, 1896, filed in the office of the Valuation Engineer, Topeka.

Locomotives	$ 1,016,050.00
Rolling stock	1,156,043.00
Tools and machinery at:	
Albuquerque	100,101.50
Gallup	11,125.43
Winslow	17,477.39
Flagstaff	238.12
Williams	9,825.07
Ash Fork	1,092.33
Peach Springs	2,160.85
New and second-hand material, Mechanical Department	21,638.65
Supplies on storekeeper's books, except Road Department supplies and car lumber	77,158.62
Car lumber in Albuquerque yard	11,319.00
Legal expenses	56,300.00
Material yard expense	84,450.00
Engineering	305,000.00
Management and miscellaneous expenses	205,000.00
Interest account	541,236.95
Taxes, one year	74,107.93
Insurance, one year	11,628.24
Total	$13,068,142.49

APPENDIX B

NET PROFIT FROM THE LAND GRANT

The following figures show the net profit by years made by the Atlantic and Pacific or the Santa Fe Pacific from the land grant.* (Letter "D" indicates deficit.)

1881	$ D7,665.89		1888	$ D1,085.93	
1882	D12,160.17		1889	D17,000.57	
1883	D5,251.23		1890	3,108,497.58	
1884	559,331.88		1891	7,163.35	
1885	92,406.98		1892	D23,489.50	
1886	105,665.22		1893	23,216.50	
1887	39,724.43		1894	D39,376.76	

* These figures are the annual receipts of the land department less disbursements. They omit intercompany payments for the so-called Frost lands, amortization of that portion of the Atchison's purchase price of the A&P RR Company's Western Division which might be considered as being for the land grant, and the Atchison's loss of revenue because it had to handle government traffic at reduced land-grant rates. Figures 1930 and prior were compiled by the auditor's office and forwarded by Collinson to Engel on April 24, 1931, LCA 3131. Figures 1931 and after are taken from the annual report of the Railroad Land Commissioner, LCA 12286, *passim.*

1895	$ 24,227.03	1924	$141,346.97
1896	D866.75	1925	96,154.14
1897	1,353.10	1926	41,133.74
1898	D5,483.15	1927	95,795.61
1899	14,824.71	1928	106,432.17
1900	D13,592.48	1929	129,133.82
1901	D27,680.02	1930	30,657.73
1902	D19,283.20	1931	D18,907.79
1903	890,442.13	1932	D39,676.19
1904	708,634.91	1933	4,404.74
1905	776,580.91	1934	4,200.80
1906	219,734.60	1935	307,820.51
1907	188,111.70	1936	223,168.09
1908	68,011.50	1937	179,255.14
1909	53,678.57	1938	69,519.15
1910	875,894.59	1939	73,089.39
1911	423,431.72	1940	377,943.89
1912	241,838.27	1941	106,839.50
1913	745,477.66	1942	205,991.16
1914	213,625.53	1943	274,321.03
1915	23,527.06	1944	259,559.70
1916	14,524.43	1945	156,793.79
1917	1,704,831.22	1946	527,201.22
1918	388,007.74	1947	630,311.74
1919	382,632.16	1948	551,063.70
1920	242,322.20	1949	434,432.96
1921	359,603.40	1950	478,045.03
1922	371,963.98	1951	97,555.67
1923	198,056.02	1952	185,642.02

Total through 1890	$ 3,862,462.30
Total through 1896	3,853,336.17
Total through 1900	3,850,438.35
Total through 1910	7,584,564.04
Total through 1920	11,964,782.03
Total through 1930	13,535,059.61
Total through 1940	15,715,877.37
Total through 1945	16,719,382.55
Total through 1952	19,623,640.89

APPENDIX C

DIVIDENDS DECLARED BY THE SANTA FE PACIFIC RAILROAD*

The profits earned were not always paid out as dividends immediately; they were distributed in conformity with the Atchison's general fiscal policies and needs.

1906	$ 320,000.00	1927	none
1907	200,000.00	1928	$ 200,000.00
1908	100,000.00	1929	100,000.00
1909	none	1930	none
1910	240,000.00	1931	200,000.00
1911	240,000.00	1932	none
1912	200,000.00	1933	none
1913	200,000.00	1934	none
1914	120,000.00	1935	400,000.00
1915	none	1936	240,000.00
1916	1,200,000.00	1937	100,000.00
1917	700,000.00	1938	100,000.00
1918	700,000.00	1939	none
1919	750,000.00	1940	200,000.00
1920	400,000.00	1941	200,000.00
1921	300,000.00	1942	none
1922	400,000.00	1943	200,000.00
1923	none	1944	350,000.00
1924	200,000.00	1945–51	none
1925	100,000.00	1952	1,000,000.00
1926	none		

Total through 1952, $9,520,000.00

* LCA 5390, *passim*. The above represents all the dividends paid by the Santa Fe Pacific while it was merely the Land Department of the Atchison. Also, it had two old notes in favor of the Atchison which it paid off, $248,761.75 in 1904 and $649,382.68 in 1905. There is nothing to indicate what these notes were for. Prior to June 30, 1916, the Atchison treated all dividends from the Santa Fe Pacific as coming out of profits. On that date the Atchison began counting all dividends as liquidation of the Santa Fe Pacific's assets and therefore of the $4,000,000 worth of SFP stock. At such time as the $4,000,000 was liquidated, all further dividends were to be treated as coming out of profit. (Engel to Jones, January 23, 1923, LCA 5390.)

APPENDIX D

GROSS RECEIPTS FROM RENTALS*

12 months ending June 30		1922	$ 83,252.57
1904	$ 4,189.25	1923	108,300.98
1905	2,619.72	1924	114,154.23
1906	4,188.12	1925	97,787.49
1907	7,821.05	1926	97,636.01
1908	10,991.75	1927	156,365.52
1909	15,425.42	1928	102,375.31
		1929	91,840.43
6 months ending Dec. 31		1930	78,318.73
1909	$ 9,788.24	1931	67,069.45
		1932	53,586.65
12 months ending Dec. 31		1933	70,799.64
1910	$26,135.02	1934	69,136.78
1911	20,931.84	1935	87,448.47
1912	28,312.48	1936	84,870.42
1913	27,633.99	1937	78,195.05
1914	30,426.12	1938	75,091.35
1915	29,749.43	1939	84,186.15
1916	45,522.39	1940	80,372.87
1917	56,346.88	1941	77,862.78
1918	60,651.86	1942	65,443.34
1919	91,966.06	1943	68,938.07
1920	101,628.59	1944	47,932.24
1921	96,593.58	1945	32,178.95

Total gross receipts from rentals, 1904–45, $2,644,065.25

* Compiled from records in the office of the Atchison's Auditor of Disbursements, Topeka. On December 31, 1909, the "Frost" rental account was changed so that the fiscal year ended on December 31, but the "Grant" account was not so changed until the end of 1917. During the interval, the author has arbitrarily assumed that one-half of the "Grant" rental for the year fell in each six months' period. After 1945 the railway received only a small amount of rental because, thanks to the 1946 sales campaign, so much of the grant was under sales contract. The auditor, after 1945, discontinued his separate rental account and included the money received in a miscellaneous income account.

APPENDIX E

GROSS RECEIPTS FROM LAND SALES, INCLUDING INTEREST AND LIEU RIGHTS*

12 months ending June 30			
1903	$1,005,909.40	1925	$ 70,135.35
1904	774,774.78	1926	30,358.62
1905	835,431.20	1927	31,059.57
1906	249,078.78	1928	99,439.97
1907	201,058.99	1929	166,132.93
1908	103,163.80	1930	54,014.83
1909	99,559.93	1931	59,408.62
1910	902,597.72	1932	67,123.14
1911	436,329.68	1933	65,541.29
1912	124,099.76	1934	53,327.51
1913	801,236.93	1935	238,701.08
1914	239,253.19	1936	262,750.33
1915	57,955.11	1937	218,556.17
1916	121,992.64	1938	86,494.43
1917	1,315,042.97	1939	93,900.16
		1940	394,300.10
6 months ending Dec. 31		1941	86,212.34
1917	$415,328.25	1942	196,299.33
		1943	244,878.80
12 months ending Dec. 31		1944	233,860.13
1918	$275,076.58	1945	181,491.34
1919	295,032.74	1946	500,550.63
1920	344,654.27	1947	679,546.58
1921	366,247.75	1948	603,440.77
1922	383,433.01	1949	499,022.84
1923	178,394.95	1950	495,714.27
1924	93,482.79	1951	271,033.36
		1952	283,175.23

Total gross receipts from land sales, 1903–52, $15,885,604.94

* Compiled from records in the office of the Atchison's Auditor of Disbursements. On December 31, 1909, the "Frost" sales account was changed so that the fiscal year ended when the calendar did, but the "Grant" account was not so changed until the end of 1917. During the interval, the author has arbitrarily assumed that one-half of the "Frost" sales revenue for the year fell in each six months' period.

APPENDIX F

GROSS RECEIPTS FROM TOWN LOT SALES*

12 months ending June 30

1904	$1,732.50
1905	1,945.00
1906	3,277.50
1907	3,485.00
1908	3,454.82
1909	3,625.00
1910	5,750.00
1911	5,982.25
1912	5,569.00
1913	4,410.00
1914	3,749.50
1915	1,655.00

1916	$ 35.00
1917	2,489.00

6 months ending Dec. 31

1917	$ 525.00

12 months ending Dec. 31

1918	$ 112.50
1919	1,325.00
1920	290.00
1921	25.00
1922	D925.00

Total gross receipts from town lot sales, 1904–22, $48,512.07

* TSW 7249, *passim.* (Letter "D" indicates deficit.)

APPENDIX G

THE SIZE OF THE GRANT*

The railroad and the government never agreed on how much land the company was entitled to under the 1866 granting act. In 1885 Williamson of the A&P multiplied the 559.5 miles constructed between Isleta and the Colorado River by forty sections per mile and obtained an answer of 14,323,200 acres. His figure, an oversimplification, was certainly not correct. The railroad did not run in a straight line between the points but curved about considerably, resulting in Williamson counting some land twice. In 1887, on what basis it is impossible to say, he wrote the acreage was 14,182,400 acres. Jones of the Santa Fe Pacific adopted the figure of 14,325,760 acres, which he found somewhere in the A&P records. Both he and the railroad auditor tried to check the accuracy of this amount, but neither met with any success. The United States General Land Office never announced how much land the A&P had earned.

The government and the company never agreed on how much acreage the

* Williamson to Register and Receiver, Prescott, June 13, 1887, TLB; Jones to Engel, February 16, 1916, and February 16, 1919, LCA 3131; Collinson to Britton and Gray, December 29, 1931, LCA 3131; Dale McGrath to Hemenway, December 28, 1942, LCA 12484. The United States General Land Office method of adjusting the limits and size of land grants is discussed in *Land Decisions*, V, 468.

A&P and the Santa Fe Pacific received. The United States set the quantity at 13,375,356.02 acres as of 1923 and, later revising its figures, said the total to 1931 was 13,426,775.83. The railroad disagreed, saying the last-named amount should be 13,754,692.05.

After the Santa Fe Pacific had released its outstanding land claims to the government in 1940, there was no practical business reason for determining either the exact size of the grant or the amount of land deeded to the railroad. The company officials had accurate figures on how much land they actually held title to at the moment, a much more important matter to them. They felt no sorrow at escaping what at best would have been a laborious task of plowing through old records.

The railroad auditor's office carries on its books a set of figures which are supposed to balance the grant. These figures are certainly not entirely accurate. Hemenway and Auditor Ralph Sellards think them a good approximation; McClelland and Chief Clerk Balch are much less enthusiastic. The figures, for what they may be worth, are as follows:

Estimated area of the grant		14,325,760.00
Losses because the railroad line ran not straight but with curves		571,067.95
Acreage in the place limits of the grant		13,754,692.05
Acreage taken for right of way	15,978.85	
Appropriated by others before 1872 map of location filed	1,415,276.86	
Mineral losses	154,680.52	
Total losses	1,585,936.23	
1872 losses made up	1,205,567.26	
Mineral losses made up	38,949.40	
Net losses		341,419.57
Available for disposition		13,413,272.48

It is worth remembering that the railroad never selected some of the indemnity land and even a few acres within the place limits to which it was entitled because the tracts were of such poor quality they were not worth having. The company, in 1940, had a suit pending to decide its right to the odd-numbered sections within the Hualpai reservation. The total amount of land available in 1940 from which the railroad was entitled to pick enough to bring its grant up to the full amount given by Congress was 1,057,050.89 acres, and it was to all this that it relinquished any claim in order to enjoy the rate benefits provided by the Transportation Act of 1940.

BIBLIOGRAPHY

1. MANUSCRIPTS

Records of the Santa Fe Pacific Land Department. This study is based primarily on these records. They consist of tract books, maps, contracts, leases, and, most important, eight hundred letter boxes containing incoming and outgoing correspondence between 1901 and the present. The files concerning annual grazing leases prior to 1938 have been destroyed. Otherwise, there is every indication that the correspondence is complete, and this is also the understanding of the present employees of the Land Department. The only index existing for this material is useless from the viewpoint of a historian and it was necessary to read all the correspondence. Important policy matters were sometimes discussed in the most unpromising-looking files and, therefore, no sampling method could have been used. The records are located in the office of the land commissioner at Albuquerque and in the Stationery Warehouse at Topeka.

The correspondence between 1897 and 1901 was misplaced when the office of the Land Department was moved from Los Angeles to Topeka. Attempts made by officers of the railroad to locate this material in 1905 and 1915 were fruitless.

Correspondence of the Atlantic and Pacific Land Department. Outgoing correspondence, apparently complete, from 1881 to 1897 is preserved in eighteen large letter-press tissue books which are stored in the Stationery Warehouse at Topeka. There is no index and so it was necessary to read all the letters.

Records of the Auditor of Disbursements, AT&SF Ry. At the Topeka office of this official the accounts of the Santa Fe Pacific are audited. For this book various monthly and yearly summaries were consulted, but no attempt at a more detailed study of the accounting records was made.

Records of the Secretary, AT&SF Ry. At the Topeka office of this official copies of all contracts and leases made by the Santa Fe Pacific are preserved. Except in two cases where the correspondence was not clear, these were not examined.

Records of the Valuation Engineer, AT&SF Ry. At the Topeka office of this official is the letter giving the estimated cost of reproducing the Isleta-Needles line in 1896.

Manuscripts at the Arizona Pioneers Historical Society, Tucson. "The Arizona Wool Growers Association, 1898–1909," by E. S. Gosney, and the MS of W. C. Barnes's autobiography, part of which was published as *Apaches & Longhorns,* are deposited here.

Manuscripts at the National Archives, Washington. These contain several packages of letters about the A&P written to and by the Secretary of the Interior as well as the outgoing correspondence of the Lands and Railroad Division of the Secretary's office. These records were of especial use in preparing Chapter II. The archives also contain the records of the United States General Land Office and the Bureau of Indian Affairs, but a sampling of the correspondence available showed very little additional information not already disclosed by the railroad records.

Manuscripts at the State Library of Arizona, Phoenix. The library has in its files "The Moqui and Navajo Scrip Case," by Mulford Winsor, the first draft of an article never completed in final literary form.

2. LOCATION OF PRINTED MATERIAL

Arizona Pioneers Historical Society, Tucson.

Harvard College Library, Cambridge.

The Huntington Library, San Marino, California.

Library of Congress.

McKinley County Court House, Gallup.

Public Library, Los Angeles.

Southwest Museum, Los Angeles. The "Munk Library of Arizonana" in this institution is by far the best collection of books and pamphlets on the subject to be found anywhere.

University of Arizona Library, Tucson.

University of New Mexico Library, Albuquerque.

University of Southern California Library, Los Angeles.

3. PUBLICATIONS OF CONGRESS

Congressional Globe, 26th to 42d Cong., 1860–73.

Congressional Record, 43d to 63d Cong., 1874–1914.

"Forfeited Grants Atlantic and Pacific Railroad Company," *House Reports,* 48th Cong., 1st sess., No. 1663.

"Forfeited Grants Northern Pacific Railroad," *House Reports,* 48th Cong., 1st sess., No. 1256.

"Forfeiture of Lands Granted to the California and Oregon Railroad," *House Reports,* 48th Cong., 1st sess., No. 793.

"The Range and Ranch Cattle Business of the United States," *House Executive Documents,* 48th Cong., 2d sess., No. 267.

"Forfeited Lands Granted Atlantic and Pacific Railroad Company," *House Reports,* 49th Cong., 1st sess., No. 193.

"Atlantic and Pacific Railroad Lands," *Senate Executive Documents,* 49th Cong., 2d sess., No. 2.

"Cattle Grazers on Public Lands," *House Executive Documents,* 50th Cong., 1st sess., No. 232.

"Land Titles in New Mexico and Colorado," *House Reports,* 52d Cong., 1st sess., No. 1253.

"Public Forest Reservations," *House Reports,* 54th Cong., 1st sess., No. 1593.

"Rights of Purchasers Under Mortgages," *Senate Reports,* 54th Cong., 1st sess., No. 737.

"Establishment of Forest Reservations," *Senate Documents,* 61st Cong., 2d sess., No. 21.

"Granting Certain Privileges to the Santa Fe Pacific Railroad Company," *Senate Reports,* 57th Cong., 1st sess., No. 1760.

"Rights of Certain Small-Holding Settlers," *House Reports,* 58th Cong., 2d sess., No. 1203.

"Report of the Public Lands Commission," *Senate Documents,* 58th Cong., 3d sess., No. 189.

"San Francisco Mountains Forest Reserve," *House Documents,* 59th Cong., 1st sess., No. 613.

"Public Land Situation in the United States," *Senate Documents,* 59th Cong., 2d sess., No. 310.

"Contracts in Forest Reserve Timber Lands," *Senate Documents,* 61st Cong., 2d sess., No. 612.

"Survey of Conditions of the Indians of the United States," *Hearings* before the Subcommittee of the Senate Committee on Indian Affairs, 71st Cong., 3d sess.

"Survey of Condition of Indians," *Senate Reports,* 72d Cong., 1st sess., No. 25.

"Navajo Indian Reservation," *Senate Documents,* 72d Cong., 1st sess., No. 64.

"The Western Range," *Senate Documents,* 74th Cong., 2d sess., No. 199.

"Walapai Papers," *Senate Documents,* 74th Cong., 2d sess., No. 273.

4. FEDERAL LAWS AND DECISIONS

Land Decisions, Vols. 1–57.

Opinions of the Attorney-General, Vol. 16.

Statutes-at-Large, Vols. 14–46.

United States Reports, Vols. 115–340.

5. OTHER PUBLICATIONS OF THE UNITED STATES

Agricultural Statistics, 1936–39.

Agricultural Yearbook, 1925.

Annual Report of the Commissioner of Indian Affairs to the Secretary of the Interior, 1874.

BARNES, W. C., "Stock Watering Places on Western Grazing Lands," United States Department of Agriculture *Farmers' Bulletin,* No. 592 (1914).

BARNES, W. C., AND J. T. JARDINE, "Live Stock Production in Eleven Western Range States," United States Department of Agriculture *Report,* No. 210 (1916), Part II.

BENTLEY, H. L., "Cattle Ranges of the Southwest," United States Department of Agriculture *Farmers' Bulletin,* No. 72 (1898).

CHAPLINE, W. R., "Production of Goats on Far Western Ranges," United States Department of Agriculture *Bulletin,* No. 749 (1919).

FLORY, E. L., AND G. C. MARSHALL, "Regrassing for Soil Protection in the Southwest," United States Department of Agriculture *Farmers' Bulletin,* No. 1913 (1942).

GRIFFITHS, DAVID, "Range Improvement in Arizona," United States Department of Agriculture Bureau of Plant Industry *Bulletin,* No. 4 (1901).

——, "Range Investigations in Arizona," United States Department of Agriculture Bureau of Plant Industry *Bulletin,* No. 67 (1904).

JARDINE, J. T., AND MARK ANDERSON, "Range Management on the National Forests," United States Department of Agriculture *Bulletin,* No. 790 (1919).

JARDINE, J. T., AND L. C. HURTT, "Increased Cattle Production in Southwestern Ranges," United States Department of Agriculture *Bulletin,* No. 588 (1917).

LEIBERG, J. B., T. F. RIXON, AND ARTHUR DOWELL, "Forest Conditions in the San Francisco Mountains Forest Reserve," United States Geological Survey *Professional Papers,* No. 22 (1904).

PARR, V. V., "Beef-Cattle Production in the Range Area," United States Department of Agriculture *Farmers' Bulletin,* No. 1395 (1925).

PARR, V. V., G. W. COLLIER, AND G. S. KLEMMEDSON, "Ranch Organization and Methods of Livestock Production in the Southwest," United States Department of Agriculture *Technical Bulletin,* No. 68 (1928).

POTTER, A. F., AND F. V. COVILLE, "Grazing on the Public Lands," United States Department of Agriculture Forest Service *Bulletin,* No. 62 (1905).

Report of the Governor of Arizona to the Secretary of the Interior, 1878–1910.

Report of the Secretary of Agriculture, 1935.

ROTH, FILIBERT, "Grazing in the Forest Reserves," *Yearbook of the United States Department of Agriculture* (1901), pp. 333–48.

WOOTON, E. O., "Carrying Capacity of Grazing Ranges in Southern Arizona," United States Department of Agriculture *Bulletin,* No. 367 (1916).

———, "Factors Affecting Range Management in New Mexico," United States Department of Agriculture *Bulletin,* No. 211 (1915).

Yearbook of Agriculture, 1933–35.

6. PUBLICATIONS OF STATES

Annual Report of the State Land Commissioner of Arizona, 1915–40.

"Arizona and Its Heritage," University of Arizona *Bulletin,* Vol. VII (1936), No. 3.

Arizona State Engineering Commission, *Report Based on Reconnaissance Investigation of Arizona Land Irrigable from the Colorado River* (Phoenix), 1923.

BUEKMAN, T. E., "The Taylor Grazing Act in Nevada," University of Nevada Agricultural Extension *Bulletin,* No. 76 (1935).

GARCIA, FABIAN, AND S. C. YOUNG, "Results of Irish Potato Experiments in the Bluewater, New Mexico, Irrigation District," Agricultural Experiment Station of the New Mexico College of Agriculture and Mechanic Arts *Bulletin,* No. 218 (1934).

LINNEY, C. E., FABIAN GARCIA, AND E. E. HOLLINGER, "Climate as It Affects Crops and Ranges in New Mexico," New Mexico College of Agriculture and Mechanic Arts *Bulletin,* No. 182 (1930).

New Mexico (Territory) Bureau of Immigration, *Bernalillio County, New Mexico.* Santa Fe, 1901.

———, *Illustrated New Mexico.* Santa Fe, 1883.

———, *McKinley County, New Mexico.* Santa Fe, 1902.

———, *New Mexico.* Santa Fe, 1894.

———, *Sandoval County, New Mexico.* Santa Fe (1901?).

———, *San Juan County, New Mexico.* Santa Fe, 1902.

———, *Socorro County, New Mexico.* Santa Fe, 1901.

———, *Valencia County, New Mexico.* Santa Fe, 1902.

New Mexico State Land Office, *New Mexico: Its Resources . . . Its Attractions.* Santa Fe, 1916.

PICKRELL, K. P., AND E. B. STANLEY, "An Economic Study of Range Sheep Production in Arizona," University of Arizona College of Agriculture *Bulletin,* No. 134 (1930).

THORNBER, J. J., "Grazing Ranges of Arizona," University of Arizona Agricultural Experiment Station *Bulletin,* No. 65 (1910).

WALKER, A. L., AND J. L. LANTOW, "A Preliminary Study of 127 New Mexico Ranches in 1927," New Mexico Agricultural Experiment Station *Bulletin,* No. 159 (1927).

WILSON, C. P., "The Artificial Reseeding of New Mexico Ranges," New Mexico Agricultural Experiment Station *Bulletin,* No. 189 (1931).

WOOTON, E. O., "The Range Problem in New Mexico," New Mexico Agricultural Experiment Station *Bulletin,* No. 66 (1908).

——, "Trees and Shrubs of New Mexico," New Mexico Agricultural Experiment Station *Bulletin,* No. 87 (1913).

WOOTON, E. O., AND P. C. STANDLEY, "The Grasses and Grass-Like Plants of New Mexico," New Mexico Agricultural Experiment Station *Bulletin,* No. 81 (1912).

7. NEWSPAPER AND MAGAZINE FILES

Albuquerque Journal-Democrat, January 1, 1901, to October 6, 1903.

Albuquerque Morning Journal, October 7, 1903, to October 31, 1903; June 1, 1907; September 6, 1918.

Albuquerque Tribune, February 20, 1933, to March 31, 1934.

Arizona Champion (Flagstaff), January 1, 1887, to May 16, 1891.

Arizona Daily Journal-Miner (Prescott), 1901; 1902.

Arizona Democrat (Phoenix), June 3, 1909.

Arizona Gazette (Phoenix), 1901; June 3, 1909; March 28, 1928.

Arizona Journal-Miner (Prescott), 1886; 1887; January 19, 1889; April 9, 1889, to end of year; 1909; 1924.

Arizona Republican (Phoenix), 1901; October 23, 1903; June 4, 1909; January 26, 1913; May 18, 1920.

Berkeley Daily Gazette, January 13, 1936.

Coconino Sun (Flagstaff), 1891; 1892; 1893; 1894; 1895; 1896; January 6, 1900, to October 19, 1901; September 5, 1903, to December 26, 1903; March 13, 1914, to March 5, 1915; December 26, 1919; January 2, 1920; January 7, 1927, to December 30, 1927; December 28, 1928; 1933. (Note especially the 45th anniversary pioneer edition, November 25, 1927.)

Daily Enterprise (Phoenix), January 1, 1902, to June 30, 1902.

Dunbar's Weekly (Phoenix), 1914; 1915.

Evening Herald (Albuquerque), 1913; 1914; 1915.

Gallup Herald, 1928.

Gallup Independent, 1914; 1915; 1927; 1934.

Holbrook Argus, 1904.

Holbrook News, July 2, 1915, to June 30, 1916.

Holbrook Tribune, 1920.

Holbrook Tribune-News, 1926; 1932; 1933; 1934; March 11, 1938.

Hoof and Horn (Prescott), 66 scattered issues, 1885–89.

Los Angeles Express, February 11, 1910.

Los Angeles Times, December 8, 1926.

McKinley County Republican (Gallup), January 5, 1905, to January 29, 1906; February 15 and March 5, 1908; 1913.

Mohave County Miner (Kingman), 1888; 1900; 1914; 1920; 1921; 1922; 1923; 1929; 1935; 1941; June 15, 1944; June 14, 1945.

Nation (New York), 1897; 1898; 1899; 1900; 1901; 1902; 1903; 1904; 1905.

New Mexico State Tribune (Albuquerque), 1925; 1933.

New Mexico Workers' Chronicle (Albuquerque), June 2, 1920.
Northern Arizona Leader (Flagstaff), December 26, 1919; January 2, 1920.
Outlook, 1897; 1898; 1899; 1900; 1901; 1902; 1903; 1904; 1905.
Prescott Journal-Miner, July 11, 1912; February 3, 1914, to February 28, 1915.
Prescott Weekly Courier, 1885; April 26, 1919; June 26, 1920.
Prescott Weekly Journal (formerly *Prescott Weekly Democrat*), 1883; 1884.
Santa Fe New Mexican, 1923; 1924.
St. Johns Herald, 1892; 1893; 1894; 1900; 1908; July 6, 1916, to June 28, 1917; 1922.
St. Johns Observer, March 12, 1927; 1930; 1933; 1934.
Southwestern Stockman, April 6, 1894, to March 29, 1895.
Southwestern Stockman Farmer and Feeder, January 18, 1901, to October 18, 1901.
Southwestern Stockman-Farmer, July 2, 1915, to June 30, 1916; 1922; 1923.
Topeka Daily Capital, September 26, 1913.
Topeka State Journal, January 21, 1905; April 7, 1928.
Washington Evening Star, July 1, 1897, to September 30, 1897; January 1, 1898, to March 31, 1898.
Williams News, 1903; 1904; February 3, 1912, to December 28, 1912 (less ten issues); February 12, 1914, to December 31, 1914; 1920; 1927; 1932.
Winslow Mail, January 25, 1900, to May 16, 1901; March 7, 1908, to September 25, 1909; January 31, 1914, to May 29, 1915; 1921; 1933; 1934; 1941.

8. OTHER BOOKS AND ARTICLES

A considerable number of books, pamphlets, and articles were consulted as background material. They are listed completely in the Ph.D. thesis out of which this study evolved. The following are especially pertinent:

BRADLEY, G. D., *The Story of the Santa Fe*. Boston, 1920.
GATES, P. W., *The Illinois Central Railroad and Its Colonization Work*. Cambridge, Mass., 1934.
HEDGES, J. B., *Building the Canadian West*. New York, 1939.
HILLYER, C. J., *Atlantic and Pacific Railroad and the Indian Territory* [Washington, D.C.]. 1871.
HASKETT, BERT, "Early History of the Cattle Industry in Arizona," *Arizona Historical Review*, VI (1935), 3–42.
———, "History of the Sheep Industry in Arizona," *Arizona Historical Review*, VII (1936), 3–51.
MARSHALL, JAMES, S*anta Fe: The Railroad That Built an Empire*. New York, 1945.
MORRISEY, R. J., "The Early Range Cattle Industry in Arizona," *Agricultural History*, XXIV (1950), 151–56.
MOSK, S. A., *Land Tenure Problems in the Santa Fe Railroad Grant Area*. Berkeley, Calif., 1944.
Opening of the Atlantic and Pacific Railroad and Completion of the South Pacific Railroad to Springfield, Mo., May 3, 1870. Springfield, Mo., 1870.
OVERTON, R. C., *Burlington West: A Colonization History of the Burlington Railroad*. Cambridge, Mass., 1941.
PEFFER, E. L., *The Closing of the Public Domain*. Stanford, Calif., 1951.
WATERS, L. L., *Steel Trails to Santa Fe*. Lawrence, Kansas, 1950.

INDEX

Abbott, F. H., 93

Abeytas Community Allotment, 149 n.

Acoma, New Mexico, 4

Act of June 22, 1874, lieu exchange: not generally used, 71; transacted, 75

Act of March 4, 1931, lieu exchange, 76

Addicks, Mr., 55

Agua Fria project, 89–92

Ainsworth, Charles F., 89–92

Albuquerque, New Mexico: AT&SF RR reached, 29; headquarters for land commissioner, 42, 143

Apache County, Arizona: irrigation project, 109; land taxed, 41, 116, 120–21, 151–52

Apache Indians, 4

Apache Lumber Co., 101 n.

Apache Ry., 101 n.

Arizona: geography of northern, 2–4; history, general, 6–7; history, livestock, 8–18, 43–44, 124–25, 143–45; irrigation project aided, 109; land leased, 115, 149; land sold, 16, 70, 98, 107–8, 127; land survey opposed, 40; land taxed, 41, 116, 120–21, 128, 136, 151–52; Navajo lieu exchange opposed, 94–100

Arizona Cattle Co.: land bought, 48; timber bought, 52; timber sold, 51

Arizona Central Bank, 101 n.

Arizona Lumber Co., 51–52, 101 n.

Arizona Lumber and Timber Co., 110–11

Arizona Wool Growers Association, 59

Arkansas Valley Town and Land Co., 85

Ash Fork, Arizona, town lot sold, 50, 111

Ashurst, Henry F., 95–96

Atchison Topeka and Santa Fe Railroad: A&P RR, early rival to, 22; A&P RR revived, 29–33; Aztec Land and Cattle Co. investment, 46 n.; bankrupt, 53; California cities entered, 32; Frost lands secured, 33; line connection at Deming, 29; line surrendered to Southern Pacific RR, 32; New Mexico reached, 29

Atchison Topeka and Santa Fe Railway: A&P RR property secured, 53; Bluewater project aided, 127; Frost lands managed, 53; land-grant rate losses, 152; lines proposed, 82, 85; or-

ganized, 53; Santa Fe Pacific Development Co. organized, 55; Santa Fe Pacific RR organized, 53–55; timber bought, 128, 149; rates, allegedly secret, 110; traffic solicitation, 150; trespass on Santa Fe Pacific RR property, 112

Atlantic and Pacific Railroad: artesian wells sunk, 50; charter and amendments, 19–24, 26, 34; coal land conserved, 52; colonization discouraged, 49; construction, 22–23, 32, 161–62; financial difficulties, 25–26, 33–34, 53; indemnity strips withdrawal canceled, 37; irrigation considered, 49–50; Kinsley trust, 33; land donated, 50; land grant authorized, 2, 20–21; land-grant forfeiture, 34–37; land grant in Missouri, 27–28; land-grant profits, 52, 162–63; land grant of South Pacific RR secured, 27; land-grant surrender, 25; land leased, 49; land sales, unsettled claims, 47, 118–20; land sold, 33, 44–49; land surveys sought, 26, 37, 40–41; land title sought, 26–28, 37–41, 118–19; line, Needles-Mojave, secured, 32; livestock in grant area, 43–44; organized, 22; Pacific RR of Missouri leased, 23; Perrin, dealings with, 47–48, 118–20; personnel, 42, 44, 50; property split, 53; reorganized, 25–26, 29–32, 53; rival lines, 19, 21–27; South Pacific RR purchased, 22; taxes paid, 41; timber sold, 51–52; town lots sold, 50–51; traffic agreements made, 23, 29; trespassers opposed, 39, 43, 52

Ayer, Edward E., 51

Ayer Lumber Co., 51

Aztec Land and Cattle Co.: forest lieu land exchanged, 62; history, 13, 46–47; land claims adjusted, 47, 118–20; land leased, 129, 141; land sold, 47, 107; timber sold, 51

Babbitt, George, 111

Babbitt brothers: land bought, 107; lieu selections opposed, 101

Baker, William F., 62

Balch, Mildred H., chief clerk, 143, 168

Ballinger, R. A., lieu selection considered, 91; railroad business car used, 121 n.

change executed, 58–69; Hualpai controversy, 135–40; irrigation boom opposed, 108–9, 126–27; irrigation projects fostered, 89–95, 99, 109–10, 127; Laguna lieu exchange executed, 87; land, coal, sold, 110; land, farming, sold, 108–9, 126–27; land, grazing, sold, 104–8, 125–26; land, irrigable, sold, 109–10, 127; land commissioner, appointed as, 55–56; land commissioner, events while, 55–142; land-grant size estimated, 167; land-grant solidification sought, 116; land leased, 113–15, 128–29, 140–42; land titles sought, 63, 117, 129–30, 135–40; lieu rights sold, 66–68, 72, 73, 75–76, 85, 86, 87, 89, 92, 93, 98, 101; Moqui lieu exchange executed, 89–93; Navajo lieu exchanges in Arizona executed, 93–102; Navajo lieu exchanges in New Mexico executed, 82–88; Navajo reservation expansion opposed, 133; Perrin, opinion of, 119; personnel employed, 103, 123–24; range deterioration considered, 121–22; Sandy lieu exchange executed, 75–76; Seaberg, relations with, 77–79, 81; small holders' lieu exchange executed, 71–74; taxes paid, 116, 120–21, 136; timber sold, 110–11, 127–28; town lots sold, 111–12; trespassers opposed, 88, 128; United States Forest Service, land managed with, 114–15; Weber, Fr., relations with, 80–81; Zuñi lieu exchanges executed, 82–85, 87
Jones, W. A., 82

Kansas Pacific Railroad, 21
Kenna, E. D., 81
Kingman, Arizona, boom, 126–27
Kingman Locating Co., 127 n.
Kino, Fr., 11
Kinsley, Edward W., land trustee, 33, 48

Lacey, J. F., 65
Laguna, New Mexico, 4
Laguna Indians: lieu exchange, 87; reservation conflicted with A&P RR land grant, 39
Lake Pleasant Dam, *see* Agua Fria project
Lamar, L. Q. C.: A&P RR land grant partly forfeited, 35; indemnity strip withdrawal revoked, 37
Land commissioner, railroad, *see* Collinson, W. B.; Hemenway, E. O.;

Jones, Howel; McClelland, C. B.; Maginnis, A. P.; Sterry, C. N.; Williamson, J. A.
Land control, *see* Range control
Land donated: A&P RR, 50; SFP RR, 111, 148
Land exchanges: summarized, 156–57; *see also names of exchanges*
Land grants, railroad, *see these railroads*: Atlantic and Pacific, Illinois Central, Northern Pacific, Santa Fe Pacific, Southern Pacific, Union Pacific
Land grants, Spanish and Mexican: A&P RR land grant, conflict with, 38; Court of Private Land Claims adjusted, 7–8, 38, 71; purchased, 16; small holders' lieu exchange, 71
Land lease policies: Arizona, state of, 115, 149; A&P RR, 49; Aztec Land and Cattle Co., 129, 141; loans, security for, 144; New Mexico, state of, 115, 149; New Mexico and Arizona Land Co., 115, 149; Northern Pacific RR, 115; SFP RR, 113–15, 128–29, 133, 140–42, 144, 149–50; Southern Pacific RR, 115; Texas, 115; Union Pacific RR, 115; United States Forest Service, 114–15, 129, 150; United States Grazing Service, 145, 150; Wyoming, 115
Land sales contracts, terms of: A&P RR, 45–46; SFP RR, 104–5, 126
Land sales and sales methods: A&P RR, 28, 33, 43–51; Arizona, state of, 16, 70, 98, 107–8, 127; Aztec Land and Cattle Co., 47, 107; Nevada, 107–8; New Mexico, state of, 16, 70, 107–8; New Mexico and Arizona Land Co., 107; Northern Pacific RR, 49; SFP RR, 103–12, 125–28, 134, 146–48, 150; Seaberg, Hugo, 106; Southern Pacific RR, 107; Union Pacific RR, 48–49; *see also* Lieu rights
Land speculators, *see* Speculators
Land survey: A&P RR problems, 26, 37, 40–41; Aztec Land and Cattle Co., 46, 118; forest lieu exchanges, 63–64; Indian Territory, 26; Northern Pacific RR policy, 116; SFP RR problems, 63–64, 116, 120; taxes, affected by, 41, 116, 120
Land title: A&P RR sought, 26–27, 37, 40–41, 118–20; Hualpai case cast doubts, 139; SFP RR sought, 63, 70–

71, 86 n., 117, 129–30, 135–40, 167–68;
SFP RR surrendered, 152
Lane, Franklin K.: Navajo lieu exchange considered, 95, 98; railroad business car used, 121 n.
Lauterback, Edward, 47 n.
Leaden, Thomas, 73
Lieu rights: inspection methods, 74 n.; SFP RR sold, 72, 73, 75–76, 85–86, 87, 89, 92, 93, 98, 148; SFP RR surrendered, 152; SFP RR used, 76, 82–86, 129, 134, 145–46; selection, mechanics of, 63–64, 70–71, 74 n., 86 n., 94 n.; summarized, 156–57; *see also names of exchanges*
Lind, John, 65
Little, S. G.: land bought, 48; land claimed, 118
Little Colorado River, irrigation projects, 49, 94–100, 109–10
Little Silversmith, 135 n.
Livestock, *see* Cattle, Goats, Range management, Sheep
Longworth, Nicholas, 92 n.
Los Angeles, California, 32
Lumber: cutting methods, 51–52; kinds of, 3; production centers, 3; sales by A&P RR, 51–52; sales by SFP RR, 128, 148–49
Lyman Dam, 109–10
Lyon, Albert E.: field examiner, employed as, 103, 123 n.; Navajo lieu selection inspected, 94, 97–98

M. E. Leverich and Co.: lieu rights dealer, 77; Moqui lieu rights bought, 92; Navajo lieu rights bought, 93, 98
McClelland, C. B.: field examiner, appointed as, 123; field examiner, events while, 123–53; Hualpai reservation appraised, 136–37; irrigation boom opposed, 126–27; land commissioner, appointed as, 143 n.; land leased, 128–29, 149–51; land sold, 126–27, 146–48; land title sought, 129–30; trespassers opposed, 128
McKinley County, New Mexico, coal land, 4, 52, 110, 148
McKinley, William, 58
McNary, Arizona, 4
McPhaul, Mr., 82
McRae, T. C., 36
Magdalena, New Mexico: lease meeting, 113; oil leases, 142

Maginnis, A. P., 55
Map of definite location, filed, 24
Marmon, R. G.: land agent, 103 n.; land appraiser, 83
Martin, D. M., 109
Martinez, Paddy, 151 n.
Melczer, Mr., 91
Mercantile Trust Co., 46
Mexican Central Railroad, 51
Middle Rio Grande Conservancy, 127
Midwest Refining Co., 142
Mineral land: A&P RR land-grant provisos, 20–21, 75, 117, 129–30; A&P RR preserved, 52; lost mine legend, 150 n.; SFP RR leased, 150–51; SFP RR lost, 130; SFP RR sold, 110, 148
Mirabel, Ramijio, 113 n.
Missouri, land grant assigned to South Pacific RR, 27
Missouri Kansas and Texas Railroad: A&P RR connection, 23; Britton and Gray employed, 56
Missouri Pacific Railroad, 23
Mitchell Brothers, 52
Mohave County, Arizona: aerial gunnery school, 151; cactus experiments, 122; goats raised, 129; Hualpai Indians, 4, 116, 135–40; irrigation, 108–9, 126–27, 148; land boom, 126–27; land leased, 113–15, 128–29, 149–51; land taxed, 41, 116, 120–21, 128, 136, 151–52; mineral lands, 4, 130, 150; recreational lands secured, 148; Sandy lieu land exchange, 75–76; stockmen nearly bankrupt, 126
Mohave County Miner: advertisements, realtors', 127 n.; lieu land discussed, 101 n.
Mondell, F. W., 65
Moody, W. A., 96
Moore, Charles L., field examiner, 103, 123 n.
Moore, Leroy O.: lieu rights dealer, 77; Navajo lieu exchange negotiated, 86–87; Navajo lieu rights bought, 87–88, 93
Moqui (Hopi) Indians: location and history, 4; lieu land exchanges, 89–93
Morgan, J. T., 35–36
Mount Taylor National Forest, *see* Cibola National Forest
Murphy, W. J., 61

National Academy of Sciences, 57
National Park Service: lieu land ex-